Praise for Aneesh Chopra and *In*

“As the federal government’s first Chief Technology Officer, Aneesh Chopra did groundbreaking work to bring our government into the twenty-first century. Aneesh found countless ways to engage the American people using technology, from electronic health records for veterans, to expanding access to broadband for rural communities, to modernizing government records. His legacy of leadership and innovation will benefit Americans for years to come.”

—President Barack Obama

“In an industry where market forces don’t naturally foster innovation, Chopra has uncovered the playbook for improvement. Regardless of party or politics, *Innovative State* is a must read for anyone with a passion for fixing the problems facing modern government.”

—Clayton M. Christensen, Kim B. Clark Professor of Business Administration, Harvard Business School, and author of *The Innovator’s Dilemma*

“Aneesh Chopra has been the leader of the movement to use technology to revolutionize government in the same way technology has been used to transform other aspects of our lives.”

—Walter Isaacson

“We’ve seen how new technologies have dramatically changed the media industry, and Chopra shows how we can use them to remake our government.”

—Arianna Huffington

“Chopra has been one of those people who has taught me the most about how we can build a better government with the help of technology . . . Aneesh Chopra is a rock star. He’s a brilliant, thoughtful change-maker. He knows technology, he knows government, and he knows how to put the two together to solve real problems.”

—Tim O’Reilly, chairman of O’Reilly Media

"Aneesh Chopra is the real deal, focused on both inspirational ideas and effective implementation. In *Innovative State*, he shows how government can serve people better by adopting new approaches to information technology. If you believe in government, or even if you're frustrated by it, read this book—it will give you hope."

—Peter Orszag, former director of the Office of Management and Budget

"Chopra starts by offering a brief but compelling history of government-enabled technological innovation in the United States . . . [He] offers great examples of bringing new kinds of talent into government . . . [and] provides useful insight about using the toolkit that he describes."

—*Stanford Social Innovation Review*

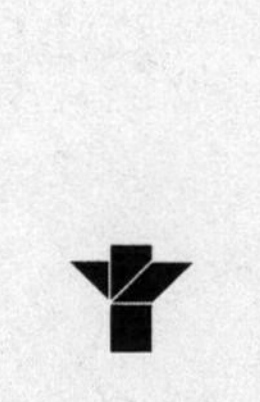

Innovative State

Innovative State

How New Technologies Can Transform Government

Aneesh Chopra

With Ethan Skolnick

Grove Press
New York

First published by Grove Atlantic, May 2014

Printed in the United States of America
Published simultaneously in Canada

FIRST PAPERBACK EDITION, June 2016

ISBN 978-0-8021-2134-9
eISBN 978-0-8021-9346-9

Grove Press
an imprint of Grove Atlantic
154 West 14th Street
New York, NY 10011

Distributed by Publishers Group West

groveatlantic.com

16 17 18 19 10 9 8 7 6 5 4 3 2 1

Contents

Prologue

Government doesn't work. At least, many in the United States have come to that conclusion. They are convinced that our government is too big, too slow, too inefficient—altogether too incompetent. Or they are simply disheartened by hyper-partisanship and political discord. Congressional approval ratings have sunk to historic lows, so low that Senator John McCain has quipped a number of times that, in terms of supporters, "We're down to paid staffers and blood relatives."[1] And, at this stage, even if they won't say so, some of them are probably teetering too.

From shutdowns of the federal government to brinksmanship over the debt ceiling and credit default, and from the clunky roll-out of Healthcare.gov to the embarrassing revelations around scheduling doctor's visits for veterans, it's understandable why many Americans have become convinced that the big challenges we face in the twenty-first century are insurmountable.

I'll admit that, at times, I've found it difficult to disagree. While serving as our nation's first Chief Technology Officer, I witnessed my share of stubborn situations across a litany of government agencies, the approach to which seemed to confirm the most cynical beliefs. Many of those circumstances were made worse by a patchwork approach to problem solving that too often relied merely upon throwing more manpower at an inefficient process, rather than rethinking the process itself. Truth be told, for too long, that's how the not-so-nimble American public sector has set out to solve lots of problems, often not so successfully or sustainably.

We can be smarter than that. We have been smarter than that.

Throughout our history, it has been more often the case that the U.S. public sector has led, not followed, the private sector in harnessing the full power and potential of new technologies to keep us safe, grow our economy, and serve our public mission. From deploying the earliest forms of automated computation to conduct the U.S. census, to the application of modern manufacturing techniques to shore up our nation's defense, our public sector has pioneered the use of technologies that later found their way to transforming the broader economy. Not the other way around.

We are returning to that form, as an innovative state—a government for the twenty-first century, one that engages its diverse society, encourages participation, and rewards partnerships focused on problem solving. It also means fostering a state of innovation, searching for the roads not yet traveled, and applying new tools and technologies that may allow for the achievement of more with less.

An innovative state focuses on the public/private interface, with emphasis on opening government data to the public and encouraging its use; convening the private sector to adopt standards that allow greater competition, especially in regulated sectors of the economy; paying for results through prizes and challenges, rather than paying for promises through procurement processes; and injecting an entrepreneurial mindset in the government by attracting and retaining top talent.

The journey began on the first full day of President Barack Obama's first term when he issued his Memorandum on Transparency and Open Government[2] and it accelerated when he extended an invitation to the nation's leading CEOs a year later.

More than 50 of them[3] accepted President Obama's invitation to the opening session of the Forum on Modernizing Government in January 2010. There, he asked for their input, in an effort toward imitation. "I know that many of you have felt these challenges in your industries and in your businesses—some of you have felt them quite acutely," the president told the assembled experts. "But I also know how you've managed to meet them, and managed through them—experimenting and innovating and finding new ways to increase productivity and better serve your customers. We're here today because I believe your government should be doing exactly the same thing."[4]

Few would disagree with that sentiment. Leaders in the public and private sectors from both political parties have embraced the ideology of an innovative state. One that leaves behind the tired arguments about government scope and size, arguments between those who enthusiastically espouse bigger and those who staunchly support smaller, arguments that create adversaries and animosity but little advancement. This isn't about bigger. This isn't about smaller. This is about smarter.

Despite the highly polarized debate on Obamacare, overwhelming majorities in both houses of Congress voted in 2015 to fix the way Medicare pays doctors in order to reward delivering better care and opened up the vast treasure troves of Medicare data so the private sector can help patients find the doctors that are right for them.[5]

In education, overwhelming majorities in both houses of Congress voted in 2015 to fix the way schools hold teachers accountable and to expand high-quality public charter schools, or learning startups.

And in 2014, Congress passed the DATA Act with a unanimous vote in the Senate and only one vote in opposition in the House to standardize reporting on where the government spends its money.

Making America again an innovative state, a smarter state, is what this book is about. This book is for government employees who feel stifled by budget bickering and political posturing, yet still believe in the spirit of public service and the possibility of bettering people's lives. It is for entrepreneurs who have shied away from assisting the government on account of bureaucratic hassle, but still believe they can contribute something significant to the search for solutions. Above all, this book is for concerned citizens of different political affiliations who have lost some confidence in government, but still believe it can be a force for good.

Chapter 1

The Next Paradigm

This may not seem plausible to those who are disillusioned by government, who view the institution as the perpetual problem, hopelessly dysfunctional, intractable, and ineffective.

At many times throughout our history, government *has* gotten it.

There have been robust periods during which government-sparked innovations informed private sector actions and energized private sector growth, not the other way around. There are numerous stories of an American public sector, from its perch of leadership, successfully applying new technologies and new organizational techniques to carry out its core public missions—such as establishing and maintaining the country's infrastructure, providing for the nation's defense, and delivering needed services and benefits to veterans and the poor.

Or, even, delivering the mail. This may come as a surprise while you wait and wait and wait on line to ship some socks to Saginaw, but the U.S. Postal Service has shown considerable innovation and creativity at some stages—repeatedly refreshing its methods, from steamboat to locomotive to airplane, in order to continue year-round universal mail service.[1] In the middle of the nineteenth century, it even used its buying power to repurpose the horse as a delivery vehicle—subcontracting for the Pony Express, which circulated mail to the western states via land routes in half the time.[2] That flourished for about 18 months, or until people gravitated toward another means of communication: the telegraph.

The telegraph itself was a by-product of government leadership. Federal, state, and local government support for waterways, highways, and runways has traditionally been critical to the takeoff of new transportation technologies, with vehicles ultimately emerging to exploit the new transportation grids. But investing in infrastructure has meant more than paving a road or digging a canal—the government has been an active player in the research and development (R&D) sphere, enabling or designing new forms of infrastructure, notably those related to communications. In 1843, Congress provided Samuel Finley Breese Morse with $30,000 in seed money for an experimental 38-mile telegraph line between Baltimore and Washington, D.C. The experiment succeeded on May 1, 1844, when the first message was sent by Morse code—news that the Whig Party convention in Baltimore had nominated Henry Clay for president.[3]

Throughout the nineteenth century, the U.S. Army pioneered in two areas of manufacturing—interchangeable parts and mechanization —as it made guns and weapons in its factories as well as ordered them from those of contractors. These innovative techniques came to be known as the "arsenal system," spreading from military factories to revolutionize old industries like sewing and create new ones like bicycle and automobile manufacturing.[4] The military was ahead of the private sector curve in other matters. Consider the pension program for Union veterans of the Civil War, which has been called the first national welfare state program. An early case of "information overload" inspired the federal government to build a massive Pension Building in Washington, D.C., between 1882 and 1887, to be inhabited by clerks processing pension claims. The building's architect, Montgomery C. Meigs, also invented an ingenious labor-saving device—a metal track on each floor along which office boys moved more than a ton of documents each day by using poles to shove baskets of paper that were suspended by rods.

Understandably, this history is of little consolation if you are still waiting on line at the post office—or airport security or the Department of Motor Vehicles—or worse, as we chronicled earlier, if you are waiting for word about your veteran benefits. There's no disputing that American government, while accomplishing much that has gone unnoticed, has also rightly earned a good share of the cynicism and criticism that has come its way.

Its failures and foibles have given rise and fuel to the unyielding ideologues who loudly assert that smaller—and less engaged—governance is invariably the ideal. And when those cynics cite the Framers for support, that's not empty rhetoric. The truth is that our founders did focus on limiting the power of the federal government in the lives of Americans—and no one complained. For most of America's first century, government played a tiny role in daily life. A diffuse country where most Americans lived on farms disconnected from one another had little use—and little desire—for an activist, big federal government. When the distance your horse could take you was the circumference of most of your life, decisions in state capitals and Washington, D.C., had little impact on ordinary people. In the years just before and especially after the Civil War, that began to change.

First, Americans moved west in earnest, and we became a continental nation with a larger set of concerns. New lands needed to be managed, and a country with grand ambitions needed infrastructure that only the government could help bring about such as the transcontinental railroad and the aforementioned telegraph. Second, the country was undergoing a rapid period of industrialization, with millions of American moving from farms to cities, from the fields to factory floors, and from mom-and-pop farms and shops to large corporations, very similar to what

China is experiencing today. The rise of companies like Standard Oil in the last third of the nineteenth century, followed by U.S. Steel and others in the early twentieth century, began to concern many Americans. Those Americans saw those companies' apparently unlimited economic power, and saw a society rapidly changing—and not always for the better. The independence, imagined or romanticized, of the yeoman farmer toiling in his fields gave way to millions of Americans working for companies built on the management principles of the day—hierarchical, top-down, and large—or losing out to those large entities in the marketplace. Crowded slums, oppressive sweatshops, dangerous factories and mines, forced child labor, companies exercising monopoly power, and harmful products being churned out by these factories were exposed by the crusading muckraking journalists of their day.

More needed to be done to limit the unchecked economic power of the new breed of big businesses and banks. At the time, however, American government—of any kind—didn't appear to be ideally equipped for such an assignment. On the local level, urban bosses dominated the politics of rapidly growing cities and were predominantly focused on divvying up the spoils of power, ignoring the needs of their residents in much the same way that businesses ignored those of their workers. Things weren't operating much better at the federal level. In the early 1870s, the federal government employed just 51,020 civilians, of whom 36,696 were postal workers—and there, too, a spoils system rewarded political cronies and party hacks with the few government jobs. Nor was the federal government on the cutting edge of technology, especially as compared to the private sector. Consider the typewriter. In 1887, a report published in the *Penman's Art Journal* noted that typewriter usage had proliferated in the private sector to such an extent in less than five years that the instrument had gone from curiosity to critical infrastructure "in almost every well regulated business establishment."[5] In contrast, the federal government had failed to incorporate the productivity tool at all.

It would take considerable time for the technology gap to close, but on the management front, pressure built for something to be done, to enable the government to take a more constructive role in limiting unchecked economic power. Then came the thunderbolt event of 1881, the assassination of President James Garfield by Charles Guiteau, a political supporter angry about being denied an ambassadorship.[6] That inspired progressive reformers to fight for a regularized and bureaucratized government where officeholders were insulated from politics. With this new "civil service" in place, government became more professionalized and ready to act.

In 1887, the Interstate Commerce Commission was established, the first major attempt of the federal government to oversee the national economy. The bill creating the commission, signed by President Grover Cleveland, stemmed from the widespread belief, especially among western farmers, that railroads were systematically abusing their power, in terms of setting rates on shipments. Railroads had to set "reasonable" rates and, in an effort to curtail corruption, were restricted from giving preference to any person, company, location, city, or type of traffic. Three years later, with Benjamin Harrison in the White House, the federal government took another major regulatory action, the Sherman Antitrust Act, passed to bust up the big monopolies.

These were the first national accomplishments of the emerging progressive movement. And by "progressive," don't think of how it's used in Washington today, as a euphemism for "liberal" and a description of the political philosophy of many in the Democratic Party. The progressive movement of the late nineteenth and early twentieth centuries was not a partisan effort—it flowed through both political parties. It carried along

Republicans like Teddy Roosevelt and Democrats like Woodrow Wilson, and it had devotees in small towns and big cities. But it united its adherents with a vision of a government that was brought up-to-date: a massive, hierarchical, bureaucratic enterprise to check the massive, hierarchical corporations. The progressive push set the stage for the twentieth century to be the bureaucratic century, in both the private and public sectors.

But again, it didn't all happen at once. While the first decades of the twentieth century saw the birth of new federal agencies (such as the Department of Labor and the Federal Trade Commission) and even the passage of important new laws to protect workers, regulate the quality of food and drugs sold, and oversee banks, it took the trauma of the Great Depression to create the building blocks of the federal government we know today.

Faced with a society in which at least one in four Americans were without work, Franklin D. Roosevelt said, "It is common sense to take a method and try it: if it fails, admit it frankly and try another—but above all, try something." He and his fellow New Dealers tried many things—some worked, some did not. But what they did do, without any argument, was remake the way in which Americans thought about the role of government. The New Deal doubled the percentage of the national economy devoted to government, and led to an alphabet soup of new government agencies: the SEC, FCC, CAB, NLRB, NRA, WPA, and CCC.[7] World War II then accelerated the growth in the size and scope of government as the nation mobilized for war. Government spending jumped from $9 billion in 1940 to $98 billion in 1944—the year Americans landed at Normandy. Rationing of certain foods and other essential goods such as gasoline, metal, and rubber was instituted. While industries were not nationalized, the government took an active role in directing the economy through a range of government organizations such as the War Production Board; the Supply Priorities Allocation Board; and the Office of Price Administration, which implemented new price controls on goods. Once victory was in hand, the most direct controls on the economy mainly abated; what remained was an enlarged defense establishment (what President Eisenhower would later characterize as the "military-industrial complex"), the New Deal agencies and programs, and the large bureaucracies to carry out their missions.

Though the two parties found much to fight about in the postwar years, there was a basic consensus about the role of government for much of that time: economic security would be provided to people through rule-bound bureaucracies, which, whatever their faults, would be fair and equitable in their treatment of people. As present-day government reform gurus David Osborne and Ted Gaebler put it: "[The government] delivered the basic, no-frills, one-size-fits-all services people needed and expected in the industrial era: roads, highways, sewers, and schools." Similar to those in the private sector, these large organizations had to collect and organize millions of records, without the computing power that we have sitting on our desktops and bouncing around in our pockets today. The result was an apparatus that, for the most part, was a "government of clerks"—tens of thousands of them. At times, it could be maddening dealing with the red tape, but in an era that moved slower and in which large, impersonal, hierarchical organizations were the norm, it was accepted: if you waited to go to your bank for the three hours it was open on Wednesday to make a deposit, you were not necessarily shocked that you had to do the same for a passport or marriage license. As the economy boomed and tax revenue continued coming in, this system worked. And from the GI Bill to the Interstate Highway System to federal home loans to the space program, the postwar government did amazing things that helped to create an American golden age.[8]

But that was short-lived. As America encountered more turbulence in the 1960s and 1970s, trust in government plummeted.

Historians have long debated the core causes of that decline, though there's no denying it was a time of traumatic, transformative events that shook people's belief in institutions of many kinds: from the struggle for racial equality to the assassinations of the Kennedy brothers and Martin Luther King Jr. to the stunning lack of transparency throughout the war in Vietnam and the investigation of the Watergate affair.[9] Parents whose children were drafted into a conflict of unclear purpose and no defined end certainly had cause to lose some faith in the government. But, so, too, did those who were simply sending their kids to school, in hopes of a better future. There was a growing belief that government was no longer delivering the requisite results in the areas of education or employment. As the National Commission on Excellence in Education found in its seminal 1983 report, *A Nation at Risk*, SAT scores had been on a steady decline from 1963 to 1980, about 13 percent of all 17-year-olds were functionally illiterate with the rate as high as 40 percent in some minority communities; and the number of students needing remedial math courses in colleges and universities jumped by 72 percent from 1975 to 1980.[10]

Even high school graduates with passable skills found good-paying jobs in short supply. The factories, foundries, and plants that powered the postwar boom in the Northeast and Midwest started to chase cheaper labor and sunnier climes in order to keep up with global competitors—taking jobs with them. A quarter century that saw rising incomes across the board came to an end in the early 1970s and was replaced with stagnating incomes for households even as women left the home and entered the workforce. Oil shocks and inflation battered the economy, and modern-day muckrakers exposed the problems with the air we breathed, the water we drank, and even the toys we gave our kids. In the ensuing years, cities, from Newark to Cleveland, Baltimore to Detroit, started to become trouble zones, with violent crime more than doubling during the 1960s, and welfare rolls increasing by 43 percent during the 1970s.[11]

So, as the 1960s of moptops and Beatlemania slowly turned into the 1970s of bellbottoms and *Saturday Night Fever*, something else changed: Americans' view of government, as many citizens began to identify an inverse relationship between its size (expanding) and its effectiveness (diminishing). Much of that growth was on account of entitlement programs intended to support the populace, programs such as Social Security, Medicare, and Medicaid that were widely popular;[12] according to data from the Congressional Research Service, such mandatory spending represented less than 30 percent of total federal spending in 1962, ballooning to 45 percent of total spending by 1980.[13]

No matter. The American people, fed up with rising tax rates and a declining payoff, started to disengage from their government. In 1964, 76 percent of those polled said that they trusted the federal government to do the right thing just about always or most of the time. By 1972, 53 percent expressed that view. And by 1980, only 25 percent did. In the mid-1960s, less than half of Americans agreed with the notion that people in government waste a lot of taxpayers' money. By 1978, that figure had grown to more than three-quarters of those polled.[14]

Around that time, some of those people started to strike back.[15] In June 1978, voters in California—a state that had invested millions of dollars in the previous decades to create world-class public universities, miles of new highways and roads, and a vast new water system—passed Proposition 13, which constrained the rate of tax increases on property. This marked the start of a taxpayers' revolt that spread across the country as 13 states passed efforts to limit taxing and spending and 23 state legislatures called for a constitutional convention to consider a balanced-budget amendment to the U.S. Constitution. On Election Day of that year, the Republican Party—with a reinvigorated antitax, small-government faction—gained three Senate seats, 12 House seats, and six governorships. In 1980, a former actor named Ronald Reagan rode that rebellious wave into the White House in a win that would have been absolutely unthinkable a decade earlier.

Addressing the country after being sworn in on a cold January day in 1981, Reagan said: "In this present crisis, government is not the solution to our problem; government is the problem."[16]

Reagan's election was a victory for those on the right who challenged the New Deal orthodoxy. Resolutely free market and antigovernment, these conservatives believed that reducing the size and scope of government—from taxes to regulations—would unleash the "creative destruction" of the marketplace. In addition to the tax cuts and regulatory rollbacks the Reagan administration undertook, it also launched an effort to cut the fat out of Washington.

In 1982, President Reagan appointed businessman J. Peter Grace to lead a commission to "work like tireless bloodhounds to root out government inefficiency and waste of tax dollars." For two years, 161 corporate executives and community leaders led a group of 2,000 volunteers to comb through the catalogues and catacombs of the federal bureaucracy to find waste and mismanagement. Issued by the Grace Commission, *The President's Private Sector Survey on Cost Control* made 2,478 recommendations, which it predicted would save $424.4 billion over three years. It issued 47 volumes totaling 21,000 pages—all of which did little more than gather dust.[17]

Part of that was because the Democratic Congress was uninterested in cooperating with a Republican president's plans to slash the size of government. But part of it was that the Grace Commission was not solving the right problem.

When you hear about a revolutionary, you usually think of a South American guerrilla wearing a beret or an eighteenth-century

Frenchman taking to the streets and storming the barricades. But in late-twentieth-century Washington, a revolutionary was more likely to come in the form of Jim Pinkerton—an ungainly, six-foot-nine-inch 32-year-old working in a midlevel job in President George H. W. Bush's White House.

Jim Pinkerton was a most unlikely choice to help lead an intellectual revolution. Graduating from college in 1979, he had rushed to volunteer for Ronald Reagan's presidential campaign and became one of a cadre of young people swept into the federal government when Reagan defeated President Jimmy Carter the following fall. By 1988, Pinkerton had become the protégé of George H. W. Bush campaign manager Lee Atwater, a legend of smashmouth politics, who made Pinkerton the Bush campaign's director of opposition research, its master of dark arts. He was the man who brought Willie Horton to the attention of the Bush campaign. A murderer who had raped a woman after Democratic presidential candidate Michael Dukakis gave him a weekend furlough, Horton became symbolic of the candidate's lack of strength on crime. In a campaign better known for its brutally negative attacks than real substance and ideas, Pinkerton was on the front lines, and was indispensable.[18]

Pinkerton was rewarded for his work on the campaign with a critical post in the incoming Bush administration in 1989—the position of deputy director of domestic policy at the White House. Occupying a domestic policy job in an administration fixated on the foreign policy challenges surrounding the end of the Cold War, the invasion of Panama, the crackdown at Tiananmen Square, and the first Gulf War was a little like being the famous Maytag repairman: you ended up with a lot of time on your hands. In between meetings on agricultural subsidies and disability policies, Jim Pinkerton came to a realization: twentieth-century government just wasn't working.

The problem was not only that government had grown overweight; it had become antiquated in a rapidly changing world.

As factories were being padlocked and the personal computing revolution was taking shape, government was not simply resisting downsizing, it was resisting updating. The very paradigm was under question—and had to be rethought. "Even the most conservative President in recent American history, Ronald Reagan, couldn't put a dent in the welfare state," Pinkerton would say. "So the issue becomes, how do we make it work better?"

At that moment in Washington, others from both parties were coming to the realization as well. One of them was Elaine Kamarck, a Democratic policy wonk with a PhD in political science from Berkeley. Together, she and Pinkerton launched what they called the New Paradigm Society, a highfalutin' name for what amounted to a series of dinnertime bull sessions on topics such as education reform and housing policy. Pinkerton and Kamarck invited academics like Bill Galston from the University of Maryland and Amitai Etzioni of George Washington University as well as journalists such as Joe Klein of *New York* magazine and Paul Gigot of the *Wall Street Journal*; even politicians—HUD Secretary Jack Kemp and former Arizona governor Bruce Babbitt—occasionally joined them. Backbench Congressman Newt Gingrich was also a regular.

Much of the Bush administration had little use for the theoretical musings of the New Paradigm Society. Richard Darman, the powerful director of the White House Office of Management and Budget, derided the focus on "empowerment" as "effete," and claimed the term itself too reminiscent of the "power to the people" calls of the radical Black Panthers. "In the real world," he said in a public speech attacking the New Paradigm Society, observers "might simply dismiss it by picking up the refrain, 'Hey, brother, can you paradigm?' "[19]

But Pinkerton and his fellow travelers had hit upon some very real challenges with what government had become. They had looked back over the past decade and seen how the New Deal manner of governing—the centralized bureaucracy—no longer was working. In *What Comes Next*, a book outlining his views, Pinkerton identified five "bugs" with this "operating system":[20]

1. Parkinson's Law: in the words of the late British author C. Northcote Parkinson, "work expands to fill the time available for its completion."[21] It is the opposite of a more productive organization; less with more, whether in number of employees or man hours per employee. At the end of the nineteenth century when about half of Americans lived on farms, the Department of Agriculture had just 2,019 employees. By the 1990s, when only 1 in 40 Americans lived on farms, the department had more than 100,000 employees.[22]
2. Peterism or the Peter Principle: in which people who consistently fail somehow manage to keep their jobs, or keep getting promoted, nonetheless. In 1990, out of 2.2 million federal civil servants, only 403 were fired for incompetence.[23]
3. Oligarchism: the bureaucracy comes to make its self-preservation the overriding priority. Reams of studies support what I saw firsthand in government: no department—whether the National Institutes of Health or the Pentagon—relishes slashing its own budget. Extraordinary effort and leadership are required to make the slightest dent.
4. Olsonism: named after the economist Mancur Olson who observed that the rise of interest groups can lead to a small number of committed individuals asserting an outsized impact on decisions. Any individual earmark or slice of Congressional pork is too small to bother the entire country, but the company or community benefiting from it will fight like mad for its inclusion.
5. Information Infarction: bureaucratic decision making fails because a bureaucracy cannot know all the relevant

> information. In top-down, hierarchical organizations, those on the frontlines have little incentive to present information that threatens the status quo. And when they do learn new, relevant information, it often takes too long for it to travel up the chain, be considered, and trickle back to have an impact.

As I know from my advisory work in the private sector, these were problems not necessarily unique to government. If you could travel back in time and ask an engineer at IBM or an assembly-line worker at a General Electric plant in the 1960s about their jobs and bosses, they, too, would drone on about bureaucracy and red tape. The difference is that as times got tough in the 1970s and 1980s, large companies began to reinvent themselves—moving from top-down to flat structures, relying on teams and networks to solve problems, putting quality first, and utilizing the latest in information technology to deliver for their customers.

And, as management guru Peter Drucker pointed out, these large companies had no choice. From automobiles to steel, rubber, and consumer electronics, the industries that powered the phenomenal growth in the U.S. economy from the late nineteenth century and into the middle of the twentieth were all dealt heavy blows with the "oil shocks" of 1973 and 1979, as well as competition from abroad, which exposed their fundamental weaknesses in a changing world. Unsurprisingly, these large companies contributed nothing to U.S. job growth during the two decades between 1965 and 1985. In fact, between 1970 and 1984, the Fortune 500 had permanently lost (that is, not counting recession-driven unemployment) between 4 and 6 million jobs, while the country added upwards of 40 million jobs. This was a 180-degree turnaround from the period before that (1945 to 1970) when large companies—as well as large government agencies at every level—created almost all the new jobs. To Drucker and others, it was "entrepreneurial management" that was growing new, innovative, competitive companies, rejuvenating older ones, and powering the U.S. economy.[24]

Pinkerton and the New Paradigmers believed that government had to reinvent and reengineer itself too. "Why can't we use technology to create a citizen-driven, desktop, user-friendly, 800-number government?" Pinkerton asked in the fall of 1991. As the 1990s began, the man who brought the world Willie Horton found a willing audience and some allies in an unlikely place: the Democratic Party.

The revolution came first in local and state governance. By 1982, state and local governments had lost nearly one of every four federal dollars they received in 1978.[25] With the deep recession of 1982 and the requirement that many had to have a balanced budget, state and local governments had to get creative. What ensued was public sector innovation all across America—from the decision in Indianapolis to outsource, or put up for private sector competition, the delivery of many services; to St. Paul, Minnesota, creating private, nonprofit corporations to redevelop its neighborhoods; to the state of Illinois reimbursing nursing homes based on quality of care delivered rather than the number of seniors kept under care. These mayors and governors had no time for the philosophical debates between the postwar, big-government liberals and the Reaganite, laissez-faire conservatives. They needed to get their job done—deliver services and serve their communities. The ideological means didn't matter.[26]

Innovations at the state level intrigued a group of Democrats who rejected not only the conservative paradigm of less government as the solution but also the old liberal paradigm that more government was always the answer. Known as New Democrats, their home was a small organization on Capitol Hill called the Democratic Leadership Council (DLC), run by Al From, a slow-talking, shy, bespectacled lifetime staffer, and chaired by a man who was his opposite: Arkansas Governor Bill Clinton. Clinton and the New Democrats believed, like Pinkerton did, that government had an important role to play, but it needed to be reinvented for the increasingly global, information-age economy. In its *New American Choice Resolutions*, unveiled at their May 1991 convention in Cleveland, the DLC called for stripping away "unneeded layers of bureaucracy" not because government was not needed but because "decentralized bureaucracies are no longer the best or most effective way to deliver services." Clinton and the New Democrats wanted a review of all government programs to determine if they had to be carried out by the federal government or indeed were needed at all, and supported a 3 percent reduction in the federal government's administrative and personnel expenses. Even more notably, the New Democrats' prescriptions for curbing pollution, improving education, and expanding health care—all core Democratic beliefs—relied chiefly on market mechanisms, contrary to the party's previous line of thinking.[27]

A mere five months following the DLC convention in 1991, Bill Clinton announced he was running for president, and central to his candidacy was his belief in reinventing government, which he called the New Covenant. Soon thereafter, Pinkerton left the White House to join the Bush reelection campaign. As one observer at the time put it: "His [Pinkerton's] mission is now poignantly simple: to destroy the one candidate who seems earnestly engaged with his own idea." Pinkerton was unsuccessful in that mission; in January 1993, Bill Clinton took the oath of office, and would go on to execute his vision, handing the assignment to his highest-ranking deputy, the Vice President, Al Gore.

The government bureaucrats; idealistic, private sector management experts; and newly minted White House staffers gathered to hear their marching orders from their new boss and did so with anticipation and an understandable case of nerves. They were charged with working on an initiative that was at the core of the new presidency and would be central to its ultimate success—or failure.

As Clinton and Gore had written in their best-selling campaign manifesto *Putting People First*:

"We cannot put people first and create jobs and economic growth without a revolution in government. We must take away power from the entrenched bureaucracies and special interests that dominate Washington. We can no longer afford to pay more for—and get less from—our government. The answer for every problem cannot always be another program or more money. It is time to radically change the way government operates—to shift from top-down bureaucracy to entrepreneurial government that empowers citizens and communities to change our country from the bottom up. We must reward the people and ideas that work and get rid of those that don't."[28]

Clinton and Gore backed up the rhetoric with substantive proposals. They called for a 25 percent reduction in the White House staff, the elimination of 100,000 unnecessary positions in the federal bureaucracy through attrition, and a three percent across-the-board administrative savings in every agency. Clinton's twelve years as a governor had helped teach him that it was not enough for people of good intentions to pass legislation and authorize new programs. Those programs had to be effective if they were going to have an impact. If government did not work, it would not make a positive difference. If Americans didn't believe that their tax dollars were being spent wisely, then they wouldn't trust government to spend them on anything.

To underscore the importance of this initiative, Clinton assigned it to Gore in the early days of his presidency and asked for a report of recommendations for action in six months' time. Gore's chief policy advisor? That just happened to be Pinkerton's coconspirator in the New Paradigm Society: Elaine Kamarck.

When Kamarck stepped forward to address the members of the task force for the first time, she presented them with a rationale for their work that stretched far beyond the political needs of Clinton and Gore, the need to reduce government spending, or even the important but mundane task of making the public sector more effective. As opposed to previous efforts such as the Grace Commission, the effort Kamarck led would be about the larger task of saving government itself—making it useful and relevant to a changing world.

As she put it to the assembled group:

"In the [1950s], people's experience in the private sector and the public sector was likely to be similar. You'd have to go to a bank between nine and three, you'd have to stand in a line, you'd have to deal with someone, and that was also the experience you'd have if you were getting a passport. Starting in the late seventies, the private sector discovered customer service with a vengeance. They started using computer technology to make things easy for people; the standout example is a bank ATM machine. And so while the private sector was knocking its brains out, the government just stood still. Today, if the government were a store, nobody would buy from it. If it were an airline, nobody would fly it."[29]

Under the direction of Gore and Kamarck, what became known as the National Performance Review went to work. It was guided by four key principles: cutting red tape so that government workers were now accountable for results, not just following the rules; putting customers first; empowering employees to get results, through methods such as decentralizing authority for those on the frontlines; and getting back to basics, ending obsolete programs and functions, and investing in productivity, including new technologies.

These principles sounded simple, and they were often included in standard management consulting concepts that had delivered results in the private sector. Of course, nothing is that easy in the federal government. Kamarck and the Reinventing Government (REGO) team would have to contend with such basic things as: How can you hold a federal employee accountable for results if it's almost impossible to remove them? How do you downsize while at the same time keep employees energized to do more for your customers? How can you bring new technologies into an organization that has individual agencies and offices that dwarf any business in size and have complex and burdensome procurement procedures? And how do you do all this while under the glare of Congress and interest groups, many of whom are quite pleased with the current arrangement?

The initial REGO report was presented to President Clinton in September 1993, and had 384 specific recommendations for reform. The REGO team got to work. Five years later, Brookings scholar Don Kettl would observe, "No executive branch reform in the twentieth century—indeed, perhaps in the Constitution's 210 years—has enjoyed such high-level attention over such a broad range of activities for such a long period of time."[30]

Gore was successful in bringing attention to some of the government's reinvention efforts, even if the actual savings impact was modest in some cases. He famously went on David Letterman's late night TV show and, donning safety goggles, smashed a glass ashtray to mock the complex federal procurement standards for what the regulations termed "ash receivers, tobacco (desk type)." If the procurement process could be shifted from unique (often characterized as "gold-plated") military specifications to more common commercial substitutes, the government could benefit from market competition. And perhaps costs could come down from the ludicrous levels that previous administrations had come to accept, such as spending $54 for a stapler or $435 for a hammer.[31] Gore enshrined the spirit of the efficiency effort in creating the Hammer Awards for civil servants who helped save money and reform public systems—using the prize as an incentive for change. The 1,378 public sector recipients of the award received a ribbon, a plaque, and a hammer, one that cost just $6.

In truth, these moments, while memorable to many, didn't represent the full story. Later analysis would clarify that a single hammer itself didn't cost that much, but it had been marked up in the accounting process to cover contractors' research, development, and other fixed overhead costs.

Still, it served a purpose as part of the larger narrative, as other reform measures made more of a material impact. Nearly 2,000 obsolete field offices were closed. Two hundred and fifty programs and agencies, such as the Board of Tea Examiners and Bureau of Mines, were shut down. Government subsidies for the production of wool and mohair, which were instituted to keep production up during World War II but were no longer needed, were eliminated. In all, 13 of the 14 Cabinet departments were reduced in size, and the overall federal civilian workforce was shrunk not by the 100,000 that Clinton and Gore promised in 1992 but by a total of 426,000 positions. When that administration left the White House in 2001, the federal government workforce—as measured by military and civilian personnel and not including contractors[32]—was the smallest it had been since the Kennedy administration.[33]

However, the goal of the National Performance Review was not simply to make government cost less or do less. No, that was the goal of small-government conservatives who disagreed with the very notion of federal government action. The goal of the review was to make a government that worked better—providing higher quality services to citizens treated as customers. Here, too, the effects were far-reaching, from allowing constituents to pay taxes with a credit card, to rewriting 31,000 pages of regulation into plain English, to committing federal agencies to tangible customer service standards.

By the end of the 1990s, there was some anecdotal evidence that the American people were seeing a turnaround: one 1999 survey found that 60 percent of respondents said they had noticed improvements in public service over the previous two years—a key proxy of trust in government. But ultimately, much work remained undone. The reinventing government initiative took on the challenge of how government delivers services but—due to inertia and Congressional inaction—the larger challenge of defining government's role was often left unmet.

Gore and Kamarck's attempt to reinvent government had come too early to tap the power of the latest industrial revolution: the information technology (IT) revolution. When Gore presented his initial report to Clinton in September 1993, there were a total of 204 websites in existence on the entire Internet. The World Wide Web, invented in 1989, existed largely in name only. But during the decade that followed, the world of technology exploded, driving productivity gains across the private sector.

To be fair, by 2000, REGO had pushed for the creation of more than 1,000 online forms, including IRS electronic filing, and had worked to help create FirstGov—a one-stop website for government information and transactions—with connections to 27 million web pages. And in an effort to improve the customer service taxpayers received, the IRS signed a $7.5 billion contract to modernize its computer system.

It was just the tip of the iceberg. Technology would grow by leaps and bounds, and government would struggle to keep up, with multibillion-dollar, multiyear modernization projects rarely proving to be the best way to do so. Today, each iPhone contains more computing power than existed in the entire world in 1961 when John F. Kennedy took office. Powered by advances in big data analytics, ever-expansive mobile broadband, and more secure cloud computing services, today's technological capabilities have the ability to personalize recommendations on what restaurant to try, what health care provider to select, or what higher education institution to attend. And, through a standardized set of instructions called an application programming interface (API), software products can communicate with each other with little friction, even across organizational boundaries. That allows companies to partner with others in delivering better products and services to their customers.

But none of that was available to Kamarck and her team. As she later reflected, "I never got rid of the nagging suspicion that the government we were trying to reform was . . . functioning, but hopelessly obsolete. We were operating on a corpse or rearranging the deck chairs on the *Titanic*."

With the defeat of Al Gore in 2000, it would fall to another generation of reformers to bring that power and potential to the continuing effort to reform government. As the nation's first president with an MBA, George W. Bush had promised to continue much of the Clinton-Gore Administration REGO work. And with his emphasis on a "citizen-centered," "results-oriented," and "market-based" government, Bush was operating in the new paradigm of Pinkerton and Kamarck. Bush, in particular, focused on harnessing the power of the growing Internet to open up government to the American people. He called for and created an e-government fund and the first office of e-government to coordinate these efforts, and he wanted to shift as much of government procurement as possible online to realize some of the same productivity gains and savings the private sector was seeing.[34]

Those lofty goals, like much else, were soon pushed aside after the terrorist attacks of September 11, 2001. Like the first Bush presidency, the second also became a foreign policy–focused one. Ironically, the main federal reform instituted to respond to the 9/11 attacks was one out of the old playbook: the creation of a new Cabinet agency, the Department of Homeland Security, and creating another layer of bureaucracy in the intelligence community with the establishment of the Office of the Director of National Intelligence. As the Bush administration took shape, government reform was sent to the back burner. In fact, government spending and the size of the federal government grew considerably under Bush, driven primarily by the war on terror.

The lag between our government's commitment to modernization and the continued advancements in technology grew during the remainder of the Bush presidency. Still, through the first few years of the Obama administration, the President's sponsorship of more open and innovative government shrunk the gap some in a host of areas.

Take Obama's challenge, in January 2010, to the assembled CEOs at the Forum on Modernizing Government: "If you can book dinner on OpenTable, or a flight on Southwest or United online, then why shouldn't you be able to make an appointment at your local Social Security office the same way?"

Questions like that had informed the White House's Securing Americans Value and Efficiency (SAVE) Award, which solicited ideas from frontline federal workers about how to make government more effective and efficient. Christie Dickson, a Social Security Administration employee in Birmingham, Alabama, identified a productivity drag in the system—she spent too much of her time booking appointments over the phone—and suggested online appointment scheduling.[35] While that idea didn't win the SAVE contest, it sparked a related competition, for an application that is not widely available in the private sector. Why not let veterans book physician appointments online with the same ease of an OpenTable restaurant reservation? On December 14, 2012, the VA announced an open competition on Challenge.gov, the new website President Obama launched just a few years earlier as part of his commitment to a more open and collaborative government. The VA Medical Appointment Scheduling Contest offered a chance for three teams to split $3 million if they could successfully demonstrate, in a virtual testing environment, that their innovative scheduling tools could plug in to the VA's existing Veterans Health Information Systems and Technology Architecture (VISTA) system to facilitate appointment making.

The competition gave a fair shake to the little guy (and girl)—it was made easy for smaller entities, such as startups to participate, without the burden of much overhead and bureaucracy. At the close of the entry window, it had attracted 41 competitors, many with no history of selling to the VA. Announced in October 2013, the first-, second-, and third-prize winners reflected this diversity—a startup called MedRed; a fellow VISTA-using health care provider, California-based Oroville Hospital; and a coalition led by technology powerhouse, Hewlett-Packard, which agreed to donate the prize purse to a veterans service organization. The winners now have the potential to gain plenty more than their purses. The VA health system, a nearly $50-billion-per-year enterprise, stands as a possible powerful anchor customer.

Others in the industry may gain, too, through the VA's establishment of a testing environment on open standards (a subject we will revisit later in the book). That will allow any health care system wishing to replicate the appointment service to more easily adopt the proven technology. The VA might offer more than the sort of online scheduling available for restaurants; it could even launch the health care equivalent of an iPhone app store, with ever lower barriers to entry for new innovative products competing on price, quality, and service.

While this is a fluid story, I have faith that it will deliver on its promise. And, as you will learn later in this book, similar techniques have resulted in thriving new government services that have even inspired private sector adoption, such as Blue Button, which allows veterans to download their own information safely and securely in a computer-friendly form. In this case, insurance companies like Aetna and United Healthcare replicated the government's functionality when they started providing the service to their commercial customers.

In this way, the government has an opportunity to return to its role, from earlier stages of American history, of introducing new services and techniques to the private sector. It all starts with government embracing a need for a new approach, a mindset that is consistent with the American legacy.

George Washington recognized the need for such new approaches. In preparation for his retirement from service following America's successful war for independence and six years before he would become its first President, Washington sent a circular letter to the states on June 8, 1783. Washington observed that the foundation of the United States "was not laid in the gloomy age of Ignorance and Superstition" and that "the Treasures of knowledge, acquired by the labours of Philosophers, Sages and Legislatures, through a long succession of years, are laid open for our use, and their collected wisdom may be happily applied in the Establishment of our forms of Government . . ."[36]

For Washington and the other founders, forms of government should be tried and discarded if they fail to work in favor of better, more up-to-date institutions. The Founders did exactly that. After casting off the British empire, they scrapped the first draft of America's federal government—the Articles of Confederation—for a new, stronger, more effective federal government. With Washington presiding at the Philadelphia convention in 1787, they drafted a Constitution that allowed for change.

Americans have always understood that government is not some sacred entity with which the people should not tamper. Nor is it an evil, external force. It is a tool. Like other tools, it needs to be revised and upgraded to remain useful.

From the eighteenth century to the twenty-first, we Americans have remade our federal, state, and local governments every generation or two, to solve new problems or to address old challenges better with the latest in organization and technology. What our predecessors did with the technology of the steam age and the early industrial era, we can do with the technology of the information age.

Innovation in government is not alien to the American tradition. It is the American tradition. The purpose of this book is to show how we can be true to that tradition by remaking American government once again. This is not a conceptual framework. It is a practical guide, a playbook borne of the experience I gained while serving as the nation's first Chief Technology Officer, working to instill a more open, innovative government that will meet the challenges of our day. To help put these concepts in context, and to share a bit of how I found them to be useful and effective, I'd like to take you back to some of my formative experiences.

Chapter 2

The Boy on the Chair

My father, Ram Chopra, was born in 1945, in a town called Padhana. At the time, that was India. But, two years later, when India gained independence at the price of partition with the new nation of Pakistan, his family found itself one mile on the other side of the new border. They could still see India from their doorstep but, they decided, in light of the region's violence, to flee to New Delhi with whatever they could carry. There, his father Rishi was able to find employment, largely due to his rare commodity, a college degree. And he imparted the value of education in Ram, who excelled in school and eventually earned his own degree, in engineering, at the M.S. University of Baroda in Gujarat.

It was around that time that opportunity arose elsewhere; in 1965, both U.S. houses of Congress, in bipartisan fashion, passed the Hart-Celler Act to remove the annual caps on immigrants per country, including the countries of South Asia. Still in his early 20s, my father, like so many others around the world, found the prospect of America to be irresistibly appealing.[1] So he enrolled in Villanova University's graduate program in engineering. There, he would learn skills that would help him to earn three patents on refrigeration and defrost systems, which became embedded in products that remain operational today. Grateful for the opportunities that America had afforded him, his wife (also an Indian immigrant), and his two children (myself and my younger sister Monica), he instilled, and nurtured in me, his beliefs in education and innovation. He also emphasized giving back through civic participation.

All of the above serves to explain how, in 1983, I found myself on a plastic chair in a drab room on the second floor of a nondescript local government building in my hometown of Plainsboro, New Jersey. I had identified a problem, and, at age 11, was naive enough to believe that, if I merely brought the matter to an adult in authority, it would be solved. In building our subdivision, developers had failed to separate the public from the edge of Amtrak's train tracks. After I told my father that I had seen kids my age playing dangerous games near the tracks, he took me to one of Congressman Chris Smith's town hall meetings. There, I stood up, waved my arms, got the Congressman's attention, and asked if he would do something to secure the tracks, either through government action or collaboration with our local community. He thanked me, expressed concern, and pledged to look into it when Congress took up Amtrak funding.

No fence was ever built, but my faith was not lost. And my father made sure I wouldn't stop speaking up. As I progressed through high school, he would often speak in optimistic terms about all that a determined, creative person could accomplish. More often than not he would then provide an example of those who had played some role in solving the seemingly unsolvable. One such person happened to be a pioneer in emerging technology who, like my father, was a Baroda graduate.

That person, Sam Pitroda, had begun his formal education in a single-room school with no electricity in one of the poorest villages in rural India. He would earn a master's degree in physics, specializing in electronics, by age 21. After coming to America with $400 and never having used a telephone, he would go on to create 100 patents in telecommunications, fuel a startup that Rockwell

International would acquire, and do groundbreaking work on the "electronic diary" in the early 1970s that laid the groundwork for mobile computing. Yet, what he would later achieve back in, and for, India would dwarf even his incredible feats in America.

During a trip back to India in the early 1980s, Pitroda attempted something that should have been simple; from an upscale hotel in the capital, New Delhi, he tried to call his wife in Chicago. But he couldn't get through. This caused him a minor inconvenience. For India as a whole, however, such telecommunications limitations had become a critical concern, isolating the country and, in Pitroda's assessment, endangering its ability to compete economically with the rest of the world. At the time, the country had more than 700 million people and fewer than three million telephones. Nearly all of India's 600,000 or so villages had no telephone access at all. If you wanted a line, you needed to wait, and wait, and wait. My own grandfather had experienced the interminable delays; after moving from a rural village to New Delhi in 1962, he waited nine years for a telephone line. Nor had there been much improvement in the decade since.

Pitroda wasn't willing to wait any longer for someone else to effect transformational change. For a mere rupee-per-year salary, he relocated to India to lead a monumental endeavor: extending digital telecommunications across the country, even to the least advanced and most remote areas, such as the village of his youth. He understood that the commercially available products of that time were outdated and suboptimal. They were analog systems in a world transitioning to digital. But digital systems for widespread, commercial use were not yet available in India, especially systems that could meet the country's unique requirements, with its heavily rural (and dispersed) population, and frequent power interruptions due to monsoons and other weather events. Pitroda believed a shift in mindset, from acquisition to innovation, could do the trick. Rather than invest billions in outdated technology, he organized a dedicated research and development effort charged with building India's solution on a foundation of newer digital technologies. The effort invited Indian firms to license the technology and build up a domestic manufacturing base to supply the country's telecom needs, so that everyone across its 600,000 rural villages could have access to telephone services by the turn of the century.

In a country of more than a billion people, Pitroda hired just 400 workers for a newly formed R&D lab called the Centre for Development of Telematics (C-DOT). He chose those with little or no experience but with a few key common characteristics: young (average age of 25), ambitious and optimistic, focused on possibilities rather than limitations. Free from the embedded bureaucratic restrictions of traditional government agencies, they pooled their recent engineering training and embarked on their Apollo mission. Within three years, they built four new telecom exchanges that met India's requirements. They innovated in numerous ways. For instance, they designed a refrigerator-size metal box that was able to keep telecom equipment cool and protected from the elements, without air-conditioning, and costing just $8,000. While a typical telephone equipment company would have invested hundreds of millions to design a comparable suite of products, Pitroda's innovation team spent less than $36 million. And they met their goal: every village in India got access to a telephone by the end of the century.

I must admit, some elements of the account were lost on me. Yes, I was Indian by heritage, but largely American by upbringing—I would visit India only once during my youth. We had phones in America, so it was hard to relate to the particular problem that Pitroda had addressed. Further, I didn't have an advanced understanding of the technologies involved; after all, as a high school student growing up in the 1980s, my idea of "hi-tech" was largely limited to what was needed to play Mike Tyson's Punch-Out on my Nintendo, to program at a primitive level on my Apple IIe, or to rewind a VCR tape.

Still, I appreciated Pitroda's passion and persistence, not merely in identifying a problem, but in finding a way to solve it. My father made sure that I understood another point: that Pitroda couldn't have done it alone, that his effort called for a sponsor in the Indian government, a collaborator capable of leadership and courage. After seeing the value in Pitroda's proposal, Rajiv Gandhi—son of India's then-Prime Minister Indira Gandhi—made it his cause too. While serving in his mother's cabinet, Rajiv chose to invest his political capital in pitching the project to other government officials. He tapped Pitroda, rather than someone currently occupying that bureaucratic turf, to plan and oversee the assignment. And he cleared the traditional bureaucratic obstacles to give Pitroda the power to recruit and deploy the qualified workers whom he deemed most appropriate for the assignment.

The lesson was that government could be an engine for good. I took that optimism into my years at West Windsor-Plainsboro High School, and while many of my classmates were competing in sports, I was doing so through Model UN, Mock Trials and Debate Club, and as Vice President of Student Council. My coach and mentor was the charismatic Brian Welsh, who taught an eclectic hands-on course called Introduction to Political and Legal Experience. It was a laboratory for critical and creative thinking against the backdrop of modern American democracy, and it inspired me to engage further in this area, outside of school walls.

That led to two formative experiences in the summer following 11th grade. At Boys State, a citizenship and leadership program sponsored by the American Legion, I learned the value of outreach, coalition building, and compromise, especially after I was selected to represent New Jersey as one of two Boys Nation senators, just as Bill Clinton had represented Arkansas in 1962. Through the course of a contentious Boys Nation debate about flag burning, I became acutely aware of the painful processes and significant concessions required for even incremental movement on polarizing issues. And that was just pretend. In Washington, D.C., the consequences of divisive debates were real, and I got a sense of them while serving an unpaid internship in a cramped corner of Senator Bill Bradley's mailroom. While sorting incoming correspondence into categories for Senator Bradley's policy staffers, I took note of one stack towering above the rest, the one consisting of letters calling for the repeal of the Medicare Catastrophic Coverage Act (MCCA). Curious to learn more, I dug into countless reports from the Congressional Research Service, and gained greater appreciation of the critical linkage between effective policy making and grassroots activism. The MCCA had been hailed as a victory for bipartisanship—a policy that lowered overall health costs for Medicare beneficiaries and added a new prescription drug benefit.[2] However, in order to pass the law, the entire cost of the bill was passed on to wealthier retirees, and their subsequent revolt led directly to its demise. When the dust settled, Congress' approach might have appeared correct on paper, but as follow-on surveys showed, less than 40 percent of the impacted Medicare beneficiaries even knew they would benefit from the program.[3]

After enrolling at the Johns Hopkins University, I was determined to expand my activism, and not to confine my collegiate education to a course syllabus. I engaged in a variety of extracurricular activities, from the mundane (lobbying student affairs for an air hockey table in our dorm) to the aspirational (organizing career advice seminars as sophomore class president). Yet all of these activities were confined by the technology of the times. In the early 1990s, we didn't have cell phones, we barely used campus e-mail, and we had no clue about how the nascent Internet would alter everything, socially and professionally, in the near future. We were still living largely in an off-line world, one that required door knocking and flyer posting to spread the word.

On rare occasions, that had its advantages, so long as you could be creative. That was the case during my junior year, after my college roommate Joseph Molko and I were chosen to cochair the next year's Milton S. Eisenhower Symposium, the largest student-run lecture series in the country. We recognized that our provocative topic ("The Changing Role of Sexuality in America") was no guarantee that we could afford worthy speakers and attract enthusiastic audiences—for that, we would need to raise money and awareness. We also recognized, from our own experience, that incoming students would be eager to get an early glimpse of their classmates. Facebook, as we know it today, would not exist for another decade. So we invited incoming freshmen to submit photos and biographical information for a "Freshman Profile" book, and convinced the university to include an offer for the book (priced at $20) with its regular admissions and orientation mailers. We sold a bunch of books, which helped us attract a powerful lineup of speakers, including Camille Paglia, Angela Davis, Dr. Ruth Westheimer, and Ralph Reed, and, thus, large audiences. What is most remarkable to me, in retrospect, is that we did all of this without a web page. Forget social media, and all the promotional tweeting we could have done in this era. Think of how much a short previewing blog post could have helped. But while the first widely known browser, NCSA Mosaic, was released in September 1993, the same month that our series started, the Internet was still largely a mystery.[4] Even by the time I graduated the following spring, I was only peripherally engaged with the Internet, entirely unaware how it would shape the next 20 years of my life.

In the fall of 1994, I came to New York to work for Morgan Stanley as an investment banking analyst, as part of a class of nearly 100 people who trained together before being dispersed throughout the firm. I was in the health care group, but I had friends in other divisions, including several in the technology group. They were extremely excited about one transaction they were underwriting: the forthcoming public offering of Netscape Corporation, which was commercializing its Internet browser Navigator, a descendant of NCSA Mosaic. The Internet itself had its origins in 1969, with the birth of the Advanced Research Projects Agency Network (ARPANET) in the Department of Defense and the standardization of TCP/IP communications protocol (the primary method for routing messages across the network), under the leadership of Vint Cerf and Bob Kahn.[5] With funding support from the National Science Foundation Network (NSFNET), the network spread to universities and research labs through the 1980s. During the mid-1990s, the Clinton administration removed all remaining restrictions to widespread private sector use and commercialization. Web browsers would be the vehicle for democratizing the access. My colleagues in the technology group at Morgan Stanley believed that the Netscape IPO would spark a tech sector revolution with profound implications for the economy. They would be correct. The stock popped, and demand for it fueled a frenzied race between firms intent on underwriting the next big thing.

This much was plain to me: I needed to better comprehend this new technology platform, and its potential to influence America's cultural, sociological, financial, and political landscape well into the future, or else I would be limiting my own. That became my priority upon enrolling at the Kennedy School of Government at Harvard University for a two-year program starting in the fall of 1995. Twice, at Harvard, I benefited from a little providence. First, I spotted a job posting for a course assistant for a new class, Internet Policy, Business Strategy and the Law, a unique offering that drew students and faculty from three of Harvard's most prestigious graduate institutions. After landing the position, I got to observe the presentations and debates, and got a sampling of perspectives and predictions about where this new technology was taking us. Even better, I got to tinker with that technology, while developing, coding, and updating the course website.

Second, I boarded the right bus. When not biking to campus, I would sometimes cross the Charles River aboard the M2 shuttle, which was frequently transporting an accomplished innovator and practicing emergency room physician named Dr. John Halamka who, at the time, was also a graduate student in the Harvard-MIT program in Health Sciences and Technology. One day, Halamka shared the story of CareWeb, his latest side project.

Beth Israel Hospital and New England Deaconess Hospital, like many hospitals around the country, had recently agreed to merge in order to more effectively compete. In theory, the merger made sense, since the hospitals were across the street in Boston's famed Longwood Medical Area, and the resulting entity could lower costs by consolidating staffs and pooling purchases, allowing it to support service lines that would be unprofitable to support individually. In practice, it was quite a mess. The hospitals' medical records systems could not speak to each other, meaning that physicians at one hospital could not access the thousands of records trapped in legacy databases at the other. Conventional wisdom in such cases had argued for the construction of a giant centralized, monolithic system capable of performing all the applications one would need. Yet, the estimated expense of that undertaking, somewhere north of $50 million, would have blown all the projected cost savings of the merger.

Halamka proposed an alternative, one the executive team enthusiastically authorized him to pursue. Rather than replace the uncommunicative legacy systems, why not keep them functioning in the background, but use new Internet-based technologies to publish the data in the form of a web page at the point of care, when doctors and patients needed it? At a price tag of roughly $50,000, CareWeb was, in Halamka's words, a "quick, dirty and cheap" solution that delivered "probably 80 percent" of what a centralized, monolithic system might have produced, at about 0.1 percent of the likely corresponding cost. Most important, as he knew from his own experience as a physician, the solution would satisfy most medical professionals: If you are an emergency room physician or nurse, and you can pull up a patient's problem, medication, and allergy lists, as well as any relevant testing, "that's already pretty much enough to get you started," Halamka observed.

For getting the database fix done, he was made Chief Information Officer of the newly merged Beth Israel Deaconess Medical Center, and would later add the title of CIO for Harvard Medical School. Later, he would assume a public role as an appointed leader on health IT standards committees under Presidents George W. Bush and Barack Obama. His influence upon me was immeasurable. His success, in leveraging technology to find a frugal solution, shed light on a new path.

My backgrounds in banking and policy would have led me to examine the hospitals' problem in a completely different way. Both would start with the premise that the merger needed the centralized data system and that might cost close to $50 million. A banker might try to find the least costly equity or debt financing from the private sector. A policy maker might try to sell it as a "public good" project, in an attempt to offset some of the costs through government assistance, perhaps justified by arguing there would be savings in programs like Medicaid as a result of the investment.

Nothing in my experience had taught me to think like Halamka, to reimagine the project entirely, and consider substitutable approaches that might reach the objective at dramatically less cost. If Halamka could invent a $50,000 workaround, the traditional battles over whether or not to subsidize it, or to socialize the costs through higher private sector insurance premiums, might be moot.

Halamka's innovation mindset reminded me of my father's stories about Sam Pitroda. During my two years in Boston, I had encountered a higher concentration of South Asian students than in previous stops, which allowed me the opportunity to reconnect with my heritage. As the cofounder of the Boston chapter of the Network of South Asian Professionals, I was on the steering committee of the national organization's Tryst with Destiny conference (named after the famous line in Prime Minister Jawaharlal Nehru's inaugural speech as Prime Minister in 1947), to celebrate India's 50th anniversary of independence. We unanimously chose Pitroda as the keynote speaker, agreeing that his ingenuity and passion would inspire the audience.[6]

Plus, I just wanted to hear from him in person. By the time he took the stage in August 1997, I had moved to the next stage of my life, working for the Advisory Board Company, a Washington, D.C.–based global technology and research firm that, at the time, served hospitals, financial institutions, and corporate executives. As his silver mane whipped around, Pitroda passionately took me, and the other attendees, back in time. He transfixed the audience with his telecommunications tale and, after he finished, the applause started and didn't stop for more than a minute.

"You could feel in that room so much potential," Pitroda recalled during a conversation more than 15 years later. "I got a chance to speak for almost an hour, and the audience inspired me. I knew a lot of Indian-American kids were coming of age, bright young kids, second-generation Americans, full of energy, enthusiasm, great education, great support from their parents, comfortable with themselves. I thought my message would be good for these kids, to do things for America and for the world, since the world by then had changed. This is the future of the world, not just America or India. These kids are going to create the world for everybody. Look what they can do."

While I had heard the story years earlier from my father, Pitroda's presentation seemed new to me, not just because it was firsthand, but because I was looking at it through a fresher, more sophisticated lens, one shaped not only by my Kennedy School education but my interaction with Halamka. At the Kennedy School, initiatives like the one Pitroda undertook would have been framed through the traditional battle lines of "big" versus "small" government, which would lead to spirited debates about how much money to allocate for the project and how to efficiently spend those funds. That, in turn, might lead to further disagreement about whether the service should be delivered by the government itself, or contracted out to a private firm.

What was typically missing from such a debate would be consideration of a smarter approach, one that focused on inventing a way to solve this problem for less cost and, perhaps, with less burdensome regulation. That approach required a problem solver taking advantage of the latest technologies. For Pitroda, working with the government in India in the early 1980s, that was the evolution from analog to digital telecommunications. For Halamka, working with two hospitals in Boston more than a decade later, the enabler was the evolution from point-to-point interfaces to Internet-based platforms.

What would it be for me, and my generation? There was no way to know at that moment, but over the course of my private and public careers, I would immerse myself in new technologies, using them to uncover more innovative approaches to solving problems.

Early in my nine-year tenure at the Advisory Board Company, I wrote a research study assessing the impact of Internet-based technologies on hospital and health systems. The study, written to aid hospital executives, afforded me the opportunity to revisit Halamka and profile his latest project: the New England Healthcare EDI Network (NEHEN). Halamka had been troubled by the waste inherent in the billing and payment transactions between hospitals and health care plans. Providers could burn five to 10 percent of their financial intake on endless reams of paperwork, much of it unrelated to the improvement of patient care, such as the appealing of denied claims or assembling seemingly endless documentation. Health plans, too, wasted resources in responding to those appeals.

Halamka convinced the health plans and the larger health systems that they would benefit from removing the friction from their dialogue, and that they could do so by joining an Internet-based network. That network would connect through simple open-source software in low-cost servers at the data centers of each participating institution. The result was a less expensive approach to automate a number of activities that had been performed by hand, if at all, such as checking the patient's insurance eligibility, managing provider referrals, and collecting payment. With minimal up-front investment, the members achieved dramatic savings in billing expenses, from the previous cost of roughly $5 a transaction to as low as 35 cents net of fees. Today, NEHEN processes more than eight million transactions a month.

By 1999, the booming Internet economy grabbed the attention of the Advisory Board Company's founder, David Bradley. He chose me to lead a new startup accelerator called Advisory Board Ventures. In that role, I would introduce him to promising technology companies for possible investment, while providing counsel to the existing portfolio. Our first partnership was with my close friend Reggie Aggarwal, founder of an events industry software startup, Cvent. Eventually, he would graduate from our incubator space to manage 750,000 events in 50 countries, employ over 1,000 people worldwide, and attract over $136 million in venture capital. And, by August 2013, he would raise $100 million in an initial public offering, valuing the company at more than $1 billion.

In addition to my Advisory Board Company work, I explored investment possibilities in the technology industry through Avatar

Capital, an investment club that I cofounded with my cousin, Dr. Roger Sawhney. The club selected 17 deals in which to invest a collective $11 million in the initial funding rounds, including $100,000 in a company founded by Chet Kanojia to personalize the television experience; within the decade, Kanojia sold it to Microsoft for upwards of $200 million.

In the spring of 2000, the dot-com bubble burst. I left my Advisory Board Ventures role to focus on growing a new division within the firm as it prepared for its own initial public offering. The Advisory Board Company went public in 2001 and, over the next five years, I would move up the ladder, eventually serving as Managing Director and helping to grow our software analytics business. Ultimately, the proceeds of my stock options would dwarf my professional salary. Yet those financial rewards hardly represented the ultimate endgame. Nor did achieving some private sector success steer me away from my true passion of public service. While working at the Advisory Board Company, I was a gubernatorial appointee to volunteer positions on three separate committees: the Board of Medical Assistance Services (overseeing Medicaid), the Southern Technology Council, and the Electronic Health Records Task Force.

I still was the kid on the chair, telling a Congressman about the tracks. I still took inspiration from Sam Pitroda's story of sacrifice and success. I still wanted to see what I could do for my country, which appeared on the verge of transformational change thanks to revolutionary advances in technology. In the years to come, I would gather plenty of proof of what was possible in so many settings, when people stopped looking with puzzlement, helplessness, and anger at every seemingly unsolvable problem, and instead channeled their energy, harnessed technology, and focused on what they could do. Just look at what we did in Virginia.

Chapter 3

The Virginia Model

Back in 1999, the Virginia legislature was seeking to make someone accountable for nurturing entirely new industries throughout the state, while making sure the government's internal use of information technology was effective and efficient. Virginia became the first state in the nation to create a cabinet position for a Secretary of Technology. Three men would fill that role over the next six years, and their work over that time contributed to *Governing* magazine's 2005 selection of Virginia as the "Best Managed State."

In 2006, Tim Kaine, the successor to outgoing Governor Mark Warner, chose me to be the fourth Secretary of Technology. He had a different spin on the position, one in tune with the times. By 2006, the Internet had transformed the way consumers accessed information and conducted commerce. Yet, though it had improved some services such as e-filing tax returns and renewing professional licenses, it had not meaningfully transformed the relationship between citizens and their government. Kaine assigned me to prioritize the improvement of that interface. I realized that one of the most important things government can do is remove restrictions that exist for really no good reason. On a visit to Google, for example, I learned two things: one, most people get to government websites through search engines, not by typing in their URLs or bookmarking them; and second, government, perhaps unintentionally, made it difficult for search engines to index information that the public had the right to know. Within 90 days, we initiated a no-cost collaboration to simplify and standardize the interface between search engines and government websites, making it easier for the public to find what they need. We formed a coalition of four states, two led by Republican governors (Utah, California) and two by Democratic ones (Arizona, Virginia), whereby Google, Yahoo, and Ask.com agreed on a standard sitemap protocol that the states agreed to adopt.[1] Those states then assigned their webmasters to implement the new protocol, a task that took about an hour per site. By the launch in April 2007, Virginia had tagged about 80,000 of our own web pages (URLs) for addition to the participating search engines. In the first year of the initiative, we observed a 40 percent spike in site visitors, at no cost other than the modest incremental staff effort.

One of the promising aspects of that initiative was its bipartisan backing. Before my term even started, and as it progressed, I made a point to reach out to members of the Republican-led legislature. Through those conversations, I became convinced that many in both parties viewed technology, data, and innovation initiatives from a more pragmatic prism, beyond the usual, inflexible left-right division. That was evident when those Republicans invited me, a Democrat, to partner as a nonvoting participant on the Joint Committee of Technology and Science (JCOTS), which organized small working groups that included members from the executive and legislative branches, as well as concerned citizens. More than a dozen bills endorsed by JCOTS passed through the legislature with overwhelming bipartisan support and were signed into law by Governor Kaine, including Republican-sponsored legislation to expand rural broadband access, adopt health IT standards, and permit school boards to purchase open source education resources.[2]

Democrats, while a minority in the legislature, also attempted to put their signature on the smarter government movement, with the endorsement of the executive branch. Consider the way that Business One Stop came together. Governor Kaine, wanting to buoy the state's reputation as business friendly, sought to offer every Virginia entrepreneur a single destination to complete all the forms required to start a new enterprise—a task that otherwise might involve as many as seven state agencies, such as the State Corporation Commission, the Virginia Department of Taxation, and the Virginia Employment Commission. Governor Kaine, inspired by South Carolina's presentation at a National Governors Association meeting, gave me the assignment of creating something similar.

Upon digging in, our team estimated that implementing the South Carolina model—which not only improved the user experience but also connected the existing systems within each impacted agency—would require an investment of roughly $7 million. That estimate far exceeded our available funds. So I improvised, borrowing a page from the playbooks of Pitroda and Halamka. Each reimagined seemingly insurmountable problems, abandoned the conventional costly stabs at solutions, and used the latest technologies in an effort to get most of the way, if not all of the way, there. Pitroda didn't get a phone into every house in India, but he got one into every village. Halamka didn't consolidate all of the records from the newly merged health systems in Boston, but he created a web page that appeared fully integrated to the clinician.

In the same vein, Virginia wouldn't attempt to fully integrate all of the records at agencies that interacted with businesses, but it could still make the experience less aggravating for entrepreneurs. After we agreed upon this more modest enterprise, we realized that we had sufficient resources to launch the service and pilot it for the first couple of years. That economical approach helped a Democratic Delegate, Brian Moran, make a successful case for codifying Business One Stop into law. Its bipartisan passage gave us a mandate to launch the initiative as quickly as possible—and, for that, we turned to an emerging technology called software as a service, which offered remote access to software applications that were already developed and running over the Internet, without needing to rebuild them within our government data centers. Such "on demand" software, part of a new generation of services that would be known as cloud computing, had been made possible by the declining cost of information processing, and the increasing speed and capacity of information transmission.[3] On account of procurement hassles, it took us longer to select one of those firms, Salesforce.com, to support our Business One Stop application then it would take for our small team to build the newer, smarter forms on its service.

The team created a web-based questionnaire that was absent the typical annoying, duplicate queries, because it had eliminated 75 percent of the redundant data fields from other forms. And it was able to tailor the questionnaire based on the entrepreneur's initial answers; if a user indicated an intention to sell alcohol, for example, he or she would receive additional questions from the Alcohol and Beverage Control agency.

Our version of the Business One Stop stopped short of what South Carolina had implemented. In South Carolina, the online forms were automatically routed to all the appropriate agencies. In Virginia, an entrepreneur was still required to print out his or her completed form, and mail a copy to each corresponding agency. Still, that seemed a small inconvenience, considering how close we came to the overriding objective. After all, it cost us $150,000, not $7 million, and we still delivered significant time savings (an average of three to five business days) to the customer.

Early in my tenure as Secretary of Technology, I was confident we were on course to repeat as Best Managed State, due to the

Governor's commitment to improved government performance. For some of our actions, we used the newer technologies, such as cloud computing, which played a role not only in the Business One Stop, but also in our rapid deployment of a dashboard to track progress on agency expenditures related to contracting with minority and female-owned small businesses. For other actions, we relied simply on more prudent and frugal management; for instance, the Governor had operational reviews to confront costs related to printing, travel, energy, communications, water, mail, and so forth. In many cases, we would spend a nickel to save a dime, and we did generate tangible savings.

But I also became convinced it wasn't sufficient to become slightly more efficient. We needed to progress from reactive to proactive government. For that, we needed an innovation mindset and strategy, every bit as much as private sector companies did.

In a 2006 *Businessweek* survey, 72 percent of senior executives named innovation as one of their top three priorities. And for good reason. Historically, companies that failed to innovate tended to fall apart—or, at the very least, stall.

That was the finding of my former colleagues at the Corporate Executive Board, in their study of 600 large corporations ($1 billion to $5 billion in revenue) that operated during the period of 1950 through 2005.[4] The study defined "stall" as the moment when a firm's revenue growth across a 10-year period flips to a decline over the next 10 years. By that definition, 90 percent of the surveyed companies had experienced a stall, and those stalls were as powerful as they were prevalent, marked by an average 13 percent decline in revenue growth within the first year and much steeper stock market losses. By digging deeper into the data and interviewing key corporate leaders, the CEB found that, in spite of the seeming suddenness and unpredictability of the outcomes, the most common root causes were actually identifiable, and several were clearly preventable. More specifically, the overwhelming culprit was management failure, and one of the top reasons for such failure was the inability to innovate. In other words, management could do something to alter an organization's fortunes before it went down the same dark hole as Eastman Kodak, one of the closely studied corporations.

For nearly a century following its founding in 1880, Eastman Kodak had represented the best of American business, a transformational company admired worldwide for its innovations in still photography as well as motion pictures. Kodak had adjusted so often, remaining relevant in so many generations, that it was expected to thrive forever. This was especially true in the 1960s and early 1970s, as Kodak enjoyed dramatic sales growth due to the revolutionary Instamatic camera. In 1976, according to *The Economist*, Kodak accounted for 90 percent of film and 85 percent of camera sales in America.[5]

Yet, even at that time, Kodak wasn't nearly as healthy as it seemed on the surface. Behind the scenes, the company was setting itself up for failure, with its inability to manage its innovation pipeline. It chose not to license patents for Xerox-like photocopying technology. It chose not to sell the VCR—after inventing the device for recording and replaying television shows—because it didn't believe people would pay an estimated retail cost of $500. Then, as it began to stall, Kodak made its worst choice of all, blowing a golden opportunity to revitalize the company. After inventing digital photography within its labs and prototyping this revolutionary product, Kodak chose not to invest in further commercialization, due to the fear of cannibalizing its established traditional film photography business. It made a decision to go with what got it to the top, at the risk of going nowhere from there, even as some of its executives warned of irreversible shifts in the industry. It took a while, with Kodak's revenues peaking as late as 1996. But eventually, the stall became a free fall. A firm that had once employed well over 100,000 men and women would dwindle to a sliver of that workforce. Former peers, such as Canon and Fuji, darted ahead; software companies such as Adobe emerged, exploiting the very sort of technology Kodak had shunned.

Kodak's demise, while regrettable, did little damage to photography enthusiasts. Customers simply chose from among the long list of companies that provided them with the products they desired. That's how a capitalistic marketplace functions.

But what if the institution that failed to innovate, and thus suffered a similar slow-speed crash, was in the public sector, where customers could not choose another option without picking up and moving somewhere else? After all, citizens can't decline government, at least not legally. The late economist Albert Hirschman outlined this distinction in his landmark work, *Exit, Voice and Loyalty*, noting that, in their relationship to government, citizens' opportunities for "exit" are limited, leaving them to exercise their "voice," often through grassroots movements to advocate for change. But too often the impossibility of "exit" has led to poor services or a lack of accountability, with government sticking to business as usual because that's the way things have generally been done.

Whether the objective was to avoid customer defection in the private sector, or constituent disaffection in the public sector, the prescription was clear. Organizations seeking to prevent a stall needed not only to establish an innovation pipeline, they would have to manage it in a way that would equip the entity to address long-term structural challenges in advance. This was what Virginia needed. And, for that, it needed leadership, which Kaine provided at the start of his second year as Governor.

To address a common public sector blind spot—self-assessment—he established Virginia Performs. That interactive website allowed citizens to examine strategic long-term plans and performance indicators in seven key areas—Economy, Education, Health and Family, Public Safety, Natural Resources, Government and Citizens, and Transportation. Over time, this would evolve to include productivity measures, to inform the public how much money it costs the government to process run-of-the-mill services like automobile registration renewals or hunting license purchases. Simple as it sounds, this program would actually represent a pioneering effort for the public sector, since few at any level of government had done this since the federal government stopped tracking productivity in 1994.

This data platform was an enabling ingredient for another vehicle, announced simultaneously, that was designed to institutionalize a permanent culture of achieving more with less. The Productivity Investment Fund (PIF) was initially seeded with $3 million and primarily focused on raising productivity by lowering operating costs and increasing efficiency, while improving customer service. It served as the Commonwealth's venture accelerator, capable of making investment decisions in just months, rather than waiting out the government's two-year budget cycle. The PIF could surface ideas, develop prototypes, and funnel the best concepts to the legislature for consideration for scaling.

With funding in place and the Governor's full endorsement, we established a process to allocate the $3 million toward the most promising projects, many of which arrived in raw form. Through a collaborative, consultative model, we searched for the underlying merits of each idea, and worked with the applicants to put their best case forward. Then, once the PIF board approved a project and funded its testing, the process would move to the next frontier: expanding even the most narrowly targeted pilot program into a sustainable statewide success. We amassed an eclectic portfolio.

Take PluggedInVA. That initiative started with Dr. Mark Emblidge, exactly the sort of entrepreneur whom the PIF was conceived to empower. Emblidge served as the president of the Virginia Board of Education and the executive director of the Virginia Literacy Foundation. Those roles acquainted him with the roadblocks that adults face without a high school diploma. Two-thirds of all new jobs require a postsecondary degree. So, long after many declare an economic downturn over and a recovery in bloom, an alarming number of these adults are doomed to remain unemployed.

As the PIF chair, I met Emblidge while making my rounds of Commonwealth leaders with whom we hoped to collaborate. At that time, he briefed me on Race to the GED, a program initiated two years earlier under then-Governor Warner in an effort to double GED recipients year over year. Emblidge shared the story of country music legend Waylon Jennings, who earned his GED by watching recordings of preparation videos on Kentucky Public Television at the urging of his mother and sister. Those GED preparation videos would be made available to participants in the Race to the GED program via the Virginia Department of Education, which had freely acquired the rights to distribute those tapes, and was making them available to those who requested it.

One part of Dr. Emblidge's story struck me as strange enough to stop the conversation.

VHS tapes?

Weren't we well into the twenty-first century? Couldn't we make it even easier for Virginians to prepare, and do so according to their own schedules? Couldn't we convince the cable companies to voluntarily upload the PBS tapes and offer free access through their on-demand platforms?

It turned out that we could, and the implementation of GED On Demand would be even easier than I expected, requiring a single phone call to two of the state's dominant cable companies, Comcast and Cox Communications. Within 90 days, each had uploaded all 39 tapes and was distributing them freely on demand, and Governor Kaine filmed a 30-second public service announcement to unveil the initiative. Cable users watched the episodes more than 6,000 times in the first three months. No muss, no fuss, no taxpayer expense, just neighbors in the Virginia community leveraging their respective assets to create a difference-making public-private partnership. While no formal measurements on results were taken, it was heartening to note that, according to the Adult Learning Panel's 2008 Report to the Governor, over two-thirds of Virginia's test takers in the years 2006 and 2007 earned a GED without direct involvement in any of the state's official training programs, but by working and studying independently, aided by tools that included GED On Demand.[6]

Emblidge wasn't through, however. Completing the GED was, at best, a minimum requirement for competing in the ever-evolving job market, especially because the GED itself was in need of an update, with a revised, modernized exam not due until roughly 2014. This called for interim measures. He found inspiration in a model at the Alexandria Seaport Foundation, where young adults without a high school diploma were enrolling to earn a carpenter's license while simultaneously earning a GED. This "contextualized" GED program blended lesson plans on carpentry with the more traditional GED curriculum, so that students could learn faster and be better prepared for the real world.

Emblidge wanted to know whether this model could work in the fast-growing software industry, so we met to brainstorm a "proof of concept." In the spring of 2008, we gathered with his research partners at the VCU Literacy Institute to contemplate a contextualized GED program, one designed to meet the unique needs of two technology firms (Northrop Grumman and CGI) that had recently announced the availability of nearly 700 jobs at two software development and data centers in the rural community of Lebanon. That was a coup for Lebanon, which had made the tough investments in broadband and other infrastructure in the hope of luring jobs of the future to southwest Virginia. Emblidge called his initiative PluggedInVA (PIVA), and, by June, his project team consisted of stakeholders from the entire adult education market, including the local community colleges, the adult education programs within the school district, a college-based technical center, and the workforce system. They sought $127,000 to design a new curriculum and to recruit the first batch of students, whose tuition would be free. That summer, our PIF Board examined myriad applications and selected PIVA for a grant. By the fall, the new curriculum was in place and, by January, the first cohort of students was enrolled. They would graduate roughly one year after the project's inception.

I attended the opening ceremonies, along with Senator Jim Webb, and saw something in that community that hadn't been apparent on earlier visits: a palpable sense of hope. I met moms who had dropped out of high school to take care of young children. I met a young man who had become entangled in the criminal justice system, and wanted to leave that behind. I met countless other people with potential who just needed a path forward.

Emblidge's team delivered the initial version of its plan on time and on budget, and began designing new contextualized GED programs in other growth fields—for electricians, entrepreneurs, and other future-forward areas. Its story would have staying power and crossover appeal, even capturing the imagination of Bob McDonnell, who succeeded Tim Kaine as Governor in 2010. In an era of austerity, the Republican McDonnell would choose to scale PIVA—offering enough funds so that every educational region within the Commonwealth would have access to a PIVA program in 2012.[7] And the program earned a $2.5 million grant from the Department of Labor to expand the number of professions it served.

While PIVA was directed at adults trying to make up for what they may have missed educationally during childhood, another

PIF-fueled initiative, Virginia Star, would work toward filling in gaps for, and expanding the horizons of, kids still in school. Its origins were traceable to one of my interns, Brian Chiglinksy, who wondered what we would do with all the computers we were replacing as part of our IT modernization program in 2008. Typically, they would be trashed. But what if they could be refurbished? And what if students, rather than technicians, received that assignment, so they could get hands-on skill development as well as an industry credential to enter the technology job market.

Tom Morris, the Secretary of Education, and I went fishing, dropping a line in the Virginia school system to see if any district would take possession of the computers in exchange for developing a computer repair program for students. We weren't aware any schools in the nation had such a program, until Chuck Drake, a Career and Technical Education (CTE) instructor at Forest Park High in suburban Northern Virginia, reached out. Our proposal sounded familiar to a program he had encountered in Seattle, Washington, in 2004, called Bridging the Gap, a version of which he had brought back to Forest Park in 2007.

Drake's program was even more ambitious and impactful than our original intention—once the computers were refurbished, they were offered to needy families on a first-come first-served basis at the Bridging the Gap celebration night. After awarding him an initial delivery of 1,000 computers, we witnessed the program in action. Some benefits we expected: kids getting trained, families closing the digital divide. One was a bonus: his school district saved money, due to the reduced need to purchase additional computers. Eager to scale the idea beyond Forest Park, we sought funding to subsidize Drake's school visits across the state. We encouraged Drake to apply for PIF funding, while explaining that the PIF would assess his application with the same fiscal scrutiny as any other. That process forced him to carefully consider return on investment, and argue that it was in the state's interests to cover the overhead costs associated with the program management. By digging into the numbers, he outlined the cost-savings potential of the venture, beyond its more obvious educational and social payoffs. After winning the grant, Drake hit the road, establishing the program in ten sites by August 2009, delivering every dollar of savings that he projected and attracting corporate partners. Microsoft even waived license fees to install up-to-date software on the refurbished PCs.

In 2010, Drake presented his first year of findings to Governor Bob McDonnell, demonstrating to the new governor that the initiative had more than met its aggressive milestones. It provided social good while doing a bit better than breaking even, producing a net return of $10,000 on the initial $245,000 of investment. The Governor was so impressed that he scaled up the program further, with an additional $425,000 to support a statewide rollout.[8]

While these accomplishments in education, at modest expense, certainly validated the model of the Productivity Investment Fund, health care was the much bigger beast, representing more than 20 percent of the state budget.[9] To be truly transformative, the PIF had to play some role not only in helping people with their health needs, but in helping to control costs in that segment of the economy.

Cost reduction had never been Dr. Karen Rheuban's overriding agenda. Her passion was ensuring that as many patients as possible, even in the most remote rural communities, got access to world-class care. We first met in 2006 when, as Secretary of Technology, I was touring the University of Virginia in Charlottesville. I dropped by her telemedicine clinic to learn more about her work in videoconferencing in health care, which was removing barriers by allowing patients and doctors to communicate face-to-face from different locations, but which—to her frustration—was not compensated under the current fee-for-service health care system.

Minutes prior to our brief meeting, Rheuban fielded a call that adjusted our agenda. A baby had been born with a heart defect, the severity of which the hospital in Lynchburg was ill-equipped to treat. Rheuban diverted from her planned pitch to attend to this more urgent matter, engaging with the staff on the other end of the telemedicine call, reviewing the relevant lab values and medical data, and rendering her decision. The child needed surgery, without delay, or he might not survive.

Her intervention, through this technology, saved a life. No pitch necessary. I got the message.

Following the PIF launch a few months later, I thought of Rheuban, and how to connect her critical work to our young initiative. Certainly we could do some good by bolstering her existing programs, which were barely surviving on grant funding. But we wouldn't necessarily fulfill the PIF's mission of generating measurable savings and efficiencies for the Commonwealth. We needed an economic rationale to act, and we identified such a trigger in some troubling statistics. While Virginia ranked in the upper echelon in many categories, such as wealth per capita and workplace quality, it was in the bottom half in national infant mortality rates. The leading cause of infant mortality, according to the Centers for Disease Control (CDC), was preterm birth—defined as delivery prior to the 37th week.[10] According to the March of Dimes, Virginia graded a C in preterm birth rates, and some regions of the state were worse than that; the rural Shenandoah Valley had a rate more than twice the CDC target for the country. Rheuban had firsthand understanding of this problem, since many pregnant women from that part of the Commonwealth were delivering early at the University of Virginia Health System, often resulting in admissions to the Neonatal Intensive Care Unit.

While we were blessed to have a state university that supported such a world-class NICU, these admissions were extremely costly to Medicaid—and thus, by extension, taxpayers. Each week that a child remained in the mother's womb and avoided the NICU would save the state roughly $44,000.

We needed earlier intervention, so mothers at higher risk could take preventative measures to avoid early deliveries that strained the system—and in the worst case, led to infant death. In examination of the Shenandoah problem, Rheuban learned that many of the residents there lacked access to a "high-risk" OB/GYN specifically trained to treat those pregnancies that were most precarious. The typical political battle on this matter would likely come down to a fight over subsidies between those who deem health care a right and those who deem it a privilege. Those who deem it a right might argue that it was imperative to get a high-risk OB/GYN to set up shop in those communities; those who deem it a privilege might argue against the government essentially bankrolling the physician's salary.

Rheuban was positioned to argue for an alternative path that could achieve comparable outcomes at a much lower cost. It wouldn't require anyone moving anywhere, merely a modest investment in the telemedicine technology that she had championed, as well as fair compensation to the physician providing the virtual visit. Her hypothesis caught the attention of the PIF board, which approved a pilot study for $136,000. The early results were startling. Rheuban's interventions achieved a roughly 25 percent reduction in preterm birth rates in rural localities over a three-year period, largely because patients missed fewer appointments, down from 11 to 4.4 percent. That was enough evidence to convince Governor McDonnell to sign a law requiring insurers to reimburse doctors for telemedicine services.

We didn't need much more evidence that the PIF was serving its purpose, and yet the stories kept coming. In its first six years, and over the course of two gubernatorial administrations, one Democratic and one Republican, it would sponsor more than forty projects, and deploy more than $4 million, including savings that were reinvested into new enterprises. It would simplify the Medicaid application form for seniors. It would lower the permitting costs for mining companies. It would allow the tax department to scan millions of checks rather than the old way of getting them to the bank for deposit (via an expensive courier service), saving hundreds of thousands of dollars. It would save thousands more by switching the software in a K–12 school system from Microsoft to Google. It would give parents web access to quality rankings on preschools—since passing third-grade reading was a known precursor to later success, and earlier childhood education was critical for getting students ready to learn.

All told, the Productivity Investment Fund would deliver a 4-to-1 return on taxpayer investment, and advance key outcomes through innovation.[11] The PIF had originated in a Democratic gubernatorial administration. But its ability to appeal to both sides of the political spectrum was again illustrated when Fred Malek—assistant to Republican Presidents Richard Nixon and George H. W. Bush—endorsed the fund in his report on reforming government, during McDonnell's Republican gubernatorial administration.

Smaller? Bigger? Rather, a sterling example of smarter. Our work had left Virginia better prepared to confront the challenges of its future. I believed that it had done the same for me.

Chapter 4

Opening the Playbook

In late August 2008, I was in Colorado for the Democratic National Convention, not as an official delegate or sponsor but, rather, as a guest of Governor Kaine alongside many others from his cabinet. With Virginia in Presidential election play for the Democrats for the first time since 1964, and in light of Governor Kaine's early endorsement of Illinois Senator Barack Obama, we were receiving the royal treatment—prime seats at everything from former Charlottesville bartender Dave Matthews' rousing concert at Red Rocks to Obama's electrifying acceptance speech at Invesco Field.

It was a festive time for the Virginia delegation, even independent of the perks. Just days earlier, our work had been flatteringly profiled in the *New York Times Magazine*, with an article heralding the Virginia Model as a living example of how Obama's vision for the country might unfold. Obama's economic adviser, Austan Goolsbee, noted that Virginia validated an innovation strategy that called for investments in human capital, R&D, and modern infrastructure to transform a once bottom-of-the-pack state into an economic powerhouse. Over the past 50 years, no other state had hiked its per capita income higher.[1]

While in Colorado, I met Julius Genachowski, Obama's former Harvard Law classmate and among his most trusted advisers on technology matters, and who—at a forum held on the sidelines of the convention—quipped that Senator Obama had mandated that his staff insert a default paragraph about the importance of harnessing technology into every speech. This resonated with me. After all, the integration of technology was an important element of the Virginia Model, whether investing in electronic health records and rural broadband or increasing government transparency and efficiency. I would draw from the lessons of Virginia when Genachowski asked me to assist in outlining responsibilities of a prospective new position in the White House, Chief Technology Officer.

Obama won the state of Virginia, and won the White House. A couple of weeks after the election, Genachowski invited me to serve on the Technology, Innovation and Government Reform (TIGR) working group of the transition team. Organized under Genachowski's leadership, TIGR would advise the President-elect on implementing his campaign vision about modernizing government. The TIGR team was, in itself, an innovation. Presidential transition teams are typically designed to operate as a mirror of the existing government, with a bevy of advisers specializing in each of the respective cabinet agencies and departments to prepare briefing memos for the incoming appointees of those particular agencies and departments. TIGR couldn't be assigned to a specific cabinet agency or department, because that agency didn't yet exist. Rather, it undertook an assessment of the technology and innovation opportunities across each of the respective agencies, in order to deliver a twenty-first century government that is more open and effective.

TIGR benefited from a running start, because its membership reflected two important constituencies. Many were key holdovers from the Clinton administration, those who had embraced the REGO, or Reinventing Government, model. They offered history and context. Others, including myself, were on the front lines of the most innovative technologies deployed in the private sector, and in the public sector at the state and local levels. We could readily identify the growing gap in the use of technology between the federal government and the outside world. Together, we began fleshing out a concrete agenda for the Obama administration to execute over its first 100 days, highlighting the need for a Presidential memorandum that would set the tone for a new operating culture in Washington. The memorandum would direct the Cabinet and agency heads to take actionable steps toward more transparency, participation, and collaboration—utilizing Internet-based technologies from cloud computing to mobile broadband to meet those aims.

While writing our recommendations, we recognized the unique challenges of the moment. The country was firmly in the grip of a financial crisis, the national dialogue consumed by the severe recession that the President-elect would be inheriting, a consequence of a precipitous crash in housing values and the spectacular failure of risky instruments on Wall Street. On January 8, 2009, at George Mason University, a dozen days prior to his inauguration, Obama made his most direct statements to date about the sober state of the economy, the likelihood of a grueling slog toward recovery, and the need for swift Congressional action to pass a stimulus package.[2] He made the case for complementing short-term stimulus measures with investments that could create "a foundation for long-term economic growth." Understanding the citizenry's skepticism of the federal government following its mishandling of recent natural and man-made disasters and drawing upon his experience as the cosponsor with Republican Senator Tom Coburn of the 2006 Federal Funding Accountability and Transparency Act, Obama pledged that "every American will be able to hold Washington accountable for these decisions by going online to see how and where their taxpayer dollars are being spent." He called for the construction of a Recovery.gov website, to be ready for launch on whatever day he signed a recovery bill into law.

We at TIGR got that assignment with a defined mission: build on the foundation of spending transparency that Obama-Coburn had established. Vivek Kundra, my former deputy in Virginia, took the lead. TIGR operated under the President's embrace of the famous quote from Justice Louis Brandeis that "sunlight is the best disinfectant," while fully understanding that critics—in the spirit of former Wisconsin Senator William Proxmire—might produce their own versions of his infamous Golden Fleece awards for wasteful spending. We also understood that we could take two routes to improve upon previous data transparency efforts.

We knew that one option was to publish the most granular possible data, enabling the public to trace the flow of funds from, for instance, the Department of Transportation all the way down to a small town's stoplight. But we also knew the challenges of that ambition and that it couldn't be accomplished anytime close to Day 1, since it would require the accessing of hundreds of individual databases, introducing the increased risk of data inaccuracies as well as limits on the timeliness of reporting. So we determined that, in the near term, we should aim to better organize the data that we could immediately access and confidently publish. That decision informed the path toward Recovery.gov, the launch of which—overseen by Kundra, now in the capacity of U.S. Chief Information Officer at the Office of Management and Budget—coincided with President Obama's February 17 signing of the American Recovery and Reinvestment Act, and its $787 billion in stimulus.[3] That site would include maps, charts, and graphics, giving taxpayers a better sense of where the government was spending all of that money. While specificity was limited initially, we would keep pushing until users were able to drill down further and determine how the Recovery Act impacted their neighborhood.[4]

Meanwhile, President Obama continued planting the markers of open government. On his first day in office, four weeks prior to the Recovery.gov launch, he implemented the TIGR team's primary recommendation, penning a memorandum that not only called for an unprecedented level of transparency, participation, and collaboration but also defined the responsibilities for the Chief Technology Officer, a position that had yet to be filled. He directed that person to provide a new set of recommendations that would inform a more detailed Open Government directive that the President would issue to the government through his management arm, the Office of Management and Budget.

Now, who would be taking up that task? We, on the TIGR team, suspected it would be Julius Genachowski, though he would instead become the Chairman of the Federal Communications Commission. Meanwhile, I was in discussions with Health and Human Services to create and fill a similar position for that agency. That was, until I met with the head of Presidential Personnel on a Monday in April 2009. It quickly became apparent that the White House was focused on something else: vetting me for the still-vacant U.S. CTO position. For the next two days, my personal, career, and financial history underwent extensive review. That Saturday, in his weekly address, the President announced my appointment to a role in which I would "promote technological innovation to help achieve our most urgent priorities—from creating jobs and reducing health care costs to keeping our nation secure."[5]

A few hours after that aired, I celebrated at my 15-year college reunion with my closest friends and our families. Well-wishers from the tech community, including the publisher, thought leader, and entrepreneur Tim O'Reilly posted blogs and comments endorsing my nomination. The O'Reilly post best outlined our opportunity to build "Government 2.0."[6] That catchphrase drew upon the premise that government could be a platform, not unlike Amazon, Google, and Facebook—one that went beyond providing generic services directly to its customers, the American people, but invited and enabled those citizens to cocreate, personalize, and perhaps improve its offerings.

Still, my work could not begin until I received Senate confirmation. That hearing was Tuesday, May 19, and it was uneventful, but for the pace of activity that followed.[7] I was approved by the Committee on Wednesday and by the entire Senate by Thursday. On Friday, I was sworn in. This came at a time when Obama appointees were averaging more than two months for approval. I believed this had less to do with me than with the promise of the position—one that was intended to make government better not bigger, through the application of technology, data, and innovation.

My confirmation coincided with the launch of two major open government initiatives, following months of testing and development. One was Data.gov, a centralized portal available to anyone without any burdensome cost or intellectual property constraints. For this project, Kundra leaned heavily on the experience he gathered before joining the administration, when he was Washington, D.C.'s Chief Technology Officer. For the District's government, he had created a "data catalog," giving its taxpayers, in Kundra's view, "access to what was already theirs"; that meant everything from Metro bus and train schedules to school performance assessments to the credit card transactions of government officials to the addresses of companies that won government contracts. Further, that access was offered in a format that made it simple for software developers to create applications that would help citizens in their daily lives. One application, Stumble Safely, used crime data to offer suggestions about the safest bars to frequent; others gave users the nearest police stations, places of worship, and post offices.[8] Kundra's overall vision was loosely based on the ancient Greek concept of the agora, in which people congregated at a public square to socialize, conduct commerce, and petition their government. Only now, he was giving them the same opportunity through a digital public square, one that didn't require venturing anywhere other than to a website on a personal computer or mobile device, in the privacy and comfort of one's surroundings.

Kundra was convinced that by opening other data sets, on everything from health care to the environment to education to procurement, the American people would not only feel empowered as watchdogs, but would be inspired to create a fresh portfolio of services that blurred lines between the public and private sector, to the benefit of the broader economy or simply to the benefit of their fellow citizens. For instance, the Consumer Protection and Safety Commission had been compiling data on toys and other products used by children, out of the public's sight. Once that data was set free, creative thinkers could step in and utilize it in ways that few had considered, such as the creation of an application that allowed a consumer to scan a crib's bar code in a store and learn if the model had ever been recalled. And that was just scratching the surface of the potential of opening government data, as we will explore later in this book.

The second major initiative launching was meant to stimulate civic participation. The deputy Chief Technology Officer in the White House, Dr. Beth Noveck, conceived a three-part Open Government Dialogue, one that began with an online blank sheet, welcoming any ideas from the public that fit into one or more of the three categories from the President's memorandum—transparency, participation, and collaboration. The public could then vote ideas up or down to provide a raw measure of popularity. This was a form of crowdsourcing, which entails "obtaining needed services, ideas, or content by soliciting contributions from a large group of people and especially from the online community rather than from traditional employees or suppliers."[9]

That first phase, live for a full week, attracted more than 35,000 participants. Some of the requests weren't quite what we expected: the legalization of marijuana, access to Area 51 files on alien life forms, and the disclosure of the President's birth certificate, to name a few. Still, we managed to distill more than 900 ideas into 16 discrete topics worthy of further exploration. The second phase of Noveck's consultation invited public comment on blog posts elaborating on each of the 16 ideas. All told, she would surface more than 1,000 comments over more than two weeks. That would feed into a third phase: Noveck handing the pen to the American people. Using a wiki tool that offered a bit more structure on collaborative editing, we fielded 300 drafts of specific, actionable language.[10]

That all led to December 8, 2009, when I joined Vivek Kundra in unveiling the Open Government Directive, informed by many of the public-generated recommendations. The White House Communications team allowed me to introduce the directive live, via the Whitehouse.gov site. It was 11 a.m. on a workday, so I wasn't sure the broadcast would be viewed by many. Still, I was anxious, so anxious that I forgot my opening lines. The camera "red light" began to flash. I began to speak. My mind began to race. What am I supposed to say next? Can I get a do-over? This is . . . live! I began to laugh. And laugh. And I couldn't stop laughing.

For what seemed an eternity, I stumbled through the opening segment, pausing just long enough to let Kundra take the lead. For the remaining 45 minutes, I would recover enough to emphasize the key points of the directive. We were ushering in a new era of openness across the federal government, which included an insistence on the publication of government data in machine-readable, accessible form. We would execute near-term milestones to demonstrate tangible results, with the White House directing cabinet agencies to publish three "high value" data sets on Data.gov. We would be requiring government agencies to foster an ongoing culture of openness, which included the publication of open government plans, with clear milestones to hold leaders accountable.

Few, if any, White House reporters covered the event. Only a few blogs are so deeply committed to government transparency that they had it on their calendars. In fact, it might have gone unnoticed, if not for my flubs, which amused someone on the ever-vigilant research staff of *The Daily Show with Jon Stewart*.

"Today, at the White House, it was hilarious!" Stewart said, during his opening bit. He played the clip of my endless, uncontrolled cackling, and ended with a quip that has followed me ever since: "What is so funny, Indian George Clooney?"

At the time, it didn't seem so funny. I actually thought the President might fire me. But I would survive, and even come to appreciate the attention: there are worse things than being compared to international movie stars. Plus, my wife, Rohini, really didn't mind the nickname.

The open government movement had gotten off to a flying start in the Obama administration, but we recognized that it was only one element of what needed to occur. The fate of the economy was still up in the air, and the administration's assistance could not, and did not, cease with the Recovery Act.

Neither could mine. In fact, many of my priorities centered on creating more enabling ingredients for long-term, sustainable job growth. Those included initiatives to clear the path for entrepreneurs in the heavily regulated sectors of energy, health care, and education in particular; to encourage Internet commerce by strengthening privacy and security; and to double the capacity of mobile broadband across the country. And those specific initiatives became part of a larger effort, one constructed with my colleagues at the National Economic Council and called the Strategy for American Innovation.[11]

On September 21, 2009, I boarded Air Force One for the first time, to accompany the President to Hudson Valley Community College. The school was attended largely by adults, who sought the skills associated with the jobs and industries of the future, particularly in health care and clean energy. The future was squarely on President Obama's mind, even as he dealt with the immediate pressures of the acute economic recession; he wanted to do whatever he could to avert such circumstances again. So, in his address, he offered a vision for an economy without bubbles, one established on a firmer foundation than rampant financial speculation and over-leveraged consumer spending, one in which prosperity would be paved by skilled, productive workers leveraging public investments in the building blocks of innovation. Traditionally, as we outlined earlier in the book, government's infrastructure investment had been related to building roadways, railways, and runways. In the President's conception of an innovation economy, that notion of infrastructure would be broadened to include R&D; human capital, especially training in the science, technology, engineering, and math (STEM) disciplines; and digital infrastructure such as ubiquitous broadband access.

To transition ideas from the lab to the marketplace, the President called for new rules of the road, including technology-based reforms to expedite the patent approval process, which would allow for the introduction of more new products and services; streamlining regulations for new companies seeking to raise capital for growth; and instituting a new framework for global cooperation in the Internet economy through an emphasis on voluntary, enforceable codes of conduct to protect privacy and secure data. Ideally, sound public investments and market rules would spark the private sector to scale innovations throughout the economy, creating new jobs and industries and lifting incomes across an ever-growing middle class.

The President's vision even offered a path forward in solving some of the most seemingly intractable problems facing the country—bending the health care cost curve while improving quality;

transitioning to cleaner sources of energy; personalizing the learning system so every child could compete. Calling for an all-hands-on-deck approach to catalyze breakthroughs in these national priorities, the President spoke of a renewed spirit of collaboration among the public and private sectors; companies big, small, and new; citizen innovators, corporate labs, and the nation's leading research universities.[12]

Now we had a strategy. But we were missing an action plan. For that we needed to collaborate with business leaders from across the private sector. We needed some unusual, unexpected coalitions to emerge, in the name of shared progress. As noted in the prologue, we had gained some experience in this exercise in January 2010, when we gathered fifty of the most successful CEOs across a diverse set of industries for the White House Forum on Modernizing Government, to share their secrets for streamlining operations in a way that we could attempt to replicate in the federal government. At that gathering, President Obama gave a brief address, in which he called on them "to help us build the kind of government that the American people expect and the kind of government that they deserve—and that's one that spends their money wisely, serves their interests well, and is fully worthy of their trust and their respect." That meeting would result in several executive actions to close the IT gap between the public and private sectors, including initiatives to spur the use of cloud computing and mobile technologies in the name of improving access to citizen services.[13]

By December 2010, it was time to summon business leaders for another conversation. We congregated at the Blair House, right across from the White House, a place more commonly known as a site for housing and entertaining world leaders. This summit would require increased engagement from all parties, including the President, since even more was at stake. It was strictly about the economy, which was still slogging along at a pace that comforted no one, not with unemployment still above nine percent. This event came amid a great deal of noise, mainly from the Washington press corps, which had been harping incessantly and incorrectly on the President's difficulty in connecting productively with the business community, with some dismissing the meeting as a "photo op."[14] In reality, no photos were taken. No lobbyists were allowed. None but a handful of administration staff could participate. And no members of the press secured an invitation, with access restricted to a formal statement and some post-event interviews.

Rather, this was a "collaboration op," with the President seeking to strengthen the handshake between the public and private sectors to benefit the American people. For more than four hours, he spoke *with*—not *at*—twenty of the nation's leading CEOs, including those from General Electric, Comcast, Xerox, and Pepsi, on a broad range of topics, dedicating a full hour to ideas that would spark innovation and entrepreneurship. The day was split into five discussions, each of which would begin with opening remarks from two of the CEOs, followed by an intensive round of debate and dialogue facilitated by the President himself. The few staffers involved took on the role of transcribers, capturing the key points and ensuring we had an effective follow-through plan. Many of the CEOs later publicly reported, through a variety of media outlets, that they were pleasantly surprised and largely impressed.

Contrary to the widely held perception of Washington, D.C., as a place where nothing ever gets done, we collectively accomplished plenty in three key areas:

1) On patent reform, the President brokered a handshake commitment between the CEOs of Eli Lilly and Cisco, companies from two sectors—pharmaceuticals and technology—that had been at odds on the issue but were inching closer. They agreed to work together over the next 30 days to produce a compromise. With that secured, the President could move forward. In 2011, he

would sign into law the America Invents Act which, among other things, reduced the time to earn a patent decision by 40 percent, thus enabling innovators to focus on job creation and growth rather than bureaucracy and litigation.[15]

2) On startups, Kleiner Perkins venture capitalist John Doerr cited a research study that demonstrated the large proportion of job creation occurs *after* a company goes public, but that recent regulatory changes, including Sarbanes-Oxley, had the unintended effect of increasing the burdens of going public. The implication was clear—fewer initial public offerings meant fewer jobs. Could we better balance the need for regulation and disclosure with the economic benefits of more IPOs? In response, the President challenged his Treasury Secretary, Tim Geithner, to follow up this meeting by convening a broad set of stakeholders for the development of consensus recommendations to remove capital access barriers. This would ultimately lead to a component of the 2012 JOBS Act: extending the amount of time that a company had to comply with Sarbanes-Oxley, thus reducing the company's costs. This essentially created an IPO on-ramp, which several high-profile companies used the following year. That included Twitter, which raised $1.82 billion when it went public on November 7, 2013.[16]

3) On innovation, the President heard a presentation at the Blair House from Eric Schmidt, the CEO of Google, about the importance of wireless broadband to the economy, as well as about the exploding growth in mobile device usage. America had already led in the Internet economy—AOL through the dial-up era and firms such as Google, Facebook, and Twitter dominating in the broadband era. Now those firms were transitioning to a more competitive market for applications and services in this new era of smartphones and tablets.

Would these firms, and others from America, hold their own against innovators from China, Japan, Korea, and other present and future digital powerhouses, countries that had taken a more active role in preparing for mobile broadband? Details on this topic were discussed at a CTO meeting the following day. The resulting details led to the design of a National Wireless Initiative the President would announce in his 2011 State of the Union address and sign into law by February 2012. The new initiative would authorize the use of "incentive auctions" to create a private market for spectrum (the use of airwaves to transmit information like television, radio, and the Internet), thus ensuring the cell phone industry would have the resources necessary to minimize dropped calls and maximize mobile economic benefits. It would also fund the last remaining request of the 9/11 Commission—to ensure first responders had access to communications systems that interacted with one another, reducing the risk of unnecessary harm on account of errant or incomplete information. And it would invest in R&D to make it more likely that the next generation of mobile computing would be invented in the United States rather than abroad. Better yet, it would contribute billions toward deficit reduction.[17]

Some of the technology leaders who participated in the productive Blair House meeting—and helped shape the subsequent policy initiatives—lent their expertise in other areas. Eric Schmidt was one such contributor, serving as an adviser to the President on his Council of Advisers on Science and Technology (PCAST).[18] He would join his fellow PCAST members in drawing attention to the importance and opportunity associated with "Big Data," the catchphrase that acknowledges the exponential growth in digital information related to everything we do, from social networking to advanced manufacturing. Their recommendation to the President was for each federal agency to conceive and execute a "Big Data" strategy.[19] In March 2012, the President announced that six agencies, including the Department of Defense and the National Institutes of Health, were making $200 million in new commitments related to improving the tools and techniques needed to access, organize, and understand "huge volumes of digital data." As the strategy evolved, the President would more explicitly link the Big Data initiatives to national priorities, including economic growth, improving health and education, and stimulating clean energy.[20]

Through these and other measures, we were progressing toward an innovation economy, which had been among my core assignments as Chief Technology Officer.

In early 2012, I informed the President that I would be leaving the administration to run for office in Virginia, as part of a longer-term vision to implement a more innovative government in a state that, at Jamestown in 1607, had served as the birthplace of American democracy.

Weeks prior to my departure, the President invited my family to the Oval Office, where he entertained my wife and two daughters with tales of the design touches that he and Michelle had added. Then he turned his attention to me, thanking me for my service, expressing enthusiasm for my upcoming political campaign, and outlining my final assignment. He wanted me to produce a memo that not only summarized what occurred during my tenure but also organized some of the core tenets in a way that the work could outlast not only my time in office, but his as well.

That homework was in keeping with the nickname ("Chief Memo Officer") that my wife had given me during my tenure, as she watched me draft countless policy ideas and options for my White House colleagues. I framed the assignment in the form of a playbook, one that distilled complex concepts into a format that was simple to understand, with guidelines and principles to assist my successor, as well as the growing numbers of CTOs across federal agencies and at state and local levels.[21]

I had a head start, not just from my experiences inside government, but from the lessons learned during my parallel exploration of the private sector, where many of the principles not only had their origins, but had shown sustainability in their success. In fact, some could be directly traced to the professor Henry Chesbrough—with whom, in the fall of 2011, I had shared a lengthy lunch prior to speaking to his class at the Haas Business School at the University of California-Berkeley. Chesbrough had long been hailed as the godfather of "open innovation," which he had defined in his first of several books as "a paradigm that assumes that firms can and should use external ideas as well as internal ideas, and internal and external paths to market, as the firms look to advance their technology." Inside the Obama administration, I had been championing a public sector version inspired by what I knew of his private sector work, and I had been attempting to institutionalize that offshoot as part of the federal government culture. At our lunch, I explained not only how we had implemented some of those "open innovation" ideas, but how I viewed the roles of the private sector in connecting with our government work: as a contributor, a beneficiary, or a collaborator.

First, the private sector could extend the arm of government, helping us deliver services closer and closer, and faster and faster, to the place and time that citizens needed them. Second, the private sector could take a handoff from government, taking information that the public sector had previously collected for its own purposes and using it to create new commercial products and services, such as the multibillion-dollar weather industry. Third, in certain circumstances, we could join hands and remove barriers to improvements in areas of paramount importance to the American people, such as health care and education.

Throughout the rest of this book, I will further flesh out the elements that animate these three private sector roles in solving public problems. But at the outset, let's explore the origins of the private sector's use of open innovation.

According to Chesbrough, open innovation was the offshoot of a series of management innovations designed to strengthen U.S. competitiveness.

In the 1960s, Robert McNamara, the former president of Ford Motor Company who had become the Secretary of Defense, brought the concept of "systems analysis," the allocation of priorities and resources across projects based on total costs and benefits, from the Ford factories into the Defense Department. In the 1970s, the soaring success of NASA's Apollo missions to the moon surfaced innovations in program management to better identify the critical path toward completing a project and how to make the necessary adjustments when the most important activities along that path fell behind schedule. In the 1980s, the Japanese model for total quality management found American academic champions in W. Edwards Deming and Joseph Juran. That led to very intricate processes such as Six Sigma, which was attributable largely to Motorola, and relied upon specialized teams that targeted the reduction of defects, variability, and waste.

By the 1990s, the supply-chain management approach flourished through the use of software and data to strengthen the ties that bind suppliers and producers and squeeze out inefficiencies. As the Internet scaled, so, too, did the ability of firms to better manage inventories, reacting to changes in customer demand, to the point where Amazon and Dell would accept customer orders before even assembling the final product. These advancements facilitated, among other things, globalization, with the declining cost of communication creating greater cultural and economic exchange between countries. At the turn of the century, the Internet seized an even greater role in interconnecting a firm's product development assets—from customers, suppliers, universities, third parties, and individuals—along the innovation process. It even resulted in firms repurposing ideas that couldn't quite make the cut but might lead to value creation in the hands of another partner.

Procter & Gamble, as much as any entity in the corporate sphere, has embodied the evolution of management practices toward what Chesbrough labels open innovation. The company's transformation accelerated in the 2000s, catalyzed by A. G. Lafley's elevation to CEO and his mission to go beyond in-house tinkering through the customary corporate actions: more meetings, organizational shuffling, executive recruiting, or increasing demands on those already employed. Transformational change required knocking down walls, to allow for the contributions of innovators who weren't part of the payroll. It meant taking note of all the strategic, targeted innovations that raw materials suppliers had brought to P&G as well as recognizing that the company as a whole would be better off if it moved beyond those limited successes and pursued outside contributions even more broadly. It meant admitting, according to company CTO Bruce Brown, that "sometimes the best and brightest may not be employed at your company," or even in the country, and that products originating in places like Japan could lead to partnerships to produce P&G applications.

All of that ambition meant the need for something else: a culture change. "Getting people to look outside," Brown said. "Getting people to realize that there might be somebody outside of my walls who has a better idea than I do. And an organization that had traditionally always done things internally, to begin looking externally, and then also saying there might be some people who can do this better or faster than we can. Then we'll bring our expertise, with the global reach of our brand, to our ability to execute, and other strengths, to make this happen faster and better."

That meant bold leadership and a clear message that this "open" philosophy would be central to the company's operating strategy. Lafley established a goal that 50 percent of innovations would include a significant external component within the decade, and created metrics to monitor and accelerate that progress.[22] In

2002, Lafley even instituted an official apparatus to drive that innovation, one that has since served as the company's signature. It was called Connect + Develop, and it assigned 80 members of the R&D staff to take on the new title of "technology scout." They were charged with exploring externally to create a network of ideas and people that might augment or improve P&G's portfolio of products and stable of innovators. The aim was to replicate the success of the electric Spinbrush. A small group of entrepreneurs had initially developed that dental hygiene product, sold it to P&G for more than 300 times their initial investment, assisted P&G in the launch under the company's Crest name, and watched as it catapulted Crest back to the top spot in its market.

The company encouraged innovators of all types and sizes—independent entrepreneurs, government laboratories, contract laboratories, research institutes, suppliers, academicians, communities of practice, subject matter experts—to "connect" with P&G through a chance to collaborate and develop. To be considered, an idea needed to address a major, unmet consumer need; offer a new benefit to an existing P&G category or brand; or feature such elements as proven technology, a demonstrated packaging solution, or evidence of consumer interest.

The results? You might see many of them inside the cabinets or on the countertops of your home. For some of the products, P&G collaborated with companies that are competitors in other spaces. For instance, while Clorox is one of P&G's biggest competitors in the cleaning products sector, the companies share an interest in Glad, and jointly developed Glad Press'n Seal, with P&G developing plastic film technology and Clorox taking the lead in commercialization. The private sector powerhouses joined together on another initiative that ultimately led to Glad Force-Flex trash bags.

Some of the products came to the P&G family from other countries, such as the Swiffer duster, purchased in a fully formed state from a Japanese competitor; or the antiwrinkle cream Olay Regenerist, which emerged out of a technical conference in Europe, where P&G's skin-care researchers learned of a new peptide technology developed by a small cosmetics company in France for the healing of battlefield wounds.

A few of the collaborative products have allowed P&G to return to its roots. Originally a soap and candle company, P&G had not sold candles for more than eight decades, before partnering with a candle company to produce Febreze candles. Other collaborations, sometimes involving P&G taking technology and knowledge in and sometimes sending technology and knowledge out, have led to frequent expansion or improvement of existing product lines.

One collaboration stood out, not just because P&G's partner was the public sector, but because of the unlikely source of the solution. That is the story that I wanted Bruce Brown to share with President Obama when I recommended they meet in June 2011 at Carnegie Mellon University in Pittsburgh, Pennsylvania, on the heels of the President's new Advanced Manufacturing Partnership aimed at facilitating greater R&D collaboration for creating the jobs of the future and increasing global competitiveness. A few years earlier, P&G had worked with Los Alamos National Laboratory in New Mexico, tapping into the laboratory's data on nuclear physics to improve the development of diapers. Yes, diapers. Diapers are made at a rate of about 1,000 per minute. Due to that speed, the sand particles that absorb liquid are sprayed all over the place, rather than where a child would typically urinate. "You'd like to have as much of it in the crotch as you could," Brown said. "The ability to do that—in this violent reaction—that's basically you are just blowing this stuff around to lie it down in a precise pattern. It's a great technical challenge. Well, Los Alamos had all this code for how particles behave in a nuclear explosion."

Together, they applied that code to develop a software tool and then a superior product. P&G then announced that it would provide its high-performance computing models for free to small- and medium-size businesses, sparking a new industry of "on-demand" manufacturing tools.[23] Brown estimated savings of more than $1 billion over the years, including the software applications and related professional services, as a result of this Los Alamos collaboration.And the collaboration continues with a Los Alamos scientist now embedded with P&G.

Brown described the U.S. national laboratories as a "treasure trove of expertise." The Connect + Develop program, as a whole, has proven to be a treasure trove of cash for P&G. Yet even as it has spurred billions of dollars in annual sales growth, according to company disclosures, executives have been careful not to take the innovation culture for granted, with expediency always alluring.[24] "I would say it remains a challenge," Brown said. "You have to avoid greater value being placed on internal development rather than external development. That's a constant watch-out. You have to make sure you reward people who are doing external work in addition to internal work. Making sure you are clear on what's important, that you reward it correctly, that it's strategic and that it's valued and you invest it and you organize for it and you operationalize it on an ongoing basis. We fooled ourselves for a little while thinking it was Connect + Expand. It really is Connect + Develop. You usually have to do some work to make things work. This isn't something you just put in place and leave it. The Los Alamos story is a great example. They didn't have a computing program to make a diaper; we had to take it and adapt it."

The necessity of never-ending supervision and aspiration, even at one of America's most pioneering companies, left an indelible mark on Chesbrough. "What I've learned from companies like P&G and many others," he said, "is that before you can really effectively innovate in any open way beyond the boundary of your own firm, you have to become more open *internally* within your firm."

The respect for internal talent was embodied in the widely told stories of Jeff Bezos, the founder and CEO of Amazon.com. Bezos didn't want his employees operating in a culture where they were concerned about getting the approval of superiors for every decision, fearful of stepping out of their boxes, out of line, and into trouble. Rather, he espoused the corporate value of Bias for Action. He encouraged initiative and risk taking with his Just Do It awards, through which he would honor employees for implementing their thoughtful ideas without seeking permission—even if the resulting project didn't succeed. Their reward? He would read an employee's accomplishments aloud, invite the employee onstage for a handshake, and then hand that employee a used Nike shoe—a symbolic prize for having just done something well.

That, I would learn, wasn't all that Amazon did internally.

Bezos was participating in the company's Customer Connection program, in which executives work with the employees in the customer service department to get a taste of that experience. He took a call from a customer whose table had arrived with its top scratched. The course of action was clear enough: send out a replacement, move on to the next call. Except that, in this case, an employee nearby revealed to Bezos that this same complaint had been lodged by different customers several times before. The consistency of those complaints hadn't been shared with anyone up the Amazon chain, simply because there was no mechanism to report such issues.

Armed with this information, the managers discovered that the problem wasn't the product itself, but what it had been wrapped and sent in. Amazon reached out to the vendor, which expeditiously improved the packaging.

That was just one issue, however. What about all the others that might crop up across Amazon's extensive assortment of available items for purchase? After all, it did not serve the overall health of a service-oriented company for critical information to stay siloed in customer service, hidden from others along the Amazon chain, who, if they knew about it, might take action.

Inspired by that single customer call, Bezos set out to improve Amazon's feedback loops by empowering all of its customer service reps, modeling efforts after the lean manufacturing principles that Toyota used on its factory floor. The automobile giant had given every assembly line worker the right to pull an andon cord when confronted with a defect, effectively stopping production until the problem was resolved, and allowing for the recording of the episode in a database so it would be reviewed for possible patterns that might be preventable. Now Amazon would give its customer service reps the authority to remove from the online catalog any product causing consistent issues for customers. That decision would prompt the distribution of a report to the manager of that retail category and motivating that manager to move on it, since sales of the product were stopped until the defect was fixed. Additionally, the company would give its customer service reps something almost as important: cover. The reps merely needed to offer their reasoning to demonstrate that they had exercised good judgment. They didn't necessarily need to be right.

Without question, making this option available to frontline workers, regardless of title, required a great deal of trust. In the process, it engendered good will, with those workers feeling their voices were heard and they had a tool to perform their jobs better. And while the retail managers may not have initially appreciated the removal of items from inventory, the benefits eventually became clear through fewer customer service contacts and fewer returns and replacements.

The message of the andon story is unmistakable. Why should an organization reserve the sourcing of innovative ideas to only a select few deemed worthy of offering such input? Why would an organization cultivate a culture in which those with knowledge to share would feel marginalized?

Amazon is a shining example of open innovation in another sense: it has produced what Chesbrough calls "a force multipler element," a phrase that has military roots and business applicability. It has done so through its visionary business decision to open its e-commerce platform to external retailers—from used-book dealers to electronic shops to clothing companies to major department stores. It has invited those merchants, some of them competitors, to use that platform to provide an Amazon-like customer experience, in terms of content hosting and order fulfillment, in exchange for a fee.

Other companies have created their own force multipliers, including Apple, which has done so through its iPhone app store, inviting hundreds of thousands of web developers to offer new services that can be monetized at attractive rates. The business prospects for those developers were strong enough to convince venture capital firm Kleiner Perkins to establish a $200 million iFund. "When a professional investor decides it's a great decision to invest their own money in startups that are going to be building things that are going to be making your platform more valuable for *you,* it's the most valuable business model of all, because it harnesses other people's money, talent, ideas, and so forth," Chesbrough said. "It's other people's money making you and your business more successful."

These examples aside, I found the concept of a platform providing a force multiplier to be best crystallized over a week in August 2011.

The President's Council on Jobs and Competitiveness held a town hall–style meeting in Silicon Valley to share an update and invite public feedback.[25] The event attracted a bevy of technology's elite, including Facebook COO Sheryl Sandberg, a former Treasury Department official in the Clinton administration. Sandberg explained how, early in its rise as the world's most utilized social network, Facebook chose to unleash the power of its platform to the public. It published an application programming interface (API) to extend access to a user's data to third-party developers, accompanied by the appropriate privacy and security permissions and protections. As with Amazon, this decision would serve as a "force multiplier," inviting entrepreneurs and innovators to invest their time and resources to enrich the customer experience for Facebook's customer base, in a way that would generate revenue for their company as well as for Facebook.

Sandberg shared the latest accounting, in aggregate, of the job impact of this new "Facebook economy." While the company's official head count was approximately 2,500 employees—most based in Palo Alto, California—she found over 30,000 Facebook Developer openings on a popular job search board. None of the people filling those positions would ever appear on Facebook's balance sheet or Human Resources list. Rather, they would come from, and remain at, firms like the gaming startup Zynga and its smaller kin, focused on building services through the Facebook API.

This sort of job explosion was unconstrained by geography, meaning that, while the bulk of those jobs were in the United States, the apps economy as a whole is as global as the Internet economy, making it America's race to win or lose. The tech industry trade association, TechNet, published a study in 2011 estimating the size of the apps economy at almost $20 billion and 466,000 jobs—which just scratches the surface of its potential. The study also included a map of America to demonstrate the dispersed nature of these jobs, with all 50 states represented.[26]

It didn't take long for me to find some of them. Four days after Sandberg's insights at the Silicon Valley event, I was on Main Street in Blacksburg, Virginia, for a stop on the administration's annual Rural Tour. My colleagues fanned out across the country, participating in state fairs or, in my case as CTO, visiting university towns with a hunger for growing new industries. Blacksburg is home to Virginia Tech, a world-class research institution with the motto of "Invent the Future" and a welcoming place for entrepreneurs engaged in the Internet economy. That included the dozen firms headquartered in TechPad, a startup incubator on the second floor above a popular Main Street bar.

During my visit to TechPad, I encountered a Virginia Tech sophomore, Nathan Latka, who had already begun hiring in the Facebook economy for Lujure, later to be renamed Heyo, which developed fan pages for small businesses. Latka had started the service in his dorm room and, to that point, had one employee. The following March, after leaving the White House, I would return to TechPad to check in on his progress. It was remarkable. By tapping into a real need, Heyo was on pace to generate $1.7 million in revenue by year's end, making his company profitable. He was up to 14 employees and, to meet the insatiable customer demand, was in the middle of a funding round to raise another $500,000, for hiring more employees, aligning with strategic partners, and empowering small business owners. One partner was David Clark, an Idaho man who had quit a high-paying job with Yellow Pages to launch Social Media Gurus, which consulted with small businesses on social, mobile, and web strategy. He leveraged the Heyo tool to support well over 200 small businesses in the development of their fan pages, mobile apps, and websites.

By September 2012, just over a year to the day Sandberg shared her insight on the jobs impact of Facebook's decision to open its social graph API, staff of Heyo would be standing side by side with Virginia Governor Bob McDonnell, announcing a commitment to hire 50 workers in Blacksburg over the next two years, dramatically outgrowing the office space at TechPad.

There's another promising phase of open innovation, one in which the lines between company and customer blur, as customer engagement along the chain compels the rapid design of service features to meet clear needs. This trend, in Chesbrough's view, is another element that differentiates open innovation from earlier management innovations, in that "customers, voters, citizens, users are not simply passive recipients." Rather, they are "prosumers, producer-consumers, or people who are actively engaged in cocreating." Chesbrough covered this phenomenon in our conversations and in his most recent book, *Open Services Innovation*, as it related to digital music and the shrinking distance between artist and audience. In the old days, captured in many a movie, traditional record companies would send talent scouts to smoke-filled clubs in search of the next big act and, after uncovering performers with promise, would sign those artists up to long-term deals, create their packaging and marketing, promote them to radio stations, release their albums, and send them on multicity tours.

"Most of the time these bands didn't make much of a dent, but sometimes one would break through, and that one breakthrough would kind of cover the cost of all those who didn't," Chesbrough said. "But in the digital music environment, that vertical chain of value added between the artist and the consumer has really been disaggregated."

The music production chain is now disrupted at each step by new websites, applications, and companies that serve as a loose confederation of music services, all aimed at aligning the interests of those who create music and those who influence and enjoy it. The public doesn't need to wait for a compact disc and a marketing campaign; it can now unearth new songs and styles through the likes of Last.fm, Pandora, and YouTube, and spread the word through social media and trendsetting sites. The public can even help fund the rise of musicians on sites such as Kickstarter or ArtistShare, with sponsors allowed to watch recording sessions and gain access to extra material that the artist has produced. Ideally, when the two parties are in it together, artists will get better feedback and audiences will get better music.

While Chesbrough's description of the music industry was in reference to, and in the prism of, private enterprises, I was struck by how much this philosophy of looking and getting beyond boundaries animated a view that President Obama had articulated in shaping our open government vision. That was the principle, borrowed from Austrian economist Friedrich Hayek, of knowledge being "widely dispersed," and that, to solve problems, we should harness the power of technology and innovation to tap into it.[27]

Mitch Kapor, the legendary founder of Lotus Development Corporation, saw these concepts clearly, and spoke of them in the context of an important public policy issue—health care reform. He had come to the same core conclusion about health IT that Chesbrough had drawn from his study of the legacy music industry: that value could be created through a more active consumer. He had come to another conclusion: that there was "a yawning chasm" in mindset and capability between those participating in the lightning-fast Internet economy and those operating in the health IT space.

He tried to bridge that gap while keynoting the Health Information Technology Platform symposium on the Harvard Medical School campus in September 2009.[28] A group comprised of nearly 100 health IT leaders gathered to propose practical, actionable steps to create a health IT platform. From Kapor, they heard that to improve health through the use of IT, "It would have to be along the open innovation lines, because it was just never going to get there otherwise. Just never, ever happen."

He left the audience with clear takeaways, centering on the need for open standards, decentralized architecture, and even a role for government—all concepts that fit neatly into the open innovation framework. Concerning that government role, he envisioned a light federal approach, similar to the one that governs the Internet, with no single government entity running it from up top. The Internet operates through a decentralized multistakeholder network comprised of leaders in the public, private, and academic communities. The U.S. government simply serves as a facilitator, to insure that information flows across boundaries. It does so through its support for the Internet Corporation for Assigned Names and Numbers (ICANN)—essentially the address book for the Internet. Kapor believed that the government could build on the foundation of the Internet and serve as a facilitator for the safe, secure, free flow of health information. That meant using its convening power to achieve consensus on a set of technical standards and encouraging an early "critical mass" of users from the private sector to participate.

Even more important than the government's role on the technical front was its responsibility to alter the payment system in health care. More specifically, it needed to shift the reimbursement model to reward providers who focused on keeping patients healthy, rather than just treating them after they are sick. Such a change would create market opportunities for new products and services that can assist providers in identifying patients who should be prioritized, because of their risk of illness, and then find better ways to reach and monitor them. (That payment reform authority would become law when the Affordable Care Act was passed in March of 2010.)

This health Internet would be different and better from what was widely available already: the hundreds of health apps downloadable on app stores but lacking access to full personal medical records. It would capitalize on the freeing of that data to unleash a prosumer model, in which patients not only provide the data but also constructively interact with medical professionals along the chain. That could alter the way in which health care is delivered. For instance, a patient might wish to share lab results from the emergency room with his personal doctor for better care coordination, reducing the need for unnecessary additional tests.

The vision of a health Internet marketplace was a natural extension of Chesbrough's open innovation framework, applied in government. After participating in the Harvard meeting, I returned to Washington with Todd Park, then the Chief Technology Officer of the Department of Health and Human Services, as its advocate. As we will recount in depth in Chapter 5, it led to the birth of the Health Data Initiative and contributed to the creation of more than 200 products and services (according to a McKinsey & Company estimate) in its first three years.[29]

Through my experience, I accumulated considerable evidence that the open innovation model, so effective in the private sector, also works in what Chesbrough dubbed "the mother of all services," the government. And it works in much the same manner that culture creation, maintenance, and expansion advanced P&G; that tapping into frontline workers assisted Amazon; and that the force multiplier of standardizing open interfaces propelled Facebook. Just as the private sector achieved more with less and then replicated and scaled those achievements, the government could use those same open innovation principles to achieve more innovation and better outcomes, with less taxpayer investment. It could cut through some of the tired debates about the size of government.

"A more open, innovative government isn't really described as either big or small, but rather how government can be effective . . . as a partner to the private sector, not as a replacement for it," Chesbrough said. "This isn't an argument for going from 2,000 to 50,000 government workers. It's using 2,000 government workers to create a platform that invites 50,000 external participants to build on top of it."

Government's role in the economy should be, in Chesbrough's view, to "do enough to liberate or harness the energies of the private sector"—and in doing so, bring the two together.

"These [open innovation] initiatives have the effect of giving more information to more people sooner," Chesbrough said. "Instead of distancing people from government, they have a way of connecting people to government, and, indeed, empowering people through data and information from the government to improve services in their own lives, from the local city block to the regional and national levels."

But how would we give some permanence to these connections, specifically at the federal level, so they would outlast any administration? How would we institutionalize a culture change, taking a page from, among others, Procter & Gamble? How would we guide successors on choosing and shepherding open innovation projects, whether that meant freeing data, fostering collaboration for the lowering of barriers to entry, or engaging third-party application developers to act as force multipliers?

Those were the questions that I attempted to answer in crafting the aforementioned, in-house memo that President Obama assigned—and in the related version that was released to the public. I called that version the Open Innovator's Toolkit, a compilation of case studies where government agencies had successfully applied these open innovation principles through the use of four different policy tools. The four tools represented not an expansion of government, but an expansion of the available options—often within existing authorities and resources—for policymakers to deploy from any level of government, anywhere in the world. They were designed to give policymakers the license, impetus, and ability to break down the walls between the government and the best and brightest entrepreneurs, so all parties could speak a common language.[30]

These four tools are:

Open data. This entails enabling the public to access more of the information that is stored in digital file cabinets throughout the government, not simply for the sake of transparency, but so it can be incorporated in new products and services to help businesses grow.

Impatient convening. This refers to government's role inviting the private sector to work collaboratively on standards that lower barriers to entry and increase competition, especially in public and regulated industries such as energy, education, and health care.

Challenges and prizes. This involves casting a much wider net to solve a particular problem than available through traditional, often cumbersome and wasteful government procurement; and paying for actual results rather than flashy proposals.

Attracting talent. This includes recruiting entrepreneurs into the government, to team up with similarly skilled public officials in a startup setting, to produce breakthrough results in a tight time frame.

These four concepts, collectively, open the way for a new paradigm in American government, not the small agrarian state matching the early republic, nor the bureaucracy that grew after the Civil War, nor the inefficient relic of the New Deal, but a twenty-first century government that elevates the role of everyday Americans.

The open innovation story is, at its core, about those everyday Americans, those worthy of the "wise and frugal government" that Thomas Jefferson envisioned in his first inaugural address.[31] They deserve a way of thinking that empowers rather than divides, that confronts challenges rather than creating them, that solicits all types of expertise rather than espousing tired approaches. They deserve an American democracy that isn't defined by the playing of political games, but by the way it allows its citizenry to play a constructive role.

Open innovation is about handshakes and handoffs: the handshakes between powerful, enabling entities that allow for the handoffs to those with the hope, ambition, inspiration, and ideas to make our country better, in every conceivable way.

Chapter 5

Open Data

Thomas Jefferson was something of a weather nut. Well prior to 1776, he made careful observations and kept meticulous records of meteorological events at assorted Virginia locations, especially at his Monticello residence, where his routine included two weather records per day—once when he woke at dawn, often the coldest time of the day, the other between 3 and 4 p.m. when he had found it to be the hottest.[1] In July of that year, he was in Pennsylvania, for a rather momentous occasion in American history: the signing of a document he helped craft, the Declaration of Independence. Yet he still found time to squeeze in a visit to a nearby merchant to purchase a thermometer and then document Philadelphia's morning, afternoon, and evening temperatures in his diary. For the record, at 1 p.m. on July 4, Philadelphia's conditions were clear and mild, with a high of 76 degrees.[2]

Jefferson later took his weather passion overseas. While Minister to France from 1785 to 1789, he sought the most accurate instruments available, to compare readings with those in his home country, and validate the viability of America's agrarian ambitions. According to the *Thomas Jefferson Encyclopedia,* "His initially patriotic motive was to topple one of the two 'pillars' of the theory of degeneracy of animal life in America advanced by the Comte de Buffon and other European scholars—America's alleged excessive humidity. Also in his role as champion of the North American continent, Jefferson began in Paris to compile a record of the ratio of cloudy to sunny skies. After a five-year residence in France, he had proved to himself that America completely eclipsed Europe in the sunshine contest and he appreciated more than ever the 'cheerful,' sunny climate of his native country."

After winning his first of two Presidential terms in 1801, Jefferson incorporated weather observation into official government duties. He did so most famously with the Lewis and Clark Expedition in 1804, instructing the western-bound explorers to observe "climate as characterized by the thermometer, by the proportion of rainy, cloudy & clear days, by lightening, hail, snow, ice, by the access & recess of frost, by the winds prevailing at different seasons . . ."

Over the next few decades, other leaders began to promote greater weather data collection. During the War of 1812, James Tilton, the Surgeon General of the Army, called for his fellow hospital surgeons to do so. During the 1830s and 1840s, James Pollard Espy, a meteorologist known as the Storm King, secured state (Pennsylvania) and federal funding to expand and equip a network of weather volunteers. In 1849, Joseph Henry, the first Secretary of the Smithsonian Institution, found a way to capitalize on exciting new technology: the commercial telegraph, which had been introduced four years earlier.[3] Henry established a novel public-private partnership, convincing many telegraph companies to waive transmission fees on all weather recordings sent to the Smithsonian's forecasters for analysis. Within a decade, after receiving the cooperation of telegraph stations from New York to New Orleans, Henry was able to produce a daily weather map for nearly 20 cities, and share it for publication in the *Washington Evening Star*.

Still, the federal government remained small, and there was no formal weather agency at the start of the Civil War. Nor was there one by its end, even as government was growing some in size—in

1862, the Department of Agriculture was founded, and from 1861 through the end of the decade, the number of federal workers nearly tripled.[4] Then, on February 9, 1870, several months before the founding of a more heralded agency—the Department of Justice was formed to handle the postwar surge in litigation—President Ulysses S. Grant signed Congress' joint resolution to create the Division of Telegrams and Reports for the Benefit of Commerce.[5] That agency, operating under the U.S. Army Signal Corps, was charged with making meteorological observations at military stations "and other points in the States and Territories," while using magnetic telegraph and marine signals to give notice "of the approach and force of storms." Two decades later, President Benjamin Harrison initiated the transfer of weather-related duties to the Department of Agriculture on the civilian side of government.[6] Through the passage of the National Weather Service Organic Act of 1890, the new U.S. Weather Bureau was directed not only to collect data but to "publicly distribute weather information useful to sectors of the nation's agriculture, communications, commerce, and navigation interests."[7]

That mandate and mission of openness remained consistent throughout the next several decades, even after the U.S. Weather Bureau's move to the Commerce Department in 1940, and even as advancements in technology transformed the means of weather collection. The evolution in data-gathering instruments can be traced from kites (late nineteenth century) to upper air balloons (early twentieth century) to reconnaissance airplanes (1920s), all the way to radar and satellites—the remote sensing tools that were initially developed to serve the military but co-opted by weather data collectors in the late 1950s and early 1960s, respectively.

In 1970, thanks to President Richard Nixon's order, the U.S. Weather Bureau was renamed the National Weather Service (NWS) and moved to another new home—the Commerce Department's National Oceanic and Atmospheric Administration

(NOAA).[8] NOAA would eventually become a behemoth, one now with an annual budget in excess of $5 billion, much of that utilized by the NWS to deploy weather-monitoring satellites, run its national and regional centers, and run its local forecast offices.[9] As that has occurred, a robust private weather industry has emerged alongside, using the government data but providing greater customization and analysis in forecasting—for the likes of airlines, utilities, and agriculture firms—than the NWS, with its limited staffing, can always offer. For instance, since 1976, New York–based CompuWeather, with its staff of certified meteorologists, has provided forensic work to document past weather events for the purpose of insurance companies and attorneys validating claims, while also providing forecasts for film production companies so they know where and when to shoot.[10]

These two growing enterprises have benefited from refinements in policy, to reduce the natural tension between them. In 1978, NOAA adopted a policy that it would not "provide specialized services for business or industry when the services are currently offered or can be offered by a commercial enterprise."[11] Over the next three decades, the agency would further clarify the parameters of its partnership with the private sector, while endeavoring to make forecasting more relevant and precise. In 2004, it tweaked its data format from a proprietary one to an open Internet standard called XML, lowering barriers to entry and thus expanding the base of potential participants.[12] Now, more than 50 percent of the members of the American Meteorological Society are employed in the private sector.[13]

Through it all, NOAA's mission has remained the same: "making data easy and affordable . . . creating a more informed public, providing unbiased information . . . and giving the commercial weather industry an opportunity to flourish."

No entity has flourished quite like The Weather Channel. Incorporated in 1980 and launched in 1982 as a cable network to disrupt the more traditional model of accessing weather data since the 1950s—which was through your local television station's news broadcast—The Weather Channel's strategy was built on a simple understanding. As current CEO David Kenny put it, "Weather is personal, weather is very local." Most people wanted to know what the weather was and would be where they lived, not necessarily anywhere else. They also wanted to know it consistently and *frequently*, without waiting for the local news at six or 11. That required taking the available government data, sorting it by ZIP code, and delivering it via the company's innovative Satellite Transmission and Receiving System (STARS), to homes with cable systems throughout America. It also meant doing it on a steady clock. "There wouldn't be a Weather Channel without localization every 10 minutes," Kenny said. While there have been many STARS upgrades and generations since, local updates have remained a staple, known since 1996 as Local on the 8s.

"We tell the story better, we make it more useful, we make it more relevant, and we add value to the science," Kenny noted.

That's added value to the company. According to a Magid study that was quoted in AdWeek, The Weather Channel had "150 million unduplicated consumers across TV, online and mobile" as of the fourth quarter of 2011, and it is still the undisputed leader in a $1.5 billion industry. Kenny acknowledges that this success never could have occurred without the government's open data policy. If the company had been responsible for all of the infrastructure costs, notably the necessary recording equipment, rather than merely leveraging the available government data, the channel's launch would have been long delayed, and most certainly cost-prohibitive. It might have never gotten off the ground. But there's more to it: once The Weather Channel took off on cable, the continued access to that data, at a nominal cost, left the company with sufficient resources for additional innovation in the years to come. One innovation was Weather.com, which grants users reports and forecasts, in real time, for some 100,000 locations. Then, as newer technologies provided opportunities, the company was able to create a mobile application, which, in 2013, Apple ranked as the second-most downloaded application on its iPad and the seventh-most on the iPhone.[14] Now Weather.com even produces weather sections for local broadcasters' mobile apps. And, in the winter of 2013, The Weather Channel took Local on the 8s to the next level, launching a continuous, real-time scroll of local conditions, making even the television set appear more like a mobile app.

"All of this comes from open data," Kenny said.

The Weather Channel doesn't just take. It gives back. Every year it voluntarily communicates more than 100,000 National Weather Service alerts to its audiences, to assist the agency in its public safety mission. Its team of scientists puts many models and findings back in open source for meteorologists at the NWS (and throughout NOAA) to study, apply, and send back for further conversation, adaptation, and application.

"There's a whole meteorological community," Kenny said. "It's always been this sort of mutual mission of science that's kept us going. So I think this is a living thing. It's not just that they post the data, and we repurpose it. We think it's important that there be continuing collaboration."

Both sides—public and private—share knowledge and opinions in times of major weather disturbances, or even in the aftermath, in order to identify areas for improvement. Such reviews occurred after the Eyjafjallajökull volcano in Iceland paralyzed European air traffic in 2010. A Weather Channel subsidiary met with the Met Office in the United Kingdom as well as the London Volcanic Ash Advisory Center to exchange, blend, and align forecast techniques and practices. The result was that, when another Icelandic volcano erupted a year later, the impact on air traffic was considerably less.

As technology advances, more knowledge can be gained—even about which way the wind will blow. The Weather Channel's latest initiatives speak to what's possible at the intersection of technology, open energy, and weather data. It has long been known that the clean energy sector, wind farms more specifically, could dramatically improve productivity and profitability by optimizing how to angle wind blades based on real-time changes in weather. Historically, however, this has not been possible, because the changes in wind patterns simply occur too quickly. But now, by using new technologies such as cloud computing, The Weather Channel is able to fully exploit the data, by creating algorithms that better predict those patterns. Late in 2012, Kenny said The Weather Channel was already selling that product inside and outside the United States as a pilot and was planning to release version 2.0 in 2014, in the hopes of aligning data, decisions, and energy markets so they could move as fast as the wind.

"We're crossing new thresholds in terms of data and the ability to manage 'Big Data,'" Kenny said. "It may not have been useful to release it in the past, but it is incredibly useful today."

More than useful. Necessary. That's why other governments and businesses worldwide call upon The Weather Channel to share its data assimilation and computing models; the general mission is the same for all of those entities, real-time data, wherever and whenever, even if the immediate plans for that data are different.

"What's clear to me is the nations that figure out how to use their data and share their data and put it in the grid give their businesses and citizens a leg up versus nations that don't," Kenny said. "If I look at the disparity in weather information that's given to African farmers and farmers in Kansas, it's huge. It makes a difference. But that gap will change and close in time as data becomes available. And you compete on the basis of data and information as a nation."

Kenny deems it much too early to declare a winner on wind, even as some countries—such as those in Scandinavia—have integrated it heavily into their policy. He is certain, however, that data will be critical to making any such policy work.

"People pay us a price for our interpretation of free data, because we interpret it in a better way," Kenny said. "But at the core of it, data collection and data availability and speed in the use of modern technology will increasingly create competitive nations. And nations that don't necessarily have natural resources to compete upon can change their competitiveness by the way they use information and provide it."

When we tell the open data story, we're not just talking about the weather.

Even prior to our nation's founding, governments have been collecting data on the population here, through surveys. The British government did so to count the number of people in the colonies in the early seventeenth century. And, under the direction of then-Secretary of State Thomas Jefferson, the U.S. federal government took its first official census in 1790, with another occurring every 10 years since.

This has become an extensive and expensive enterprise: the 23rd census, conducted in 2010, came in under budget and still cost roughly $13.1 billion.[15] Through all of those decades, government agencies have collected additional data for a host of purposes—holding regulated entities accountable, conducting research on key social and economic trends, processing individual benefits, and so forth. The methods of data analysis have evolved over that time as well. In 1886, an employee of the U.S. Census Office named Herman Hollerith invented an electrical punch-card reader that could be used to process information; a decade later, Hollerith formed the Tabulating Machine Company, which in 1924 became International Business Machines (IBM). One of his colleagues, James Powers, developed his own card-punching technology and founded his own company, the Powers Tabulating Machine Company, which merged with Remington Rand in 1927. For decades IBM and Remington Rand, tracing their ancestry in part to innovative government employees, dominated the developing computer industry.[16]

As the government collected all of this data, the public developed a greater desire to access it. The enactment of freedom of information laws has allowed the public to make specific requests through a federal agency, with those requests subject to a number of exclusions and exemptions. We might not have these laws at all if not for the long-standing advocacy of the newspaper industry, as well as the yeoman efforts of John Moss.[17] The California Congressman championed transparency measures in the 1950s and 1960s in response to a series of secrecy proposals during the Cold War. Moss encountered sustained, stubborn resistance from both parties, but eventually persuaded enough members, including Republican Congressman (and future Defense Secretary) Donald Rumsfeld, to become allies. In 1966, they got a bill to the desk of a long-time opponent, President Lyndon B. Johnson. Johnson did sign it, along with a statement that he had "a deep sense of pride that the United States is an open society," even as the statement also focused on all of the exemptions for national security. Over the next two decades, and in response to events such as the Watergate scandal, Congress would amend and strengthen the bill, and it remains the law of the land.

Even so, the Freedom of Information Act (FOIA) has had its limitations.[18] It has frequently resulted in needless delay and work, the latter on account of the information's release in inaccessible formats. The agencies responsible for collecting data have conceived their systems with their own needs in mind, so that they could use that data for assorted, internal government functions. They haven't given as much thought to making the output of that data easier, in ways that could allow the public to best reuse it. That wasn't an ill-intentioned stab at secrecy; it simply wasn't seen as a requirement or priority of government.

Open innovators see data quite differently. They see it as something that should be available not by request but by default in computer-friendly, easily-understandable form. They see it as the igniter of a twenty-first-century economy that can expand industries and better lives.

They see it the way Todd Park does.

I became aware of Park's unique perspective and ability while serving on the Obama transition team in 2008. Park, the cofounder of athenahealth—a managed web-based service to help doctors collect more of their billings—served as an invaluable informal adviser for what would later become the HITECH Act, an element of the Recovery Act that offered doctors and hospitals more than $26 billion in incentive payments for the adoption and "meaningful use" of health IT. He had no designs on joining the government when he took an interview with Bill Corr, the Deputy Secretary of Health and Human Services (HHS), for the agency's new CTO position. He intended to steer Corr toward more appropriate candidates, those with plentiful—heck, *some*—public sector experience. Corr told Park, however, that he had enough people who knew government well, and that his preference was to "cross-pollinate" their DNA with Park's, so "the DNA of the entrepreneur embeds itself in HHS through this role."

Corr referenced the President's call for a more transparent, participatory, and collaborative government. To demonstrate how it would manifest itself through this position, Corr touted his department's access to vaults upon vaults of incredibly valuable data that could, in the hands of a more innovative and engaged public, better advance the mission of the agency. Then, with Park's interest piqued, the brainstorming began. "And the notion of actually working on how to leverage the HHS data for maximum public benefit was the thing that really made the role of tech entrepreneur concrete to me," Park said. "And that's what convinced me to talk my poor wife into agreeing to move across the country and jump into workaholic mode again and do this job."

After his appointment, Park explored his own sprawling agency, one with an $80 billion annual budget and 11 distinct operating divisions, including the National Institutes of Health, the R&D engine of the biotech industry; the Centers for Medicare & Medicaid Services, which provides health insurance for more than 50 million Americans; and the Food and Drug Administration, which protects the public safety. And in that research, he uncovered not only the data sets Corr had highlighted but also champions within the civil service, looking for a leader in the cause. This informal activity got a more formal boost with the White House's delivery of the Open Government Directive. As related in previous chapters, that directive provided explicit instructions and deadlines for culture changes within departments and agencies. Within 45 days, Park published four high-value data sets, one more than required by the White House directive. None had been available online or in a downloadable format.[19] One of them, the Medicare Part B National Summary data file (representing payments to doctors) had previously been available only on CD-ROM and for a $100 charge per year of data. Now, that was available for free and without intellectual property restraints, and the same was true for the other three sets Park published: the FDA's animal drug product directory; the compendium of Medicare hearings and appeals; and the list of NIH-funded grants, research, and products. By the 60th day, Park had launched an open government web page, inviting the public to comment on which data sets should be made more accessible and to offer input about each agency's overall open government plan.

Yet it wasn't just what Park was doing. It was the way he was thinking, a way that would later lead me, while grading agency performance, to point to his HHS team as a model for other agencies to replicate.[20] He understood, better than anyone, that data alone wouldn't close the gap between the American people and their government. Rather, true change would come from the improved *use* of that data in the furtherance of a personal goal, such as finding the right doctor; understanding the latest research on a patient's condition; or learning of the most recent recall of a food or medical product that could jeopardize a loved one's health.

Initially, Park did what other officials were doing in their own agencies, methodically inventorying and publishing additional data sets. Then he turned his attention to simplifying public access to that data and encouraging its use. After some investigation, he determined that, while there was little harm in the government creating some of those tools, the "real play" came in engaging outside entrepreneurs and innovators. The trick was not in dictating the next step, but in allowing "everyone else in the universe to actually tap into the data to build all kinds of tools and services and applications and features that we couldn't even dream up ourselves, let alone execute and grow to scale." He believed the subsequent development of simple, engaging, impactful tools would result in improving the health care delivery system.

To test and prove that thesis, Park partnered with the Institute of Medicine, a wing of the National Academy of Sciences, to host the Health Data Initiative in March 2010. It was a collaboration to spur participation. Together, they convened a contingent of accomplished entrepreneurs and innovators, drawn equally from the worlds of technology and health care, based on a philosophy that Park had drawn from someone we both considered our Obi-Wan Kenobi, the technology thought leader Tim O'Reilly. "If you are going to actually catalyze innovation with data," Park said, "if you want to build an ecosystem of innovation that leverages the data, you need to engage from the beginning, the people who are actually going to innovate on the data. Ask them: 'What would be valuable, how should we use the data, how should we improve the data?' So we brought a group of 45 folks together, and put a pile of data in front of them and said 'What do you think? What can you use this for?'"

What Park didn't fully anticipate was that one plus one would equal three. O'Reilly was a legendary figure in technology, as the leading forecaster of the economic boom that would come from social networking, even coining the term Web 2.0. Don Berwick was a legendary figure in health care, thanks to work with the Institute for Healthcare Improvement. They knew nothing about each other, let alone the other's importance to an entire community. Now, through this Health Data Initiative, they were in the same room, with the same goals. "Because of the fragmentation of society, you don't necessarily have a lot of broad connectivity of experts," Park said. "The intersection of O'Reilly and Berwick, and of their followers, was really magical. A tremendous source of energy and productivity in the Health Data Initiative and all these initiatives is bringing together the best innovators in health care and the best innovators in tech to do things together with data that neither side alone could have done."

The data sets available through HHS and other sources were voluminous and varied, rendering the permutations endless. By the end of the full-day session, the group had conceived roughly 20 categories of applications and services that the data could potentially power. Further, all left with a challenge: If they could make their conception a reality, within 90 days and without any government funding, their creation would be showcased at the first-ever Health Datapalooza, hosted by HHS and the Institute of Medicine. On June 2, 2010, they would exhibit more than 20 new or upgraded applications and services that would help patients find the right hospital or improve their health literacy, help doctors provide better care, and help policymakers make better decisions related to public health.

The ideas came from a range of sources. Some came from upstart firms, including MeYou Health. Its lightweight Community Clash card game, aimed at creating awareness of health factors in a user's community as compared to others, drew some of the longest lines.

Others originated from established powerhouses such as Google, which spotted value in one set of HHS data, quality measures for every hospital in America, posted since 2005 on a website (hospitalcompare.hhs.gov). Google's Chief Health Strategist, Dr. Roni Zeiger, saw the opportunity to bring this information to life through a more journalistic, provocative approach, one that would attract more eyeballs and influence more decisions.[21] For instance, he asked: Where in New York City should a patient with chest pain seek care? The city has an abundance of world-renowned medical centers, including one that President Bill Clinton had chosen for his heart operation. While most of us rely on anecdotal advice from our doctors, friends, and neighbors when selecting a hospital for life-saving treatment, Dr. Zeiger demonstrated the potential of relying more on empirical evidence. He did it quickly and at little marginal cost, downloading the national HHS file freely available in computer-friendly form and uploading it to a Google cloud-based tool called Fusion Tables, a free service that simplifies a user's ability to visualize, manipulate, or share data. He then selected roughly half-a-dozen measures, from heart failure mortality rates (within 30 days) to clinical statistics such as satisfaction surveys, such as whether a patient got a quiet room, zooming in on results in the New York City area. Then he published a screen shot of a map on his blog, with hospitals clearly marked, next to their corresponding "heart-friendly" and "patient-friendly" scores that he had derived from the data.

"It was just the beginning," Park said of the 2010 inaugural event.

Over the next couple of years, the Datapalooza earned must-attend status among health care innovators, with the audience increasing more than fivefold and the number of submissions increasing more than tenfold, with 242 companies and nonprofits competing fiercely for 100 showcase spots. The growth was reflected throughout the participant spectrum, with mature and emerging firms, student teams, and even celebrities all presenting their prototypes that had the dual benefit of advancing the HHS mission.

Aetna, a mature firm looking to offer a more personalized experience for customers calling in to its nurse call center, designed an IT cockpit. When a customer called a nurse, a series of applications opened on his or her screen, providing location-specific government data—related to everything from environmental factors to quality measures—in order to guide advice. In this way, a patient discharged from a hospital in Georgia could get tailored assistance from a nurse in Ohio, from the booking of appointments at the best place to seek treatment to the latest evidence from the National Institutes of Health on managing the condition. "This helps the patient use a bunch of public information, but does so through one of the oldest and most effective user interfaces ever designed, which is called, 'Talking to another human being,'" Park said. "The point is that in the open data revolution, the innovations happening on top of open data are about much, much, much more than the apps. The apps are real, but you also have information in rich human services."[22]

The startup Healthagen was intent on reducing unnecessary emergency room visits which, according to the nonprofit National Quality Forum, waste nearly $40 billion per year. So it added a new dimension to its already-popular iTriage smartphone application. That application, created by two emergency room doctors, had allowed users to input information about their symptoms, read about possible remedies, and learn whether they could seek care for the condition at a lower cost, outside of the hospital. The firm's new iteration leveraged the smartphone's Global Positioning System (GPS) capability to offer a local list of health centers subsidized by the government for lower-cost care. It even allowed users to book appointments. Already, iTriage has been downloaded nearly 10 million times in more than 80 countries and, as of this writing, had a 4.5 rating (out of 5) from users on Apple's app store. "Better yet, there have been testimonials, including 'this saved my life, because I got help for something I didn't realize was life threatening,'" Park said. Healthagen grew so fast that Aetna acquired the company in December 2011 and continued investing in product improvements. The application recently integrated a Centers for Disease Control data set to improve the symptom analyzer.

Student teams also made contributions, notably a pair of emergency room residents from the Johns Hopkins University. They used data from the Centers for Disease Control's bio-surveillance program and built Symcat, a more accurate resource for patient self-diagnosis than was available through websites such as WebMD. While WebMD provides high-quality reference medical information, Symcat can—with the assistance of the user providing symptom and family history information—actually estimate the probability of certain conditions. It's the difference between telling a user what cancer is and telling that user whether there's a reasonable chance that he or she has it. The application won a $100,000 Robert Wood Johnson prize and catalyzed the formation of a company.

Somehow, though, it was a larger-than-life celebrity, Jon Bon Jovi, who made this movement seem the most real.[23]

The activist musician took center stage as one of the first speakers at the 2012 Datapalooza.[24] Roughly two minutes into an unusually stiff performance, he tossed aside his script as if it were a busted guitar, preferring to riff from the heart.[25]

Bon Jovi spoke slowly, softly, and passionately about his JBJ Soul Kitchen restaurant in Red Bank, New Jersey, where diners leave donations of whatever they can afford and, if they can't afford anything, volunteer their labor instead. He then spoke specifically of one man who worked in the kitchen so late one night that Bon Jovi and his wife suspected, correctly, that the man had no place else to go. After a frustrating attempt to find an available bed online, Bon Jovi came to believe that those with limited resources—and a reliance upon public transit—would have virtually no success hunting down comfortable shelter in suburban New Jersey. Nor would anyone who wanted to use the Internet help.

Bon Jovi continued his story by recounting the January 2012 event that he had attended as a member of the President's Council for Community Solutions. I had attended, too, to announce the tech program associated with the Summer Jobs + initiative. At a bathroom break, we—two guys from New Jersey with quite dissimilar backgrounds—met in the hallway. He asked if he could apply open data concepts to the homelessness issue, and that brief discussion, followed by brainstorming, had led to the Project Reach developer challenge. The challenge called upon the public to use open data from the Departments of Veterans Affairs as well as Housing and Urban Development to address veteran homelessness through an OpenTable-style application that provided information about bed, clothes, food, and medical assistance at and around New Jersey shelters. It had produced five formidable finalists, and a punch line to Bon Jovi's speech.

"The power of 'we' allows us the opportunity to truly make a difference," he told the Datapalooza audience.

Without question, Bon Jovi's star power had made a difference, too, as was illustrated when he left the dais to a chorus of applause from the standing-room crowd of 1,500. Still, Bon Jovi couldn't upstage the man who presented more than an hour earlier, wearing glasses and a suit. In an article about the event, a

Forbes.com reporter expressed surprise that Todd Park, not the global superstar, received the really raucous response. But it didn't surprise me. He hadn't sold millions of records or starred in more than a dozen films. Park had, however, risen through the ranks to succeed me as the nation's Chief Technology Officer. And he had energized two communities—in the technology and health care spaces—with his infectious energy and irrepressible passion. Rather than wow with wonk speak, he peppered his presentation with colloquialisms like "awesomeness" and closed his address with "Rock On!" In settings such as this, he was invariably the one who left the crowd calling for encores.

"I just felt like I was incredibly lucky to be able to kick things off with this amazing gathering of people," Park said months later. "There are many evangelists for the movement, and I felt like, more than anything, I was channeling them. That's what is so exciting about this. It's a movement with so many leaders, powered by so much innovation across the board, around the country, people who believe the truly great innovation ecosystems are decentralized, self-propelled, and open. There were many, many, many impressive people at Datapalooza, not quite as famous as Bon Jovi, but who were just as enthusiastic. It was fantastic, really, really awesome."

I mentioned earlier that Healthagen, in its iTriage application, used GPS as a tool to provide open government data (a list of medical providers) in a more manageable, user-friendly format, based on location. But GPS itself was the product of a series of earlier open government initiatives.

The U.S. military had been tinkering with navigation systems as early as the 1940s, with independent aims and moderate success throughout the next few decades.[26] In 1973, the Defense Department designated the Air Force to consolidate the various established concepts into a comprehensive system called the Defense

Navigation Satellite System (DNSS).[27] The first experimental GPS satellite launched in 1978, with more launched by the mid-1980s, and all available only to the military.

Then, in 1983, a Korean commercial airline, en route from Anchorage, Alaska, to Seoul, mistakenly entered the Soviet Union's airspace. A Soviet fighter jet shot it down, killing 269 people. To minimize future navigational errors, President Ronald Reagan allowed civilian access to GPS. But that access came with a catch—to protect national security, he imposed a filter that blunted the accuracy, as compared to what was available to the military. President Bill Clinton, an advocate of using GPS for "addressing a broad range of military, civil, commercial, and scientific interests, both national and international" throughout his two terms, took away the restrictions prior to leaving office. On May 1, 2000, he ordered an end to the intentional degrading of GPS accuracy: "The decision to discontinue Selective Availability is the latest measure in an ongoing effort to make GPS more responsive to civil and commercial users worldwide . . . This increase in accuracy will allow new GPS applications to emerge and continue to enhance the lives of people around the world."

Propelled by the government's support, more private sector entities began experimenting in this space. Those innovators began offering a variety of commercial applications. Prices for GPS chips fell dramatically, allowing phone carriers to offer navigation as an inexpensive, standard feature in products. And the GPS industry—requiring roughly $1.3 billion a year from the U.S. Treasury for procuring satellites and furthering systems development—has grown into a $65 billion enterprise.[28] That includes an array of smartphone apps helping users find anything from an art museum to an aunt's house.

In the mid-2000s, Dr. David Van Sickle had a more critical cause in mind.[29] While working as a respiratory disease detective in the Epidemic Intelligence Service at the Centers for Disease

Control and Prevention (CDC) in Atlanta, he didn't need to dig much to identify a major problem in the health care system. That was easy as breathing—breathing for *him*, anyway. "People think about asthma, and think we must have a handle on it in the U.S.," Van Sickle said. "But the grim reality is that most patients' asthma in this country is uncontrolled. There's a higher rate of going to the hospital than there should be. We have been doing the same thing about asthma for years, and we have made basically no dent in hospitalizations. The majority of those people think they are doing fine, so no one treats them with a course correction. And, so, there's inexcusable morbidity. There's this really ridiculous gap between what we should be able to do and what we've been able to accomplish."

In his view, this has been largely a product of information gaps on both the public health and clinical sides of the equation. During his time at the CDC, including his work examining asthma outbreaks due to mold exposure in the aftermath of 2005's Hurricane Katrina, he kept coming across the same obstacles: asthma data that was often years old and long outdated by the time he saw it; data that only accounted for deaths and hospitalizations rather than informative events such as school and work absences. Due to these limitations, research at the public health level was often done by "carpet-bombing a community" rather than targeting specific, smaller areas.

These gaps made it nearly impossible to tackle the issue in any productive, proactive, expedited individual way. "You would never have to ask a credit card company to review data on an annual basis," he said. "But you have to ask public health or health care to do that? This is vastly behind where other industries are."

Nor was America an outlier. While at the CDC, Van Sickle read about an acute asthma cluster in Barcelona. "It sent a bunch of people to the hospital and a bunch of people died," he said. "The investigative team finally asked where people were when they were having symptoms. They mapped that, and finally figured out that the filters hadn't been installed correctly in the harbor silos, which meant that when people were loading soybeans, it created a potent soybean dust. It was the first time we recognized that as a powerful allergen. But it took them *ten years* to figure out what was happening."

America certainly doesn't have that sort of time for delays in discovery, not with its pressing health care cost crisis: those costs are rising sharply and seemingly without end, with an expectation they will far exceed their already-excessive current chunk of the Gross Domestic Product in the United States. According to the World Bank, the U.S. spent 17.9 percent of its GDP on health care, compared to 11.2 percent for Canada, 9.3 percent for the United Kingdom, and 5.2 percent for China.[30] There's a crying need for innovation aimed at greater efficiency, and a focus on preventative measures that will allow patients to avoid factors that could trigger a condition, and thus further strain the system. There's a need, above all, to empower doctors and patients.

That's what Van Sickle set out to do after leaving the CDC, armed with a generous fellowship from the Robert Wood Johnson Foundation to serve as a Health and Society Scholar at the University of Wisconsin-Madison.[31] "I had this great mandate to do something, to solve a problem that had always been bugging me," he said.

And he had this great tool, GPS, to use to improve public health. Early during his time in Wisconsin, Van Sickle decided to attach an asthma inhaler to electronics. The resulting device, called a Spiroscout, created a time and GPS location record of symptoms as the inhaler was used. The onset of those symptoms could be linked to a place—and thus, to the elements of exposure. If the person was using the inhaler more than twice per week, it probably meant an emergency room visit was imminent.

Van Sickle initially built a small batch of those devices, "just to show I wasn't completely crazy." He benefited from participants' understanding that, by sharing information, they might help others avoid symptoms. Still, he attempted to address privacy concerns. "It was done sensibly and protected," he insisted.

Over time, the devices became more advanced, smaller, and with better battery life.[32] He has also changed his vantage point, choosing to come at the problem from the private sector—from "industrial size, not professional size, without everything that is in the way on the academic side." He started a company, Asthmapolis, to improve asthma management and public health surveillance, striving to lower costs associated with asthma while providing a novel data stream for health improvement. By 2013, his device had earned FDA approval, his hypothesis that information could lower asthma attacks had been validated in testing in North Carolina and Kentucky, and his business had attracted $5 million in venture capital to tackle a market of more than 20 million asthma patients in the United States alone.

Patients with uncontrolled asthma spend thousands more per year than those with controlled asthma. As more health systems enter into population health contracts with insurance companies, taking responsibility for improved outcomes, there is an emerging market incentive to adopt a program such as Van Sickle's and integrate it into a physician's regular practice.

"The doctor can take the data from a daily list for the patient, make it meaningful, and get it back to the patient," Van Sickle said. "Such as, 'You should not be having symptoms every night. Here's what is going on with you.' It's personalized guidance, personalized education, captured from daily life and put to use."

At the White House, we saw the importance of Van Sickle's work. So we invited him to a June 10, 2011, event, and honored him as one of our Champions of Change.[33] These weekly gatherings were designed to bring attention to innovators, educators, and builders who, in our view, were "Winning the Future Across America," starting in their communities. Through this initiative, we came across people from a wide range of backgrounds, but who all had one thing in common: they successfully and creatively moved a cause forward, improving their communities and, by extension, the country. On June 10, our list of champions was narrowed to those who did so through the use of open data.

One of those we honored, Bay Area real estate broker Leigh Budlong—whose Zonability app allowed prospective commercial tenants in San Francisco to understand zoning limits in their area—captured the spirit of the day in an online post: "Whenever I hear people are bummed out by government, I try to tell them about this very cool and seemingly quiet movement underway . . . data is awesome and figuring out how to make it useful to a target audience is the reward."[34]

Another champion was a part-time chicken farmer named Waldo Jaquith. As a secondary sidelight from his duties as a webmaster at the University of Virginia's Miller Center, Jaquith had launched Richmond Sunlight, a volunteer-run site that kept close tabs on the activities of the Virginia legislature, including manually uploading hundreds of hours of video of floor speeches, tagging relevant information on bills and committee votes, and inviting the public to comment on legislation. Jaquith had also earned a Knight Foundation fellowship to convert state government codes across the country into online machine-readable formats; shortly after the Champions ceremony, we would hire him to design Ethics.gov.

Then there was the champion trio of Bob Burbach, Dave Augustine, and Andrew Carpenter.[35] While working together at a San Francisco education nonprofit called WestEd, they had stumbled upon an Apps for America 2 contest sponsored by the nonprofit organization Sunlight Labs, requiring the use of a data set from Data.gov. "We wanted to show government that cool things can happen when they make data available," Burbach said.

During the three-week mad dash to finish, they chose the largest-possible data set they could find: all of the content that made up the *Federal Register*. One of the government's time-honored transparency vehicles, created in 1935 by Franklin D. Roosevelt's signing of the Federal Register Act, the compendium had been designed "to bring order to the core documents of the Executive Branch and make them broadly available to the American public."[36] First published in March 1936, the "government's daily newspaper" included any government action that, by law, had to be disclosed to the public—everything from Presidential executive orders and proclamations to agency rules and regulations to meeting announcements. The publication was intended to encourage the public's participation in actions that had been proposed, and fully informing it when such actions became final.

In the decades following the *Federal Register*'s introduction in 1936, the federal government would expand exponentially in terms of the number of agencies, personnel, and programs—Social Security, Medicare, and Medicaid were among the notable new entitlements; and the Presidential Cabinet doubled in size from Roosevelt to Obama, partly due to the Departments of Health and Education. In light of this expansion, transparency became even more critical to the populace, to make sure everything was running as it should. But it became even tougher for people to turn to the *Federal Register* for that assurance, since the compendium's size and complexity grew in accordance with that of the government. It became, over the next seven decades, a rich, enormous (more than 81,000 pages in 2010), and nearly indecipherable roundup, written by regulators for consumption only by the lawyers of the regulated.

The corresponding website, initially developed in 1994, turned out to be even less accessible, due to its aesthetics. It was little more than a PDF version of the complex printed edition, and that PDF had serious problems. It was virtually unreadable, in part because agencies had to pay by the page to get content included, so they went to comical extents to shrink that content, often forgoing paragraph breaks. That site was the only means of access for people who weren't inclined to pay nearly $1,000 for an annual subscription to the hard copy, or didn't have the time to travel to a law library and sift through hundreds of pages, simply to find the one thing that impacted them. These challenges in accessing useful information, whether through the print or online mediums, contributed to well-heeled lobbyists knowing infinitely more about what was happening in Washington than the general public ever could. Certainly, the lobbyists didn't mind, since they could command thousands-per-hour fees for the dispersal of that knowledge to billion-dollar industries. So much for helping Regular Joe from Idaho.

When Burbach and his team first encountered what he called "the tons and tons of data" that made up the *Federal Register*, that data struck them as extremely meaningful: information that people could use not only to know more about how government was running, but also so they could better run their businesses without running roughshod over regulations.

But it was impossible for the technology-savvy trio, let alone the average citizen, to understand much of it. Burbach, Carpenter, and Augustine couldn't change that complex regulatory content—and, as neophytes to government, they wouldn't have known how. But that inexperience, in some ways, was actually an advantage. They came to the task without preconceptions of how the data should be presented, but they brought their expertise—drawn from their knowledge of the consumer Internet and their mastery of web development—which allowed them to envision presenting the material in radically different and simpler ways than were previously considered.

Their early prototypes were imperfect, as Burbach acknowledges. But because they weren't working inside an agency or beholden to immediate presentation to the public, they could continue tinkering, driven only by the desire to give people the search for government actions most relevant to them. At the Sunlight Foundation contest at the Gov 2.0 conference in fall 2009, their web application GovPulse won second place. They kept working on the application in their spare time, and won first place in a related competition sponsored by the world-renowned Consumers Electronics Show in Las Vegas. They returned to San Francisco, but unbeknownst to them, their work was intriguing government officials on the other coast. The archivist of the United States wanted to incorporate their innovations directly on his domain in time for a seventy-fifth anniversary event. So they formed a company called Critical Juncture, and set out to meet the aggressive 90-day timeline to reconceive and relaunch the FederalRegister.gov site.

In their efforts to democratize access, Burbach, Augustine, and Carpenter presented the material in a format with which the public was extremely familiar: one that resembled a newspaper site, divided into topical headings and sections. It also allowed users to set alerts, so they would be notified when a new government action applied to them or their particular type of small business. On July 15, 2010, the new site launched, and 11 days later, to commemorate the 75th anniversary of the act behind the *Federal Register*, the trio was honored at the National Archives. Later, the team and its government partners tore down more of the wall between the government and its citizenry. They did this by reinterpreting the existing legal requirement that any regulation that would appear in the *Federal Register* must be accompanied by a physical copy no less than one day in advance for public inspection. That provision had historically allowed those "in the know" to get a jump on important regulatory matters in advance of the general public, simply by walking into a reading room. But, why not post an electronic copy of the public inspection document for everyone to read? With that in mind, Critical Juncture built an online reading room mirroring the access rights afforded to insiders.

And true to the spirit that moved them to tinker with the documents in the first place, the team set out to publish an application programming interface to enable the next group of innovators to build on top of their work, free of intellectual property constraint or cost. To come full circle, the Sunlight Foundation, home to the initial contest that sparked their involvement, would go on to build a new tool called Scout. This innovation not only improves search capability, it expands it beyond the *Federal Register* to include any relevant Congressional documents.

"It's cascaded from an open data side project, meant to be only a couple of weeks, into something that is affecting the regulatory sphere," Burbach said. "We sort of fell into this, but it's a good example of how by using open data, you can effect change."

Open data continues to demonstrate that it can effect change outside American boundaries as well.

In September 2010, President Obama presented global leaders at the United Nations with a challenge: "When we gather back here next year, we should bring specific commitments to promote transparency; to fight corruption; to energize civic engagement; to leverage new technologies so that we strengthen the foundations of freedom in our own countries, while living up to the ideals that can light the world."[37]

His first international stop to further this endeavor was far away, but closest to my heart. The U.S. President and India's Prime Minister, Manmohan Singh, officially announced the launch of the Dialogue on Open Government aimed at delivering tangible benefits in both countries through the joint development of an open data web portal, with a goal to expand its reach to countries around the world. India was an appropriate ally. It had already built a robust technology industry. And, in 2005, it had enacted the Right to Information Act, setting goals related to more accountable and effective government.

On November 7, 2010, at St. Xavier's College in Mumbai, President Obama toured the first Expo on Democracy and Open Government. The expo featured 10 technology applications utilizing open data to empower India's citizenry, including an innovative text message service that informs voters within the final two weeks prior to an election if any candidate in their jurisdiction had any criminal records.

The highlight of the tour, however, was the latest innovation championed by Sam Pitroda, who would serve as my counterpart in the Indian government as Advisor to the Prime Minister on Innovation. Together, we would cochair the U.S.-India Open Government Dialogue. Pitroda, as noted earlier, had repeatedly left behind lucrative opportunities in America to pursue his grander mission of empowering the Indian poor, especially the rural poor. First, he set out to do so through the telephone. Then, as chair of India's National Knowledge Commission, he set out to empower them through the expansion of fiber broadband, with an emphasis on providing greater access to government data.

Now he had the chance to show President Obama how all of that infrastructure investment could impact India. Through video conferencing, he connected the President from the bustling urban campus in Mumbai to a modest local government building in Kanpura, the first village in the country to be connected through optical fiber to rural broadband service. And not just any broadband service—rather, service at speeds not available in most parts of America. After the residents held festivals and dressed colorfully in anticipation of the event, some, including local politicians and a sufficient number of English speakers, got to participate in the conversation. Such visual communication, from a major city to a remote village in a country as geographically and economically diverse as India, was an impressive feat in information technology.

Even more impressive than what the President saw, however, was what he heard. People enthusiastically shared stories about how the broadband connectivity had relieved some pressures, gaps, and difficulties in their lives. A student spoke of how, in using it for graduate education, he could stay and care for his mother rather than trekking two towns over for classes. A nurse related how the digital access to health information allowed her to target people in need of immunizations.

Then there was the farmer who, in speaking about seeds and tools, provided the true takeaway from this endeavor. His story illustrated how this access to government information—a result of open government principles powered by technological innovations—could fundamentally improve the way a society operates. In order to borrow money for a farm in India, as anywhere, a bank requires proof of land ownership. That requires traveling, by one means or another, to a distant city center and hoping that the government official turns over the necessary information. And for generations, that has often meant returning empty-handed, and then resorting to borrowing from a local lender at egregious interest rates. Yet, under Pitroda's vision of a country connected by fiber optic broadband, the villager could get what he needed without the middleman. Within weeks of his village's connection, the farmer was able to access his own data in a safe, secure manner, printing out his proof and executing a bank loan.

"These are the principles and benefits of e-governance," Pitroda said.

These were principles and benefits that the President clearly comprehended, as was evident in his comments to the villagers: "One of the incredible benefits of the technology we're seeing right here is that, in many ways, India may be in a position to leapfrog some of the intermediate stages of government service delivery, avoiding some of the 20th century mechanisms for delivering services and going straight to the 21st."[38]

Pitroda was ecstatic about the global attention the interaction received and hopeful that the spotlight would inspire the people of India to continue their efforts. More than anything, he was amazed at the President's grasp of what Indian leaders were trying to accomplish, especially as Pitroda spoke of the grand vision, to connect 250,000 rural village centers with government information in the same manner. "Most political leaders, in a short period like that, will not get it," Pitroda said. "He immediately got it; he understood that we are trying to democratize information to empower people, and it is going to result in a better democracy. That's how we are going to be different from China or anybody else."

In Pitroda's view, the fourth phase of empowerment—after telecom, knowledge, and broadband connectivity—is innovation. In that spirit, White House CIO Vivek Kundra and I returned to India in March 2011 to formalize a simple but transformative first step not only toward the implementation of the ideals of the U.S.-India Open Government partnership, but also toward the expansion of the effects of that collaboration beyond our two countries. We would do this through open sourcing of the Data.gov platform, making the platform freely available all over the world, and we would achieve that through the formation of a joint software development team of a dozen developers drawn equally from India and the United States. The developers would work in a modern manner—using Skype in lieu of face-to-face meetings; and GitHub, the leading online code repository, to coauthor and test the software program. That resulted in a beta release about a year later, a free resource available to every government in the world.

Pitroda's preference was to introduce the platform where the need was greatest, in an underdeveloped nation in Africa. He had met the President of Rwanda while giving a speech on higher education at the State Department and through continued joint efforts between India and the United States. Work to pilot the service is under way.

As we continued to work together directly, independent efforts involving other countries were ongoing and expanding, much of it a result of American leadership—dating back to the President's September 2010 challenge at the sidelines of the United Nations. By the one-year mark, nearly 40 countries had made explicit commitments to join the newly announced Open Government Partnership, and seven countries had published their specific action plans, made in consultation with their citizens. As of November 2012, 58 countries had made concrete commitments, developed in consultation with their people and with support from a growing NGO community investing in the expansion of capacity to achieve the bold goals.

There's clearly been a lot of action in open data, over just the past few years. If the journey was judged by the increase in open data sets publicly available, the graph would be shaped like a hockey stick, with the blade pointing left.

So, how do we score its success?

One could score it by the increasing number of data sets that have been made available. On its first day of operations in May 2009, the Data.gov platform hosted 47 data sets. By November 2012, it would host nearly 400,000. One could score it by usage figures—for instance, in the first 24 hours after HHS posted raw hospital list price data, it was downloaded 100,000 times.[39] One could try to count up the number of localities to which the movement has scaled, with the federal effort inspiring numerous state and local versions, in major metropolises such as San Francisco, California, and even tiny towns such as Manor, Texas.[40]

But, in actuality, the power of the movement is even harder to quantify, because what is most encouraging is the increasing share of America's brainpower that is focused on solving our collective problems, with input from those who had never intended to work on a government project.

Open innovation allows them to contribute, even if it is merely a means to another personal end. Mike Krieger, a Brazilian immigrant, was working for a startup and considering others when he began tinkering with open government data as a weekend distraction. He used San Francisco's crime information to create the iPhone app CrimeDesk, steering residents away from the most dangerous places to park, walk, or bike. While the public received that benefit, Krieger was getting the valuable technical experience he sought, and which would come in handy when he reconnected with former Stanford classmate Kevin Systrom on another potential project: "I wasn't starting from zero. I had already built an app." Together they would build the photo-sharing behemoth Instagram, which quickly attracted roughly 100 million active monthly users and Facebook's attention, with the latter acquiring it for what was heralded as $1 billion, though it turned out to be closer to $715 million.[41]

As America attempts to get and stay ahead in a variety of industries, it is benefiting from the full force of this data liberation movement in all sorts of expected and unexpected ways. Data, deployed through the latest technology, represents one of what Sam Pitroda calls "the new tools of today to solve the problems of tomorrow." They are multifunctional tools, a Swiss Army knife of sorts, with functionality in an assortment of sectors, scenarios, and situations. It is becoming a virtuous cycle: as hundreds of data sets are made available, more challenges are conceived, more online communities and entrepreneurial companies create tools for consumers, and more Datapaloozas, beyond the original that spotlighted health, sprout up to showcase the innovations and inspire others to innovate.

The Energy Data Initiative and its related challenges have targeted all areas of the energy spectrum, from fuel economy to environmental protection to consumption awareness. The Safety Data Initiative and its related challenges have focused on everything from emergency response to consumer product recalls to worker safety to drunk driving education to the performance of the body armor worn by law enforcement. The Education Data Initiative is aimed at students from preschool through college, and enables developers to empower those students, giving them better access to test scores, class grades, even federal student loan information.

On May 9, 2013, President Obama kicked off a Middle Class Jobs & Opportunity Tour emphasizing the need for middle-class job creation, the need for Americans to develop the skills to fill those jobs, and the need for American employers to provide hard workers with a fair opportunity and a decent wage. To accompany this speech, he signed an executive order for an Open Data Policy called Managing Information as an Asset.[42] It required that newly released government data be made freely available in open machine-readable formats while appropriately safeguarding privacy, confidentiality, and security. By tying these elements together—open government and jobs—he made the open data movement about more than the original purpose of transparency. It was, and is, about that transparency. But it is also about economics. It is about unleashing technology entrepreneurs to create products and services that consumers need and use, so the resulting economic activity can foster job creation.

At this stage, if anything's holding the movement back, it's awareness.

That's why the President's continuing emphasis is so significant. So are the efforts, throughout the administration, to publicize activities in this area, for those with expertise in everything from public safety to health care to education to energy to global affairs and so forth. As Todd Park noted, "If you are in these spaces and do not know this stuff is available, then it's like being in the navigation business and not knowing that GPS exists. There are big, game-changing data resources that are being made available through government action that *every* entrepreneur is going to want to know about, and some already do."

The mission?

That everybody will. And then, as Todd Park puts it, "entrepreneurs can turn open data into awesomeness."

Chapter 6

Standards and Convening

It all started on a Sunday morning in 1904. According to legend, someone dropped a lit cigar or cigarette through a cracked glass block in a sidewalk. The block functioned as a skylight for a basement. That basement belonged to the John Hurst & Company dry goods building. The blaze triggered an explosion that left much of Baltimore burning.[1]

The city could not find the means to stop the flames. More than 1,200 firefighters answered the urgent call for assistance, arriving by train from as far as New York, eager and seemingly well equipped. Yet they were largely ineffective, because their hose couplings could not connect to the fire hydrants. In fact, the couplings weren't even compatible from one building to the next. So, as the firefighters scrambled to use other methods, the fire raged for more than 30 hours, reducing 1,500 buildings on 70 blocks to rubble, killing five people, and leaving thousands unemployed.

It may not have gone on so long, or done so much damage, if compatibility had been a priority in the fire equipment industry. Instead, the market incentives led manufacturers to design entirely proprietary systems, including different couplings for each vendor. After all, a city that purchased a particular system would be entirely dependent on that system's manufacturer for any improvements or upgrades. A more interoperable system would give city officers more market choices all the way down to the spare parts level, meaning that a manufacturer would lose some leverage, and likely some margin.

The question became whether some good could emerge from the ashes. The winds of the progressive era were beginning to blow strong—the Roosevelt administration had brought a major antitrust suit two years before, the Department of Labor had been established the previous year, and the landmark Pure Food and Drug Act would pass two years later. There was an understanding that government had a role to play in protecting Americans from the dangers of their rapidly industrialized and modernized country. So, naturally, after the Baltimore fire, there was a call for stricter building codes and the use of more fireproof materials. But there was also awareness that those improvements might not be sufficient to prevent a similar calamity from occurring elsewhere. The industry needed to come together and drive toward greater standardization, so firefighters wouldn't again be stymied by intentionally ill-fitting parts.

If you owned a Betamax video recorder in the 1970s, you can probably relate to the challenges of competing formats. Its manufacturer, Sony, tried to dictate a standard for the rest of the industry. Instead, JVC formed a broader coalition to commercialize its own technology, VHS, which was not compatible with Betamax players and vice versa. VHS came to dominate the market and quickly rendered Betamax irrelevant. Nearly two decades later, history could have repeated itself in the rollout of the DVD. Initially, there were two different formats, each backed by a number of prominent companies, with Sony and Phillips on one side, and Toshiba and JVC on the other. But a new market force, the computer industry, took a leadership role in applying the lessons from the VHS/Betamax fiasco. After its Technical Working Group (TWG) threatened to boycott all formats other than a single, standardized one, the DVD manufacturers ultimately came together and produced a common standard.[2]

Consumers benefited, getting higher-quality images on a more durable disk that could hold additional material. So did Hollywood. After resisting DVD production for fears of copyright infringement, the motion picture industry felt quite differently in 2004 when its studios booked a record $15 billion on DVD sales and rentals, compared to $9.4 billion in revenues at the box office.[3] And while the creators of the original DVD standard couldn't have predicted this at the time, the lightweight nature of the product would later fuel one of the early twenty-first century's breakout companies: Netflix, which could send feature films around the country for the price of a stamp.

That's an example of the private sector succeeding in standards development and application without the influence of the government, and you can find plenty of those throughout the past two-plus centuries. But public sector engagement in this area is also as old as the American republic, with government not always content to wait for the private sector to solve a standards problem.

In his first annual message to Congress as President, back in 1790, George Washington spoke of the importance of "uniformity in the current weights and measures of the United States," and even directed his Secretary of State, Thomas Jefferson, to prepare a plan. From 1830 through 1901, an Office of Standard Weights and Measures, operating under the U.S. Treasury Department, oversaw much of the work—in collaboration with manufacturers, scientists, educators, government officials, and the public at large on standardizing everything from length to mass to temperature to light to time. But its mandate, funding and testing capacity, was modest, if not minuscule. Congress largely adhered to the 10th Amendment, leaving decisions about scientific research investments in standardization to the states, which really meant much of that work wouldn't get done.

By the turn of the twentieth century, the need for standardization was even more acute, partly due to American society's increasingly mobile and sprawling, yet interconnected, nature. Previously, most commerce had largely been relegated to the local community, because that's where people stayed: a gallon of milk was a gallon of milk because that's how the local dairy measured it, and that's what the consumer, not knowing better, came to accept. But now consumers were expecting conformity wherever they traveled. And increasingly large companies, in an increasingly large country, needed to think outside of their most proximate market and be assured that their products could compete on a fair unit of measure around the country.

The introduction of electrification served as another impetus for the government to seek greater conformity in technology. For the most possible industries to benefit, the producers and distributors of electricity needed to settle on some standardized way of measuring volts and kilowatt hours, among other things. And for that technical work, most of which would be deemed precompetitive—more commercially relevant than typical university research but not designed to advantage any single firm—some scientists and engineers argued for a role for government. According to an official historical review provided by the National Institute of Standards and Technology (NIST), "The builders of America's industrial complex had little interest in standards as such, but the scientists, engineers, and experimenters working for industry or independently found themselves increasingly hampered without them."[4]

Further, according to NIST's historical documents, "The burgeoning electrical industry showed that simple standards for mass, length and time were no longer sufficient." The nation needed uniform standards for electrical units, as well as units and standards for new discoveries such as x-rays and radioactivity.

This required research, mostly in physics and chemistry. And that meant "simple offices of weights and measures had to be replaced with more sophisticated institutions."

Finally, after nearly two decades of debate on whether the government would be overstepping into the economy by engaging in proactive standards work, the National Bureau of Standards (NBS) was finally formed in 1901, and would retain that name until it became NIST in 1988.[5] Originally directed by physicist Samuel W. Stratton and staffed by only 12 members, including a chemist, an engineer, and five technical assistants, the new agency restricted its work to that which—to paraphrase the NIST historical documents—would cooperate with university research laboratories, support private enterprise, and promote general welfare. Following the Great Baltimore Fire, the shipping industry also raised concerns about fire hoses and couplings. In response, the Commerce Department enlisted the Bureau of Standards to collect over 600 sizes and variations of hose couplings in use across the country. One year later, the National Fire Protection Association, with the support of the NBS, established a national standard diameter and threads per inch for hose couplings and fire hydrants, while endorsing an interchangeable device for nonstandard couplings. It proved a greater struggle to achieve widespread adoption; for reasons ranging from expense to inertia, many cities took years or decades to comply. Still, the overall fire hose standardization effort left a significant legacy, as one of the first major examples of the federal government responding to a crisis by galvanizing a private sector industry behind a laudable goal—in this case, public safety—and then convening government officials and scientific experts to find solutions.

But why wait for a crisis? Not long after the establishment of the fire standards, the federal government would use similar means—initiating action without imposing mandates—to achieve economic ends. It would apply its convening authority in the aviation industry, in order to spur R&D and growth.

The government had little to do with Wilbur and Orville Wright getting off the ground at Kitty Hawk, back on December 17, 1903. Rather, their flying machine—carrying a pilot, rising by its own power, descending without damage—was a credit to their imagination, experimentation, and determination. In the decade that followed; however, America failed to fully capitalize on their creativity, undermined by ongoing, acute issues of safety and reliability. In 1908, Orville Wright himself was flying above 2,000 spectators when a propeller and rudder broke, sending his plane nose first into the ground and killing his twenty-six-year-old passenger, Lieutenant Thomas Selfridge. By 1913, America ranked 14th in government spending on aircraft development and, by 1916, had produced only 411 aircraft.

It was around that time, however, that the government identified a way to contribute. In 1915, the Woodrow Wilson administration tucked the creation of a new committee into a Naval Appropriation Bill. The National Advisory Committee for Aeronautics (NACA), while low profile and modestly funded, represented a rather significant shift in the scope of government. Its 12 unpaid members were commissioned to conduct research and development on engines and wings. NACA sought to develop a catalog of wing curvatures (or airfoils), so that the appropriate shape could be safely matched with the corresponding aircraft.

This variety could not come, however, until the committee settled on a standardized way of testing each airfoil design. That breakthrough, coupled with American entry into World War I, supercharged aviation production. In just nine months spanning 1917 and 1918, the government procured more than 12,000 planes for use in that conflict.[6]

But, in the year that followed, in the absence of government demand, production again nosedived. The new Commerce Secretary, a millionaire mining engineer and investor named Herbert Hoover, was intent not to allow America to cede leadership to Europe in this promising new industry. Hoover was obsessed with efficiency—he endeavored to eliminate, from his position in government, much of the waste in the postwar manufacturing economy. That required him to reconcile his guiding mission with his conservative governing philosophy: one based on individualism, industry autonomy, and an aversion to what he deemed the traditional, intrusive models of government intervention.

Hoover would thread that needle through convening rather than coercion, and his vision of an "associative state."[7] He eschewed the top-down planning approach widely espoused throughout Europe, instead using the state's power to encourage the formation of voluntary and flexible trade associations that represented dozens of industries and saw value in cooperation, even among fierce competitors. Those associations would remain independent of the government, but would benefit from the government's "friendly interest," allowing access to its scientific research experts. They would work together to unlock opportunities and achieve growth, by identifying the technical barriers in a particular industry, designing standardized and simplified parts and procedures to address those issues, and attempting to validate their assertions and methods with the help of a government lab. In this sense, the government wouldn't be getting in an industry's way, so much as clearing a path, enabling that industry to grow and thrive, through the recognition and implementation of the best possible practices.

"We are passing from one period of extremely individual action into a period of associated activities," Hoover told the U.S. Chamber of Commerce in Cleveland. "We are upon the threshold, if these agencies can be directed solely to constructive performance in the public's interest."[8]

This is the approach that Hoover would apply in aviation. Hoover was aware of NACA's standards for wing designs in advance of the war, and their positive impact on the safety of military airplanes. And he was concerned about the collapse in airplane production following the armistice, from 21,000 per year to a total of 263 in 1922. After casualties associated with poor aircraft design, militarily and commercially, America needed to reduce the risk to commercial operators and potential investors, and relieve the worries of would-be passengers, which meant elevating and expanding upon the safety work that NACA had initially done. Hoover called for the organization of a trade association called the Aeronautical Chamber of Commerce, and pushed for the passage of the Air Commerce Act of 1926, to better coordinate government's capacity to collaborate with that association, opening research laboratories for the purpose of technical breakthroughs and safety upgrades. The two leading manufacturers of that era, Douglas and Boeing, wholly adopted various NACA standards, in their production of the popular DC-3 and 247 aircraft. Those standards, and their subsequent iterations, would play a role in aircraft acquisitions for World War II. Standardization also set the stage for the commercial aviation boom that continues through this day. According to Bureau of Transportation statistics, commercial airliners currently employ more than 500,000 Americans on a full-time or part-time basis, more than 600 million passengers board domestic flights alone in the United States each year, and Boeing projected in 2013 that the U.S. would need 35,280 new planes, valued at $4.8 trillion, by 2032.

During two terms as Commerce Secretary that spanned the Woodrow Wilson and Calvin Coolidge administrations, Hoover doubled the size of the Bureau of Standards and engaged nearly 100 industries in the collective process of creation and deployment. According to his Presidential library, he was intent on insuring "that industries voluntarily cooperated in improving our national progress and improving Americans' standards of living. To Hoover, no product or industry was too mundane for review and reform: flashlight cases, lumber, chinaware, mattresses, and bricks all merited primers on elimination of waste." That's right, even bricks. Under Hoover, standardization reduced the varieties of paving brick from 66 to five. At the conclusion of Hoover's tenure—and prior to his election as President—the Commerce Department calculated that its standardization and simplification efforts had generated roughly $600 million in economic impact across America's $18 billion manufacturing sector.[9]

Over the next several decades, Commerce Department officials in Republican and Democratic administrations largely adhered to Herbert Hoover's model in their governmental approaches to affecting economic activity: avoiding the ideological extremes of industrial policy (picking winners and losers) and laissez-faire (letting everyone be). Many also embraced his belief in the power of collective action, especially that of interested parties in the same industry, with the guidance of and access to—though not interference from—the government.

In that sense, the Council on Competitiveness was a philosophical descendant of those trade associations that Hoover had called into action.[10] Nonpartisan and nongovernmental, the Council was created in 1986 in response to concerns that America was losing economic leadership around the world, notably to Asia. It consisted of an all-star team of CEOs, university presidents, and labor leaders, who came together to assess America's place in the global marketplace, identify obstacles and opportunities, and generate public policy solutions.

As technology advanced, the corporations represented in the Council encountered more challenges that required collective consideration and action. As of the early twenty-first century, several of America's manufacturing behemoths had invested millions in high performance computing (HPC), including modeling and simulation activities that were intended to dramatically reduce production times and costs, by allowing for the optimization of design prior to the physical testing stages. In 2005, the Council undertook the High Performance Computing initiative. Three years later, a Council report confirmed earlier findings that "virtually all U.S. businesses that have adopted HPC consider this technology indispensable for their competitiveness and corporate survival."[11] This report cited some examples. Boeing used HPC to reduce its expensive "live" experimental tests from 77 to 11 for the Dreamliner 787 compared to the 777. Walmart used HPC to better manage its worldwide stores from its Arkansas headquarters, in everything from determining shelf space to turning out the lights.

Still, the report noted that only energy firms among U.S. industries had truly integrated HPC into critical business functions, while suppliers to all of those top firms had lagged behind, with many not using HPC at all. It called that situation "troublesome" in light of HPC's potential to reduce costs and speed time to market; the gap is especially concerning as it comes at the same time that international firms are "driving HPC through their supply chains more aggressively." There was an explanation for the holdup: suppliers, mostly small- and medium-size manufacturers, typically could not afford to employ the expensive new technologies. Nor had the large manufacturers standardized a method for sharing computer-generated models across their respective supply chains. These issues had undermined progress, with the large firms often held back by their smaller, but essential, brethren.

How could the government help democratize access to this high performance modeling and simulation technology so America's manufacturing sector could run more efficiently and build new products more rapidly? In 2011, the Commerce Department joined the Council on Competitiveness—including General Electric, John Deere, Lockheed Martin, and Procter & Gamble—in the launch of a new public-private project called the National Digital Engineering and Manufacturing Consortium (NDEMC).[12] Seeded with $5 million, two-thirds of that from the private sector,

NDEMC ran a pilot program in the Midwest, leveraging research universities and aimed at making modeling and simulation software and training available to small- and medium-size manufacturers. The large manufacturers, such as John Deere, invited their supply chains to participate in the program—in its case, for the purpose of more cost-effective tractor parts. Others offered to help any small- to medium-size manufacturer in the hope of validating the hypothesis that access to such technologies could strengthen American manufacturing.

Nearly 30 suppliers took advantage of the initiative within the first couple of years. One was Jeco Plastics, an Indiana-based company of 25 employees, which sought to supply plastic shipping pallets to a major German manufacturer, a task that had previously fallen to a Chinese supplier. The order was contingent on making a couple of key cosmetic changes and, while doing so, not diminishing the pallets' ability to handle the required weight. Facing seemingly insurmountable cost and time constraints to make these irreversible alterations, Jeco CEO Craig Carson turned to NDEMC, and the access it afforded to supercomputers and staff at Purdue University. Testing its models rapidly and at no cost, Jeco adequately upgraded the pallets, increased the purchase order fivefold to $2.5 million, and received enough recurring income as part of a long-term contract that it was able to expand its workforce by 60 percent. Its successful experience with modeling, simulation, and analysis (MS&A) even led to additional contracts, including one with NASA.[13]

NDEMC is trying to scale the program by encouraging the development of new, low-cost software products that serve the nation's small- to medium-size manufacturers. It is also addressing the issue of standards, a necessity considering the diversity of the U.S. supply chain. For context, consider that the Department of Defense alone works with more than 30,000 manufacturing suppliers in the United States, suppliers that represent approximately 10 percent of the total number of the nation's small- and medium-size manufacturers. Many of these suppliers also provide parts and services to other manufacturers, making it impossible for them to implement a specific method for each one. As part of its broader vision of a "digital industrial commons," NDEMC is working toward standardizing programming language so each supplier can more easily share advanced models and simulations regardless of the manufacturing counterparty.[14]

Further, in May 2013, President Obama announced the launch of a program spearheaded by the Defense Department to build a Digital Manufacturing and Design Innovation (DMDI) Institute—one of three new manufacturing hubs that received $70 million in federal funding, plus an expected financial match from private sources.[15] The DMDI seeks to inject the full potential of information technology into a new, "smarter" manufacturing economy, one that allows for the safe, secure sharing of product designs, quality improvement through faster feedback loops from sensors and data analysis, and faster delivery of products. And, in conjunction with the private sector, it will address a growing array of standards activities, related to data interoperability, definitions, mapping, security, and other areas.

As President Obama said on the day of the announcement: "The economy is dynamic. Technology is constantly changing. That means we've got to adapt as well."[16]

In the Obama administration, we envisioned this approach—leading through coordination and collaboration rather than fiat—working in other sectors. Ideally, public officials would convene parties to encourage the development and deployment of standards that can spark innovation in a given sector of the economy; entrepreneurs would put those standards to work in the development of new products and services; and forward-leaning communities would serve as early test beds for those products and services.

On all of these points, we had willing partners on the legislative side, many of whom saw the value in expanding the reach of an agency that had already experienced considerable growth. Throughout the decades, the Bureau of Standards—and in its latest incarnation as NIST—had been granted greater responsibilities, capabilities, and financial resources. For instance, from 1969 to 1993, there were 79 separate pieces of law that directed the agency to conduct laboratory research and support technologies related to everything from energy conservation and recycling to the metric system to computer security.[17] And, in 2007, with the passage of the America COMPETES Act, NIST would be on a 10-year trajectory to double its budget; by 2013, it had already crossed $1 billion. That legislation also created a new, more prominent, position for the NIST director— Under Secretary of Commerce for Standards and Technology—while directing NIST to collaborate with the private sector on initiatives as varied as cloud computing standards and high performance building standards.[18]

Still, while standards activities grew along with NIST, my colleagues at the White House, including Cass Sunstein, the Director of the Office of Information and Regulatory Affairs (OIRA) and Ambassador Miriam Sapiro, the Deputy United States Trade Representative, sought to revisit the policy President Clinton established in 1998. That had directed agencies to use voluntary consensus industry standards rather than create their own. That essentially told us, as well as other government officials, what we could not do. We couldn't impose our will on others. But we needed to clarify what government *could* do, and what role it could play in assisting the private sector, to reach its own consensus on standards. And in doing so, we needed to provide some specific guidelines to federal agencies, so they clearly understood the appropriate areas and limits of intervention.

Over the course of two years, we engaged hundreds of stakeholders from the public and private sectors, and those interactions would inform the memo we created to institutionalize our approach.[19] That memo started with a clear edict: all standards activities, in the U.S. policy context, must involve the private sector. Yet it added that involvement of the federal government, either in the form of active engagement or a convening role, was appropriate "where a national priority has been identified in statute, regulation, or Administration policy" and that involvement "could accelerate standards development and implementation to help spur technological advances and broaden technology adoption.

"In these instances, the Federal Government can help catalyze advances, promote market-based innovation, and encourage more competitive market outcomes," the memo continued. "The Federal Government should clearly define its role, and then work with private sector standardization organizations in the exercise of that role."

We cited, as an example, the role that the administration had begun to play in the energy sector, since Congress authorized its involvement with the 2007 passage of the Energy Independence and Security Act (EISA). That legislation had directed NIST and the Department of Energy to convene the private sector for the development of standards that would underpin the modernization of the electrical grid.

That work was long overdue. Following Thomas Edison's invention of the lightbulb, America had embarked on what the National Academy of Engineering regarded as one of our great achievements, the construction of "an advanced and complex electrical system that would become a model for the world," thanks to public and private investments.[20] And yet, at an event in June 2011, Energy Secretary Steven Chu referenced Edison to illustrate the industry's recent stagnation. What if Edison transported in a time machine from the 1800s to the present day? He wouldn't recognize the modern manifestations of his inventions in lighting and sound recording, such as LEDs and iPods. "On the other hand, he would feel really at home with most of today's power-generating system," Chu said. "That's in the last half of the nineteenth century, and here we are at the beginning of the twenty-first century."

As Chu argued, we need a modernized electrical grid, a twenty-first-century system for the twenty-first-century economy. We need widespread implementation and ongoing expansion of a "smart grid." This is a grid that, as defined by the U.S. Department of Energy, uses information and communications technology to improve "the efficiency, reliability, economics, and sustainability of the production and distribution of electricity." Such a grid uses digital versions of millions of pieces and parts, such as controls, meters, and transmission lines, upgrades that reflect the power of modern computing and wireless broadband. While many of these remain in relatively primitive stages, the expectation is that, after testing and tinkering, this technology will fully enable real-time communication between the utility and the customer, to accelerate the recording of, and responses to, electrical demand. Real-time information about the state of the grid has value in times of normalcy and distress, for both consumers and utilities. For consumers, knowing the cost of supplying energy at a specific time, such as when demand is greatest, allows them to alter their habits, related to when to do the laundry, run the dishwasher, or merely remove a plug from an outlet. For utilities, it helps to know as soon as possible that a few solar-paneled homes in a neighborhood are requesting more energy than usual. That could speak to cloud cover, and might allow those utilities to better prepare for a surge in energy requests from other homes in the area.

Improving interactions between utilities and customers, in a way that specifically targets the efficiency end of the energy equation, is consistent with President Obama's oft-stated goal of cutting energy waste in half over 20 years, as a complement to ongoing efforts to increase and diversify energy production.[21] Yet there have been holdups, and some can be traced, at least in part, to the way in which the sector is organized. Simply, America has never had one nationalized electric utility system; instead, it has over 3,000 local and regional systems governed by local and state regulators. Each state has adopted a regulatory system with different financial incentives for the utility—from rewarding production at the lowest costs to allowing utilities to recover more money for producing costlier renewable energy. Those incentives impact both the pace of smart grid technology adoption and the effectiveness of those technologies in lowering energy usage and upping reliability, to name just two improvements.

So far, innovation has been slow. At the aforementioned June 2011 White House event, only about half the states had adopted specific policies related to smart grid technology, and most of those policies were modest. Most utilities make more money if they sell more power, not the inverse. That's their incentive. So, why should a utility invest in something that reduces power consumption to the detriment of their shareholders? And for the regulators who oversee those utilities, and whose primary concern is to keep costs down for the rate payers to whom they are accountable, why add any expense without clear benefit? The math doesn't make sense.

A few leading states have tackled the incentive problem by implementing policies to decouple the production of energy from the sale of energy services that fuel homes. Others have needed a push. That was the idea driving the White House Strategy for a 21st Century Grid, which, released on that June day, explicitly called for aligning the incentives to encourage the deployment of smart grid technologies, in the name of "a clean, smart, national electricity system that will create jobs, reduce energy use, and expand renewable energy production."[22]

To demonstrate how anyone could make a difference, Secretary Chu invited Shreya Indukuri and Daniela Lapidous to share the stage on the day he released the report. The high school seniors had raised money to install a smart energy system at the Harker School in San Jose, California, using off-the-shelf smart submetering devices, dedicated to individual buildings, as well as an intuitive online dashboard that allowed the school superintendent to learn exactly where energy usage was greatest on the school campus. With a week of installation, several anomalies became apparent, especially the excess usage in the gym. Further investigation revealed that the air-conditioning had been running over the weekend, without anyone knowing or needing it. A flip of the switch saved several thousand dollars and, over one year, Harker saw a 13 percent savings on its energy bill and a 250 percent return on investment. Lapidous proudly touted the low barrier to entry for such a campus-based "smart meter project": a cost of between $10,000 and $20,000 per school with an 18-month payback period. Then the teenager drew laughs by drawing a clear conclusion: "Even if you're not an environmentalist, it's pretty hard to argue with a 250 percent ROI."

It certainly is. And if two teenagers could accomplish so much, energy savings stories similar to theirs certainly should become commonplace, rather than seem extraordinary. But three things need to happen. First, the incentives for the utility companies need to be aligned with those of their customers, no easy task.[23] Second, those utilities need to grant access to the sort of data that even the Harker students didn't have at their disposal. Third, all 3,000 utilities need to come together to standardize the way that information is shared, so that it could be understood and implemented by third-party developers and ultimately by consumers. If all of that occurred, it might result in a vibrant marketplace, as simple and appealing as the iPhone app store, competing to aid the Harker students, and those like them, in identifying energy waste.

So NIST and the Department of Energy, represented by George Arnold and Pat Hoffman, respectively, worked together to convene the Smart Grid Interoperability Panel. That public-private partnership was led by the existing private sector standards bodies to design and deploy the necessary standards, and aided by $10 million that President Obama had allocated in the Recovery Act in 2009. The stakeholders—utility sector entities, manufacturers, and technology firms, to name a few—recognized they needed each other. Good faith, plus good leadership, can go a long way. According to Arnold, in light of the structure of the utility sector, the government "is really the only entity that can provide that coordination leadership role." NIST prioritized the panel's work by emphasizing more than a dozen areas critical to jump-starting the smart grid industry. Among them: standardizing how utilities communicate with customers on energy usage information.

By February 2011, the participants endorsed what Arnold characterized as "a very robust toolkit" of standards. Now it was time for the next giant leap: deployment of those standards in a sector that, according to Hoffman, was "ripe for an information revolution" of the sort that manufacturing had already begun to experience. Months later, I addressed a leading forum for utility executives interested in grid modernization, and raised a question: "How can we safely and securely provide customers electronic access to their energy information, thereby supporting the continuing development of innovative new products and services in the energy sector?"

The answer would come through enlisting a coalition of utility companies, those willing to implement the agreed-upon standards. It was a strategy based on what a number of insurance companies and medical providers were already working toward in the health care space: standardizing and simplifying the method in which Medicare recipients and veterans could download personal health data, through the placement of a Blue Button icon on patient-facing websites. Why not create a Green Button that would have a similar role and payoff in the energy sector—allowing utility customers to download their own usage data and do with it what they wished, including sharing it with a growing array of third party applications that competed to provide money-saving tips?

The appeal was well received, especially by those who had been quietly at work on the underlying standards and saw an opening for faster implementation. Still, the movement called for a champion, someone who understood the importance of engaging the customer to spark innovation. That champion would come from California, where policymakers had long been working to enable the utilities and their customers to benefit from more efficient usage. They had begun to do so in the 1980s through a process called "decoupling," to separate energy sales from profits, and give utilities state-approved incentives to encourage conservation and the use of renewable energy. Then, in 2011, Karen Austin came aboard as the new CIO of Pacific Gas & Electric.[24] Austin had devoted her career to recognizing, understanding, and improving customer relationships in the private sector, while establishing herself as an e-commerce retailing pioneer at Kmart and Sears, with customer-friendly programs such as Buy Online, Pick Up in Store.

I called Austin, assuming she would be receptive to the Green Button proposal. "I thought the idea was fantastic," Austin recalled. "Of *course* we should give our customers this information. Let's do it!"

Seeing it as a win-win-win, for the customer, PG&E, and the environment, she called other California utilities, including Southern California Edison and San Diego Gas & Electric, and convened a meeting within a couple of weeks: highly unusual alacrity for the typically sluggish utility sector. At the meeting, she—and I, as a government representative—would be sitting at the same table with a small group of public, private, and nonprofit leaders, not on a dais, looking down.

"A partnership," she said.

We had a brisk breeze at our back. That July, the California Public Utilities Commission, the state's utility regulator, had ordered that the utilities at least agree on a process for the design of a standard record format, making this stage merely about solidification and deployment. And, since the three utilities represented different parts of the state, they weren't competing with each other for customers but, rather, free to compete together, against the clock, toward the achievement of similar goals.

"The key was just to keep it simple," Austin said. "A lot of the standards had already been thought through but never deployed."

To Austin, the idea of not getting something done, even in the compressed time frame, "didn't cross my mind. The thought of creating separate formats, I don't know, it wouldn't have made sense to proceed that way. It was going to happen. I was comfortable that we were going to get there."

Before they left the room, they agreed upon a sketch of the key fields that a customer would need, as well as a standard record format for the data that would fill those fields. Then they assigned someone from every utility to deliver a common user interface. This was a relatively easy technical exercise, since the group adopted an existing standard that simplified the "what" and "how" data would be published and transmitted between parties.[25]

Within 90 days, I visited California once again, to celebrate a number of Green Button commitments.[26] Austin's PG&E and her counterpart at San Diego Gas & Electric announced they were live for all of their customers; the technical body responsible for the data format, North American Energy Standards Board, announced a free starter toolkit that included detailed technical documents necessary for developers to build products and services on top of Green Button data. A few startups demonstrated early prototypes of apps that personalize energy savings tips through the use of a customer's Green Button file.[27] All of this was inspiring, but incomplete. Following the presentation, an audience member asked if the utilities would be publishing their rate schedules electronically as well, so customers could make energy decisions based on specific costs at a particular moment; in California, peak time pricing is double or triple the normal rate. Austin, who recognized the value of that data, related the reality: improving access to that information might take more than a year.

In the interim, however, an entrepreneur named Jason Riley was working to prove that there were better ways of linking energy pricing and usage data. Prior to the Green Button launch, back in 2010, Riley had founded a startup called Genability on the premise that, to deliver meaningful savings, an energy consumer would need both pricing and usage data. The pricing side hadn't been a problem; with the help of contractors, he had begun manually entering utility tariff information for hundreds of rate plans into an online database, offering access to developers for a fee. On usage data, however, Riley had been stuck, since that information had been inaccessible to the public. At least it was, prior to Green Button.

I met Riley a week after the Green Button launch in California, while I was serving as a guest judge at a Cleanweb Hackathon in New York, where industry and government officials outlined specific challenges related to energy, such as the exorbitant cost of solar panel installation, and—in a bit of foreshadowing—New York City's efforts to help residents better prepare for storm surges through the visualization of climate change. The organizer's primary purpose, however, was to invite volunteer developers to spend 72 hours building prototype applications on top of a growing number of energy information services, while promising modest prizes.

With access to Genability's Electricity Pricing database, Green Button data for energy usage, and other open energy data sources, 15 developer teams completed prototypes by Sunday evening. One stood out, because, in using both Genability and Green Button data, it educated users about the most economical rate plans for them. The Watt Quiz was a simple, engaging customer survey that, after the customer uploads his or her Green Button file from the utility, helps answer a simple question, "Which tariff rate plan saves you the most money?" It showed how one family could save 44 percent simply by changing the rate plan.

The CleanWeb Hackathon scaled into an international movement, not just because developers like to tinker and gather, but because of the promise of a new business model—making money while helping energy consumers save it. Take, for instance, Simple Energy, based out of Boulder, Colorado, which partnered with San Diego Gas & Electric in its launch of the Green Button service. After using Simple Energy's Customer Engagement platform to see her family's energy usage online, Heidi Bates deputized her six-year-old son Thaddeus as the "Light Police," to run around the house unplugging unnecessary luminescence. "He really digs it," she said. The enthusiasm spread throughout age ranges; a grandmother, Josephine Gonzales, saved over 20 percent on her electric bills using the Facebook-connected platform.

Meanwhile, in Northern California, in the wake of the Green Button rollout, Austin continued coming across customers who benefited from the access to information, and were eager to share experiences. That included one couple—she refers to them as Kelly and Jim—from San Luis Obispo that had downsized to a residence half the size, expecting the energy bill to decline in kind. "When it didn't budge at all, Kelly got onto the Green Button, and took that data and then really went around her home and looked at her usage," Austin said. "She was able to cut her bill from $160 per month to about $50 per month, which was an annual savings of $1,300."

Some customers even revealed that they had taken it upon themselves to spread the Green Button word around their neighborhoods, to improve the area's overall efficiency. Understanding the power not only of the data but also the importance of presenting it in easily comprehended charts and graphs, Austin asked the board at Pacific Gas & Electric for resources to sponsor an Apps for Energy contest in partnership with the White House.[28] Nearly 50 developers applied in the spring of 2012, some small companies, some single individuals. They produced a diverse range of concepts, with first-place honors going to Leafully—a visually appealing software tool accessed through social media that breaks a person's energy footprint and environmental impact down into a corresponding number of trees saved. The second prize went to Melon.com, which combined Green Button and the EPA's Energy Star portfolio manager to give more than one million commercial buildings a "simple and affordable" benchmarking analysis, allowing managers to compare their buildings with others around the United States, comply with the law, and save money. The third-prize winner, VELObill, was a colorful, intuitive application for consumers to view utility usage, compare it to peers, find ways to save, and find local contractors who can get them closer to their energy goals.

Still, Austin was anxious to iterate further in collaboration with the White House, simplifying access for third parties and, thus, speeding the rate of innovation. My successor as Chief Technology Officer, Todd Park, would announce the release of Green Button Connect My Data, a program that would eliminate the need for customers to take possession of their own data via download in order to use third party applications. Through the Connect My Data service, that upload would happen automatically once consumers enrolled.

Austin helped winners of the Apps for Energy contest go into production in her market. One was the previously mentioned Leafully. Another was PEV4me, which, by accounting for a user's driving habits, calculates how much the user would save on gas by switching to an electric car. Another was UnPlugStuff, which assists in determining the cost of phantom usage, such as leaving your toaster plugged into the wall. In the first three months, after setting up all three with sufficient security protections, roughly 10,000 people signed up to use their services, and that was even with limited advertising during the election season.

"So far, so good," Austin said.

Austin viewed this early progress to be a product of "keeping it simple versus trying to boil the whole ocean, and getting everyone on the same page."

In this scenario, "keeping it simple" meant implementing the Green Button standard rather than attempting to account for every possible request for how to access someone's individual energy data. It also meant moving incrementally, first providing the data in downloadable form, then automating that connection.

And "everyone" meant representatives of the government *and* the private sector, not at odds with each other but in collaboration, sharing ideas and shaking hands, before handing off to entrepreneurs to innovate.

Utility executives haven't always embraced government involvement in their affairs—after all, as Austin noted, government regulation can sometimes slow the pace of innovation.

"In this case," Austin said, "government was a positive enabler for sure."

In 2013, President Obama would use the State of the Union to reiterate his commitment to the smart grid, by calling for a Race to the Top proposal which would provide financial incentives to states who adopt energy efficiency policies. As of press time, that had yet to pass, but players in this space had moved ahead anyway, with 35 utilities and energy providers voluntarily committing within the first year to provide 36 million homes and businesses with their own energy usage information in the consensus, industry-standard Green Button format.

For all the inroads we were making in the energy sector, we knew there was a need to pour our energy, in terms of standards creation and deployment, into other industries. In the Obama administration's calculus, no national priority ranked higher than health care. Thirteen months prior to the signing of the landmark Affordable Care Act into law, its technological underpinnings had been codified in the Health Information Technology for Economic and Clinical Health Act (HITECH Act), a provision of the Recovery Act that we mentioned earlier. Only weeks into his first term, the President pushed for a $26 billion incentive program that would encourage doctors and hospitals to adopt and use electronic health records. And on this rare issue, he didn't encounter much pushback from either party, since many members on both sides of the aisle—from Hillary Clinton to Newt Gingrich—agreed that, no matter how we financed the care delivery system, it needed to be modernized through the application of information technology, to improve quality and reduce costs. Congress authorized the Centers for Medicare and Medicaid Services (CMS) to pay doctors up to $44,000 and hospitals millions based on their size—but only if they "meaningfully used" certified technology in their daily work treating patients.

Why the broad consensus for intervention? Because, as the rest of the economy was surging forward, experiencing sizable productivity gains powered by the workplace application of information technology, health care was stuck on a treadmill. It was underinvested in technology, relative to comparable service industries. Even when the industry did invest or innovate, its priorities tended to be misdirected, focused on the wrong set of problems. That was partly a product of the predominance of the fee-for-service structure in the $2 trillion health care system, a structure that financially rewarded quantity over quality. The more patients a physician sees, the more tests that physician orders, the more the physician can bill. There is little incentive in the system for investing and engaging preventive and chronic disease management, care coordination, medication management, and telemedicine services (e-mail, online chats, and videoconferencing). In fact, there is actually a perverse disincentive, as healthier patients need fewer services, thus reducing provider compensation. It should come as no surprise that health care professionals have sought IT-enabled products that improved efficiency in billing and scheduling for services that will be reimbursed, but largely ignored those that might improve individual care, let alone the health of the greater population.

Consider the problem of premature births, which we described in a Virginia context in Chapter 3. The health IT industry has the capability to better predict if a mother is likely to deliver early, which often leads to admissions into neonatal intensive care units. But, when those admissions generate revenues of more than $40,000 per week, what is the incentive for a health care system to invest in that technology? Altruism alone? And, worse, even if you identified those vulnerable mothers, you would bear the costs of any preventative services that you offered, since most come with no reimbursement.

Even while pushing the health IT movement forward, proponents understood that the payoff would be limited until the payment systems aligned incentives. This was even noted early in a 2005 report by the RAND Corporation, the nonprofit global policy think tank, which estimated the potential of more than $81 billion in annual savings through the widespread adoption of electronic medical records systems, with that figure potentially doubling through additional health IT-enabled prevention and management of chronic disease.[29] The report declared that the full benefits of health IT were "unlikely to be realized without related changes to the health care system."

Lawmakers of all stripes referenced the sanguine predictions of the RAND study in advocating for incentives to encourage provider adoption of such systems, and that advocacy played a role in the passage of the aforementioned HITECH Act. They did not, however, provide the accompanying payment reform, at least in the short term. And when RAND reassessed its study in 2013, its findings prematurely rang alarm bells for many.[30] It found that the $81 billion savings had not materialized, and health costs had actually risen, ironically, in small part due to the improved billing and documentation procedures that the health IT systems had made possible. So, rather than a refuge for consensus, health IT became more of a partisan talking point for those opposed to the President's overall health care agenda and unwilling to consider the contributing factor of fee for service.

There remained a need for a more virtuous cycle in health care, one outlined by the Center for American Progress.[31] That think tank saw potential for health IT adoption, care delivery innovation, and provider payment reform to interact and flourish, with each helping to make the others work, instead of the absence of one or more of those elements stalling overall improvement. In its reassessment, RAND didn't give up hope: "We believe that the original promise of health IT can be met if the systems are redesigned to address these flaws by creating more-standardized systems that are easier to use, are truly interoperable, and afford patients more access to and control over their health data. Providers must do their part by re-engineering care processes to take full advantage of efficiencies offered by health IT, in the context of redesigned payment models that favor value over volume."

Progress in those areas was already under way.[32]

On payment models, the Affordable Care Act had included many payment reform provisions, chief among them the creation of a new Center for Medicare & Medicaid Innovation, seeded with $10 billion to run experiments on new payment models that have the potential to improve quality and lower costs. To complement the center, Congress granted a new regulatory authority. If the CMS' nonpartisan actuary certified that a payment model achieved quality improvement and cost reduction, then the

HHS Secretary could make it an option for every provider in the country.

On interoperability, the HITECH Act had tied its $26 billion in incentives for health care providers to their adoption of technologies that incorporated standards, which would be defined in three stages over the next five years. And for the standards work, we had called upon an experienced hand—my old friend Dr. John Halamka, who had engaged in the standards process across two Presidential administrations.

Under President Bush, who had pledged in 2004 that every American would have access to a personal health record within a decade, HHS would seed pilot investments for technical work to that end. As Chairman of the Healthcare Information Technology Standards Panel (HITSP), Halamka was exposed to well-intentioned actors, but also to a process primarily driven by a few senior government people and the vendor community, rather than by the doctors, insurance companies, and patients. It was also a process that lacked any economic incentives for the parties to push themselves toward the best possible performance. In the current market environment, vendors and their hospital customers simply didn't have much of a stake in making it easier to share information. The reimbursement system encourages health organizations to grow through increasing market share, an objective that would be undermined if it was easier, not harder, for patients to seek care elsewhere.

The result of such a vendor-driven approach, according to Halamka, was "basically codifying the status quo." The standards that they did create "were so cumbersome and so heavy that vendors could only successfully implement them by charging vast sums of money."

In his new role, as vice chair of the Health IT Standards Committee (HITSC) in the Obama administration, Halamka had a more formal legal foundation than during the Bush administration.

Authorized by the HITECH Act, the HITSC would benefit from greater engagement and urgency among all parties, a clearer business case to scale what works, and a more constructive governance model. It was a collaborative model that owed plenty to the insights that Mitch Kapor, the Lotus Development Corporation founder, outlined and endorsed in his aforementioned speech calling for a Health Internet. Kapor called for a less complex, more open, "light federal approach" that would encourage an early critical mass of users to participate—something like a dozen or more products and services built on the standards—thus reducing costs and time to market while fueling innovation. That's how the standards committee set about its work.

"Let's do it in an open, transparent, multistakeholder fashion that will be bottom-up rather than top-down and will be fueled by innovation, agility and low costs," Halamka said. "We'll make it a 'do-ocracy.' That is, you will be rewarded for actually achieving results. What ended up happening is that suddenly the implementation guides, instead of thousands of pages of complicated technology specs, became ten pages of simple technology specs. You saw existing Internet standards being leveraged for health care. You saw open source. You saw intellectual property freedom. And you suddenly actually got the vendors a little bit on the run, because now they were having to open their systems and enable platforms and they could no longer charge obscene amounts of money for simple tasks."

Among those tasks: downloading your own health data from a provider. That was the topic at a gathering of Internet thought leaders hosted by the Markle Foundation in New York in January 2010.[33] Participants included Todd Park, then the HHS CTO; Dr. Peter Levin, the CTO of Veterans Affairs, and a former entrepreneur in the biotech and semiconductor sectors; former Google Health leader Adam Bosworth; and Professor Clay Shirky, an author and Internet scholar.

During brainstorming, the meeting's participants decided to use a simple text format called ASCII that, if sensibly organized, machines and people could read with equal ease. Park and Levin agreed that Veterans Affairs would serve as the test case, with Medicare to follow shortly thereafter. The VA had a head start as it had the largest consolidated network of hospitals, the largest electronics records system, and nearly a million users on its personal health records platform. "There was certainly no technical challenge to doing this," Levin said.

President Obama took on some of the marketing challenge himself. With everything proceeding smoothly in production, he shared the news with the Disabled Veterans of America on August 2, 2010: "Today, I can announce that for the first time ever, veterans will be able to go to the VA website, click on a simple 'blue button,' and download or print your personal health records so that you have them when you need them and you can share them with your doctors outside of the VA. That's happening this fall."

But how many of the roughly 1.5 million veterans would use it? When asked by Eric Shinseki, the VA Secretary, Levin pulled a figure out of the air: 25,000 in the first year. "But I had no idea whether they would really want this," Levin said. "I figured the worst case scenario is, I'm out on Pennsylvania Avenue with a clipboard, getting people to sign up."

No clipboard required. By October 2012, Blue Button would serve more than 1 million downloads across all of its federal agency partners—the VA, the Department of Defense (serving active duty military), and the Medicare program—under the basic premise that any American should be able to download information the government keeps on them in machine-readable form. Its popularity in the public sector inspired adoption in the private sector, and Dr. Levin would fill a role there, too, spearheading the development of the service to convening a volunteer network of private sector developers. A coalition of health insurance companies, led by UnitedHealthcare and Aetna, would offer Blue Button services for their own members as well. In September 2013, the Office of the National Coordinator (ONC) for Health IT touted another milestone: 500 partner organizations had pledged consumer access through Blue Button in order to reach 100 million Americans, nearly one-third of the population.[34] Further, new privacy regulations, updating those originally mandated by the Health Insurance Portability and Accountability Act of 1996 (HIPAA), required any medical providers with electronic records on patients to offer them back to those patients in electronic form at a nominal fee.[35] All of this means that the country is getting closer to honoring President Bush's long-ago promise of providing personalized health records to everyone.

Those measures, while important to transform the health care system, are not sufficient. So in a parallel effort, beginning in 2010, ONC would apply the "light federal approach" to how patients and caregivers could safely and securely share health information over the Internet.

That effort began in response to Dr. Floyd "Tripp" Bradd's testimony to the HITSC about a patient who was moving to Arizona and wanted his records forwarded electronically. After receiving that consent, Dr. Bradd was able to e-mail the records in a format that the other provider—using the same software package—could import and read. But conventional e-mail isn't that secure. The data isn't encrypted, and there is no way to prove the identity of the sender or receiver. Dr. Bradd challenged us to develop a safer, more secure version of e-mail.

Two public servants teamed up to provide it. Doug Fridsma was already working inside the administration, leading standards work at the ONC. Arien Malec was taking a leave of absence from his executive position at RelayHealth to join the government on a temporary basis.

"If there are existing standards, we say, 'our job is done, we don't have to do anything else,'" Fridsma said. "If people say, 'We've got a big hole; this is a problem because everybody is doing it in a whole bunch of different ways,' then we can use our convening authority to say, 'Success is filling this gap in the standards in such a way that it works with these other things that people care about, and meets all of our policy objectives as well, but *you* guys have to tell us whether it solves the problem or not.' At the end of the day, the government's role is to convene."

Together, Fridsma and Malec led a new initiative called the Direct Project, aimed at developing a safe, secure, and cost-effective method to "push" health information between providers, patients, and other stakeholders. By standardizing interfaces, the duo hoped to achieve a 90 percent reduction in the cost of exchanging laboratory results, to name just one example.

They recognized that the road to interoperability required an incremental, thoughtful approach, with Fridsma noting that, just as people use more than one means of personal communication, cell phones, landlines, and social media, to name the most popular, "We shouldn't expect that within health care, which is far more complicated, we should have a single way of communicating either." Further, they recognized the critical need for all sorts of outside input. Rather than call upon contractors to construct a monolithic system that the community would accept, reject, or ignore, as had been done in the United Kingdom a few years earlier, it was more constructive to work with the community toward the standardization of the fundamental building blocks—meaning, structure, transport, security, and services—for electronic health record communications. "We turned the whole project inside out," Fridsma said. "We created government as a platform, if you will, a way to engage the public and let them tell us what was important and then support them in accelerating their consensus to a common solution."

This engagement approach—consistent with what Tim O'Reilly had described as Government 2.0—also squared perfectly with lessons Malec had learned in the private sector, particularly in startup companies, "that participation drives innovation and, that in the open source software, the more you share, the more you get from the community." Malec also believed that, since most health care is provided by the private sector and it would be writing the integrated software that pulls everything together, it *needed* to be part of the process. That way, the private sector would be more likely to own the responsibility for creating the solution.

"Instead of having an approach of telling people what to do, it just seemed like the right thing would be to set a challenge, set a vision, and ask people to get involved," Malec said. "We set a vision, a view of the world as it would look past the innovation, but that outcome would describe what happens and not how it happens. Then we got people together, gave them this big inspiring vision, and said we want you to be the ones to figure out how and to own how."

Malec had anticipated that perhaps a handful of hypermotivated organizations would participate in the Direct Project. That was, until he attended the annual Healthcare Information Management Systems Society meeting and got a chance to introduce the idea to tens of thousands of health IT stakeholders. "The response was overwhelming," he said. Within a month, 90 organizations wanted to participate—and thanks to modern collaboration technologies, they could do so with just an Internet connection and the occasional conference call.

The Direct team set up a series of wiki sites without restrictions on participation or observation. Then it elevated some participants, those with special interest in the implementation of a solution, to the status of Committed Members. Before and throughout the process, the government promoted some basic discussion guidelines (discouraging members from conducting side e-mail conversations) and even some policy parameters ("guard rails," in Fridsma's parlance) that were meant to keep the community moving forward toward solutions that, at the least, sufficiently conformed with technological and security realities to have a shot. The government was vocal, but not tyrannical. "Ultimately, we have just a single vote at the table," Fridsma said.

Still, the government's steering role was significant. Even when conversations became contentious, Malec kept all parties at the table. As Sean Nolan of Microsoft noted, "Arien's personality was key. He maintained the respect of a bunch of people that generally don't respect each other."

In Malec's view, plenty was accomplished.

"In one year, we had progressed from nothing to 'running code,' real-world testing, and commitment," Malec said, noting that 70 organizations implemented the work of the Direct Project in their products. "We had a model for every provider in the country sending secure information to every other provider in the country and every patient in the country; we had a path, a real path, to make that happen. We had enabling software that any software developer could incorporate into their products to smooth the path. And we had the process for process. We had a template for how to do this in the federal government—this new style of interaction between the federal government and private sector."

They had accomplished all of this at a very low marginal cost, and their work led to products that were relatively inexpensive, with a growing competitive marketplace offering unlimited Direct messaging services for less than $20 a month.

Malec returned to RelayHealth in the summer of 2011, nine months after he had planned, and not due to any disillusionment. Rather, his time in government had reinforced his belief in its unique position to see problems from coast to coast and its capability, through a handshake with—and handoff to—the private sector, to effect positive change. A little push, a lot of support. "That's a trick that I think government can replicate," Malec said. "The risk of doing the wrong thing, of trying too much and getting unintended consequences, is so small—and the risk of doing the right thing and creating the right outcome is so huge—that it's a really useful thing that government can do. And the second big idea is that when the relationship is participatory, when the relationship is open, it really does foster a sense that the government isn't a *thing*, it's what we do together."

The work went on after Malec's departure. In August 2012, the ONC announced that the Direct standards would be required for the next stage of the health IT incentive program taking effect in 2014. In response, members of the Direct community took the ball, launching an independent, self-regulatory nonprofit called Direct-Trust to ensure the agreed-upon standards are deployed in health IT. Essentially, the private sector was picking up where the government left off.

As of this writing, the open government approach utilized for Direct and other health IT standards has attracted more than 500 people representing over 300 organizations, working on one or more of 10 active programs.[36] This will give a head start to new startups seeking to compete in the health IT industry.

Will the interoperability standards adopted for 2014 deliver on their promise? Will future health IT regulations result in the ultimate objective: a true "plug and play" health IT ecosystem where innovative new products and services could be distributed as easily as apps on the iPhone app store, perhaps through an API standard?

Too soon to say. But, in May 2013, milestones were met—more than 50 percent of America's doctors and more than 80 percent of hospitals were participating in the meaningful use incentive program.[37] That represented a doubling and quadrupling, respectively, from previous participation. It appears the industry has reached a tipping point that will position the care delivery system for its most difficult chapter: achieving more with less.

"We have done more the past two years than in the previous twenty," Halamka said.

Which merely means that more can be done.

"Standards aren't standards because we say so," Fridsma said. "Standards are standards because people use them. The only standard you don't have to maintain over time is the standard you never use. Standards, good ones anyway, will continue to grow and change to accommodate new use cases and new innovations that are out there."

Sometimes, successful innovations come at the intersection of ongoing and evolving initiatives. In this case, some combination of Blue Button and the Direct Project could eliminate extra steps for patients, and make them more likely to participate. Rather than be required to download their information onto the computer after every medical development, and then determine which parts to share with which caretakers, what if patients could simply set preferences at various points of care (whether the emergency room or the pharmacy) that would automatically route medical information to other places it should go? For instance, it is useful for a primary care physician to know not only that a patient was admitted to a hospital the previous night, but also every test that was run, every diagnosis that was made, and every medication that was prescribed while the patient was there. It is also useful for the physician to know whether the patient ever picked up a prescription. This sort of knowledge is especially valuable to address one of the health care system's most troubling inefficiencies: nearly one in five Medicare patients discharged from a hospital is readmitted within one month, at a cost of nearly $17 billion to the government, and often due to inadequate patient follow-through, especially when it comes to taking the proper medication.

As was the case with energy data and Green Button, all this progress in the field of health information records could not occur without that initial enabling piece—the development of a standardized method for health IT applications to send and receive Blue Button files on behalf of patients to everyone in the health care ecosystem, with security and privacy built in. That Auto Blue Button Initiative effort, again largely driven by private sector entities, would eventually be launched as Blue Button + in February of 2013.[38] It would enable consumers to do everything from printing a physical copy of their records to sharing it with a third party application.

"All of this data more or less exists in the market," Levin said. "But getting all of it in one place, making sure your prescriptions are in the same place as your immunizations, in the same place as your radiologist images, in the same place as the last time you took antibiotics because you had a sore throat, and with all of those things now able to flow without friction between places of trust, that's what the Auto Blue Button Initiative is all about."

Technical standards aren't a sufficiently sexy topic to sneak their way into the daily senior staff briefings held in the West Wing, nor common in cocktail party conversation. Yet, someday, they might be. Look at how they were applied after President Obama announced the official end of combat operations in Iraq on August 5, 2011.

Service members, who had spent months or years in an unforgiving conflict, would be coming home. They would need jobs. The President, citing the shockingly high unemployment rate among young veterans, called upon the private sector to provide those opportunities. Corporate executives enthusiastically raised their hands, eager to assist. But this was about more than good will or gracious gestures. The veterans would need direction in order to navigate their way through all that might be available via the competitive and expansive online job listings industry. They needed to have some idea of which listings had been set aside for them.

There were essentially two options to assist them. We could create a single website, through government funding, which would provide places for every willing employer to post listings. That would have been the default. That, however, also would be redundant and burdensome for employers, most of which already had preferred methods for online job postings. Alternatively, we could engage the job listings industry in designing and deploying a standardized method to "tag" job listings associated with a veteran hiring commitment, regardless of the website they chose for those postings.

We chose the latter and started our 90-day sprint for a Veterans Day launch by calling upon the experts at Schema.org, a voluntary collaboration between Google, Microsoft, and Yahoo, that tagged web pages in a way that helped users find the most relevant and specific information.[39] Take recipes. Schema.org includes a recipe standard that reflects a consensus among many in the online recipes industry on the sort of information that is most useful to a cook, including cuisine type, calorie count, ingredients, and instructions.[40] Any website is free to add the schema to its page, enhancing its search results on the participating search engines and inspiring customers to click through and learn more.

This sounded like something we could simply and seamlessly apply to our project. I engaged the private sector online job listings industry to help design the schema. Figuring that veterans would need to know more about job descriptions, locations, and compensation, among other topics, we engaged a variety of stakeholders for further input before publishing the agreed-upon standard at schema.org by October 2011. That would give us a month to encourage the job listings industry to begin tagging relevant job listings with the standard before a Presidential announcement on Veterans Day.

On November 7, 2011, President Obama announced the launch of the Veterans Job Bank, a Google-customized search engine—built at no cost to the taxpayer in collaboration with the Department of Defense and Veterans Affairs—that any veteran could use to find the tagged jobs that were right for them, including the ability to narrow results based on military occupation code or ZIP code.[41] On that day, several job listings vendors, including Monster.com, Simply Hired, and LinkedIn, publicly pledged to adopt the schema.org standard if they had not already done so. Simply Hired, for example, had already kept track of nearly 500,000 open jobs associated with veteran hiring commitments and all of them were tagged on day one. Within a year, the job listings sites would feature more than one million veteran-tagged jobs, and shortly after that, Google would devote a day to highlighting the Veterans Job Bank on its most precious asset, the search home page.

The next step in this process was bringing the Job Bank to veterans, rather than forcing them to find it on a government website. Several technology firms volunteered to build free apps to help connect veterans with the Bank, with the reward of being honored at the Joining Forces Veterans App Showcase, featuring Dr. Jill Biden, the Vice President's wife. Originally, Twilio was not among those participating firms. Yet, upon learning about the event just one day earlier, the San Francisco cloud communications company thought it could contribute. Its CEO, Jeff Lawson, issued a "lightning challenge" to his more than 75,000 partner developers to build a more veteran-friendly interface to search for these tagged jobs, accessible on smart phones and using their technology.[42] He set the deadline for 8 a.m., Pacific time, the following morning, five hours before the event.

Tony Webster, a 25-year-old web developer, just happened to be on Twitter when the challenge crossed his feed. He had been interested in open government for a while and, although he had never served in the military, had close friends who had returned from Iraq and Afghanistan. He had heard horror stories about their job searches due, in part, to the reluctance of employers—for one reason or another—to hire veterans. Further, he had a good understanding of Twilio. So he headed to a café, intent to expeditiously create something unique before its doors closed at midnight. "I wasn't about to be up all night, because I actually had a real job, too," Webster said. "I whipped up something in four hours. Then I went home, ramped it up, and got some sleep."

His conception of HeroJobs.org wowed the Twilio judges by flipping the model. After entering their Military Occupation Specialty codes and ZIP codes, veterans received text messages, every morning, with the appropriate, veteran-committed openings in their area. Webster had no idea whether anyone would actually use HeroJobs.org, but many veterans did, and veterans' relatives told him they appreciated the ease of the service.

His application was designed just for the competition, not as a full-running site, and eventually it faded out. So, too, did many of the demonstrated apps in the showcase. But firms like Google and LinkedIn have further invested in making their applications work with the former's launch of VetNet, a portal that accesses and builds valuable services, such as networking courses and Google Hangout video discussions, on top of the jobs bank. LinkedIn would develop its own veterans page, and a discount offer for those users—a free LinkedIn premium account (a $99 value), plus a more direct path for employers to connect with the 1 million veterans already on the LinkedIn platform.

Common to all these examples is the notion of a more innovative state. That starts with smart government, government that identifies problems, convenes the interested parties and innovative thinkers, and then empowers them to address an issue. It is one of the initiatives that, for those that follow, will set a rather high standard.

Chapter 7

Prizes and Challenges

In 1861, with the Civil War starting to rage on sea as well as land, the Union found itself in very rough waters. Its strategists knew that its antiquated wooden boats were no match for the Confederacy's more modern, sturdier ironclad ships.[1] And they knew that, if they didn't upgrade their own fleet, they were sunk. That's why the Navy engaged in a procurement process, selecting three designs for further development, including one from John Ericsson. At the Battle of Hampton Roads in 1862, Ericsson's USS *Monitor* managed an important draw against the Confederate battleship *Virginia*, at least temporarily preserving the Union blockade of the Commonwealth of Virginia.

Following that modest success, President Abraham Lincoln and the Navy expanded the ironclad fleet in early 1863. But with increasing use, the Navy discovered that the vessels had a key defect: the magnetism of the iron siding interfered with compass tracking, skewing navigation so significantly that even the most capable captains often steered the ships the wrong way.

Thankfully, President Lincoln had a new vehicle to help steer them back. Starting with Benjamin Franklin's foundation of the American Philosophical Society (APS) in 1743, there had been many calls for, and attempts at, creating a national society of science, through which ready, willing, and able experts would pool their talents to tackle the nation's most pressing and seemingly intractable problems.[2] That effort gained some momentum in the 1850s, through the work of a group of influential, yet self-deprecating scientists in Cambridge, Massachusetts (calling themselves the Scientific Lazzaroni after an Italian bakery). But it was the Civil War that made such collaborative exploration really imperative, since the military began to recognize the value of scientific advice in evaluating new inventions to aid the war effort. In 1863, as he was assessing the ironclad problem, President Lincoln signed into law a unanimous act of Congress to establish the nonprofit, independent National Academy of Sciences (NAS), for work on an assortment of challenges during the conflict at hand and—assuming the Union endured—the decades to come.[3]

Fifty scientists signed up for the cause, receiving no compensation. A subset of them got to work on the Navy's ironclad assignment. The results were impressive enough that President Obama spoke of them in a 2013 speech marking the 150th anniversary of the National Academy of Sciences. "By the next year, they were inspecting the Union's ironclads and installing an array of bar magnets around the compasses to correct their navigation," Obama told the audience. "So right off the bat, you guys were really useful. In fact, it's fair to say we might not be here had you not. Certainly I would not be here."

That line drew laughter, but the story of the National Academy's founding is fodder for a serious conversation about problem solving, specifically the need for the government to be open, flexible, imaginative, and even courageous. Consider the stakes for Lincoln: he was in the midst of a conflict that could have entirely wiped out a young country. Yet, after the traditional problem-solving process went awry—with a contractor developing flawed ironclads—he adjusted, turning such a critical endeavor over to a startup with no track record. Reckless? Not really. In that case, Lincoln and Congress had drawn upon our most underutilized resource, our diverse talent in the private sector, widening the net to include the perspectives that might otherwise have been unknown or ignored, since our government has relied upon the same narrow cast of contractors, often choosing those who best know how to curry favor in the Beltway. In the instance of the ironclads, Lincoln and Congress drew upon prestige and public service as the primary motivators for time-limited participation; too often since, our government has defaulted to an external dedicated employee base which, by its nature, means greater costs.

Simply, we haven't truly learned enough of a lesson from history, so we keep repeating the counterproductive parts.

In so doing, our government has gotten bigger, more bloated, and not necessarily better. Its modern acquisition culture—accepting of exorbitant costs and lengthy delays, rarely considering novel alternatives, and leaving itself no way out—is best embodied by the F-35 Joint Strike Fighter, and the Department of Defense's ongoing, embarrassing attempts to get it in the air.[4] In 1996, the Pentagon conceived the F-35 as a radar-evading jet that would represent the pearl of the American armed forces air fleet. It contracted defense powerhouse Lockheed Martin to build roughly 2,500 jets at a cost in the $50–$60 million range apiece, for a total of roughly $125–$150 billion. Initially, according to the U.S. Government Accountability Office (GAO), the jets were supposed to be introduced in 2008, with a full rate of production by 2012.[5] Trouble with software testing, development, and integration led to numerous delays, and the projected cost of the aircraft had more than doubled by 2013, with the GAO reporting that tests to "evaluate the combat effectiveness and suitability of the aircraft in an operationally realistic environment" would not commence until 2017 or be completed until 2019, 26 years after the original contract. The total cost of roughly $400 billion—including nearly $2 billion for fixing errors uncovered in testing—would make it the most expensive government project in U.S.

history, even with Lockheed Martin scheduled to deliver about 300 fewer planes than originally promised.

This is where our procurement strategy has been taking us. Norm Augustine, an aerospace businessman and former undersecretary of the Army, saw it coming. In 1983, he quipped that, at the current exponential rate of aircraft inflation, the cost of a single combat plane would not only exceed the department's entire budget by 2054, but would need to be shared by the Air Force, Navy, and Marines. Absurd, right? In 2010, *The Economist* checked the numbers for a progress report.[6] This time, no jokes. "We are right on target," Augustine said of his dire prediction. "Unfortunately nothing has changed."

Contract spending and inflation pressures are modern realities, not just in the Department of Defense for its complex weapons systems but also in a broader set of agencies that require information systems integration and related organizational support to address everyday concerns such as affordable housing, small-business lending, and public safety measures. The Obama administration has prioritized reining in contract spending, after the Bush administration had intentionally increased it through its philosophy of outsourcing more day-to-day services to the private sector. In fiscal year 2010, the federal government achieved the first year-over-year reduction in contract spending since 1997, down from $550 billion to $535 billion, partly through canceling overdue information technology contracts at several agencies (including Homeland Security, Justice, and Treasury) and asking agencies to pool software resources. In the fiscal year 2012, contract spending was down to $516 billion.

Still, that was more than double what it was in fiscal year 2001. Such an enormous figure would typically provoke a spirited, even rancorous debate about government size and waste, regardless of whether the public or private sector was providing the work. It might even spark a discussion about scope: perhaps the government should get out of certain market areas on account of the related budgetary strain. Those are worthy conversations, but they shouldn't be the only ones, especially in an era when new easier-to-adopt technologies enable the government to explore alternate avenues. If the emphasis in problem solving is on "how," rather than simply "how big" or "how much," we might have a chance to achieve quicker, better, and, in some cases, cheaper solutions. There will always be a place for traditional acquisition methods, through which a government identifies a need, translates it into a set of requirements, and then selects a vendor with the lowest, technically acceptable bid.

But we need to make room for others.

Where can we find them?

In our history. In a bookstore.

Often, brainstorming leads to a better way to solve big problems. On the odd occasion, browsing can.

While working in the Clinton administration, as the Deputy Assistant to the President for Technology and Economic Policy, Tom Kalil stumbled upon Dava Sobel's *Longitude: The True Story of a Lone Genius Who Solved the Greatest Scientific Problem of His Time*. The best-selling book chronicled the overlooked efforts of John Harrison, an obscure eighteenth-century clockmaker, in assisting the British government to address the most vexing nautical issue of that time: the inability to accurately determine longitude while at sea, with the solution eluding the most illustrious thinkers of the era, including Sir Isaac Newton.[7]

This limitation led to numerous lost or wrecked ships, and to many lost lives, even before the grounding of four of Rear-Admiral Sir Cloudesley Shovell's ships off the Isles of Scilly in 1707, and killing roughly 2,000 sailors. That tragedy, however, provided the impetus for the Longitude Act of 1714 and its creation of the Board of Longitude, which included Newton, and which established rather substantial financial rewards for introducing methods that determined longitude within varying distances—the top prize of £20,000 was equivalent to nearly $3 million today. In opposition to the conventional thinking of scientists and engineers, Harrison, then just 21, invented a watchlike device known as the chronometer. The device was initially too expensive for widespread use, and the Board of Longitude never awarded the top prize to Harrison, though it did give smaller prizes to him and at least nine others for their minor discoveries to aid the cause. It also incrementally funded some of Harrison's continuing efforts, as did Parliament, and his work on the device until his death in 1776 set the stage for costs to come down considerably in the nineteenth century and for the chronometer to become the preferred method for measuring longitude.

Learning of Harrison's long-ago, somewhat slow-motion triumph energized Tom Kalil to start charting a new course in modern policy making.

"I call prizes an old idea whose time has come again," Kalil said.

Kalil's evangelism was based on the modern reality, best expressed by Sun Microsystems cofounder Bill Joy, that "no matter who you are, most of the smartest people work for someone else."[8] It was also based on economic austerity, since incentive prizes are awarded only to successful solutions and on simplicity, with the competition process designed to stimulate rather than stifle ambition.

Kalil asked the National Academy of Engineering to organize a workshopping event in April 1999 that attracted the former Republican Speaker of the House, Newt Gingrich, to speak on the importance of challenges and prizes.[9] It also attracted representatives of various government agencies, including one of its most innovative, Defense Advanced Research Projects Agency (DARPA), founded by President Eisenhower in 1958 with a one-page memo in response to the Soviet launch of Sputnik. DARPA was made responsible for preventing future technology-based surprises in defense, as well as for developing surprises of America's own. Over the decades, DARPA had drawn upon those they believed to be the best and brightest scientific and technical minds throughout the country. But the agency recognized that prizes may uncover untapped talent in often-unrelated areas. So DARPA worked with Kalil and the Congress to pass legislation to give it authority for prizes. Kalil left government for academia in 2001, but DARPA's experimentation in this area would continue, as one of the government's leading proponents of prize policy throughout the George W. Bush administration and beyond.

While advising the Chancellor of the University of California-Berkeley and chairing the Clinton Global Initiative, Kalil continued advocating for challenges and prizes through position papers and op-eds, declaring this as "an idea that people of both parties should rally behind," due to its ability to leverage the prize purse and, after finding a winner, attract further investment in a field. Yet, for most of the Bush administration, the government's use of prizes was modest, limited to DARPA, NASA, and the Department of Energy.

The private sector was another story. There, the prize movement was taking off, thanks largely due to Peter Diamandis. While growing up in New York, Diamandis had a fascination with space and flight, winning a rocket design competition at age 12. Even after earning his medical degree, he continued exploring space-related opportunities—from communications to transport—as an entrepreneur. In his 30s, a reading of Charles Lindbergh's autobiographical *The Spirit of St. Louis* encouraged him to get his pilot's license, while also introducing him to the role that "the extraordinary prize stuff" played in the role of the commercial aviation industry. That book related how Raymond Orteig, a New York hotel owner, issued a 1919 challenge to aviators to fly nonstop from New York to Paris. Nine teams spent more than $400,000 in competition for Orteig's $25,000 prize. Lindbergh, then a 25-year-old mail pilot, pulled off the transatlantic feat.

If Lindbergh had applied for a government grant, his proposal probably would not have survived the peer review process, given the skepticism about his undertaking. Instead, Lindbergh merely needed to convince himself that he could cover the costs and summon the guts. He explained his daring by wondering, rhetorically, "What kind of man would live where there is no danger?"

This frame of thinking appealed to Diamandis, himself a dreamer and doer who found inspiration for his endeavors not only in history —such as the Apollo missions—but from science fiction. "My mission and purpose in life was to explore a new frontier," Diamandis said. "The *Star Trek* universe painted a picture of a world of abundance, powered by technology. It offered to us, in our visioneering, a model of what the future could be like."

In 1996, Diamandis announced the first X PRIZE in St. Louis. He based it on the Orteig Prize, and made entrance exceedingly appealing, by securing a $10 million donation from entrepreneurs Amir and Anousheh Ansari. The award would go to the first private team that constructed a spacecraft capable of carrying three people to 100 kilometers above the Earth's surface, twice within two weeks. In response, 26 teams from seven countries, collectively spending more than $100 million in development work, with Scaled Composites, from Mojave, California, winning in 2004 for a vessel called SpaceShipOne (SS1).[10] Better still, the entrants' remarkable progress toward a proof of concept stimulated the imagination of countless others who hadn't been part of the competition. That, as Kalil noted, served to launch something else: "The big win was not that someone got a prize, but that Richard Branson and others said, hey, space is not just for governments anymore. There can be a vibrant commercial space industry." That industry has since exceeded $1.5 billion in public and private funding.

The government needed to more consistently achieve that sort of payback on innovation investment. That was a frontier Kalil sought to explore further, after joining the Obama administration in 2009 as the Deputy Director of the Office of Science and Technology. He and I worked on the President's Strategy for American Innovation, which included a call for agencies to increase their use of prizes and challenges as a tool for stimulating innovation. By March 2010, the White House Office of Management and Budget would release instructions to agencies, encouraging them to use prizes and challenges, even if they had yet to receive explicit authority. And by January 2011, with the reauthorization of the America COMPETES Act, Congress would cement that status, granting explicit authority for all agencies to spend up to $50 million per prize.[11]

As the prize authority scaled across the government, Kalil and I took turns attending the annual Visioneering Workshop hosted by the Diamandis' nonprofit X PRIZE Foundation. This is where prominent philanthropists, CEOs, public officials, and even celebrity activists such as Will.i.am of the Black Eyed Peas would gather, on the grounds of Fox Studios in Los Angeles, to identify critical problems and then, over a three-day period, funnel ideas from broad to specific, until they were worthy of presentation to the public in the form of measurable, actionable challenges. I joined one conversation between Diamandis and a Qualcomm executive about the possibility of developing a noninvasive, instantaneous diagnostic medical device.

Six months later, at the 2012 Consumer Electronics Show, Diamandis and Qualcomm CEO Paul Jacobs announced the Tricorder X PRIZE, named after the multifunction handheld device used for sensor scanning, data analysis, and recording data in the fictional *Star Trek* universe. The contest, with a $10 million top prize, gave entrants three-and-a-half years to develop a device capable of diagnosing 16 distinct conditions and five vital signs in a pool of people over a three-day period in late spring of 2015.[12] Within a year, more than 230 teams from 32 countries had signed up to compete for the $10 million prize, including Dr. Anita Goel, a friend running a Boston-based nanotechnology startup, Nanobiosym, with an entry that runs a genetic analysis on saliva.

Also at the 2011 Visioneering Workshop, Google chairman Eric Schmidt and his wife Wendy shared an update about a challenge that had emerged from the wreckage of one of the nation's most tragic embarrassments. In April 2010, the *Deepwater Horizon* rig had exploded in the Gulf of Mexico, killing 11 men and causing the largest oil spill in history. Day after day, for more than three months, television viewers watched oil gush into the gulf. Ultimately, a SWAT team of sorts, under the leadership of Nobel Prize–winning Energy Secretary Stephen Chu, in collaboration with British Petroleum, contributed to the successful capping of the well. Yet that still left the massive chore of slurping up all the sludge that had seeped into the water and toward the shore.

While the well was gushing, Diamandis received plenty of e-mails, asking him whether the X PRIZE Foundation considered contributing to the cause of capping the well. But he didn't believe BP would cooperate enough for his organization to play a constructive role. He did, however, see a role in the cleanup, especially since technology in such efforts had not advanced much in more than two decades. Within 24 hours, Wendy Schmidt committed to serve as the sponsor. The Department of Interior offered technical support. The Shell Corporation provided some financial support. That allowed the X PRIZE Foundation to advertise a purse of $1.4 million, with $1 million to the grand prize winner, for the teams that could prove they could recover the most oil on the sea surface, at a minimum of double the existing record rate. Roughly 350 teams preregistered, with 35 ultimately revealing their designs. Ten were then selected for testing in New Jersey at

Ohmsett, a Department of Interior facility with the largest saltwater wave tank in North America.

Diamandis anticipated that, at most, one team might achieve a doubling of the top rate through their efforts over the course of the 15-month competition. Even competitors with the deepest understanding of the industry initially thought his goal was too bold. Still, an Illinois-based company named Elastec took a shot, getting outside the box, asking its workforce of 140 to work around the clock to design a unique grooved skimmer.[13] In the official test trial, winner Team Elastec recovered oil at a rate more than *three* times better than the gold standard, at 4,670 gallons per minute and an efficiency of 89.5 percent, and more than five times what had typically been recovered at Ohmsett. Six of the other top-10 entrants achieved the minimum requirement of double the record rate. That alone would have rendered the challenge a success. But that would ignore two other important insights: first, the amount of private capital relative to the prize purse, which Diamandis estimated at 20-to-1; second, the diversity of the participants, which included teams hailing from Norway and the Netherlands; a family from Alaska that used a father's savings; and Team Vortex, led by a designer who doubled as a tattoo artist and partially funded by one of the artist's customers.[14]

"You never know where the innovation will come from," Diamandis said.

That idea, that innovation can come from anywhere, was the inspiration behind InnoCentive. Founded in 1998, and then spun out of the pharmaceutical company Eli Lilly a few years later, it is a for-profit marketplace that searches for problems in a variety of industries and then frames and poses those problems to potential solvers.

During his stint as InnoCentive CEO, from 2006 through 2012, Dwayne Spradlin attempted to perfect the art and science of challenge creation and presentation, in order to ensure that a competition would be a better tool than the tired strategies that have been tried again and again. That required paying attention to each step in a series: identifying a difficult problem, designing the applicable challenge, engaging the appropriate audience, dangling an attractive prize, and stimulating the development of a fresh, innovative potential solution.

First, in Spradlin's view, it is essential that large organizations of all kinds—commercial, government, or charitable—run a rigorous "problem management program" prior to issuing any challenges. Pointing to the old adage that asking the right question gets the questioner 80 percent of the way to a solution, he lamented that "organizations are not terribly good at this discipline today." In his view, an organization needs to identify a market need and manage "a very thoughtful process of structuring that into something that is well defined, understood; something that ties back to the strategic levers of the organization, which comprehends all the work that has succeeded and failed in the past" to shape a well-defined problem with specific associated criteria.

"Spending this time up front to thoroughly wrestle a problem to the ground before trying to solve it is not only the best use of up-front resources, it also fundamentally changes the character of the problem-solving efforts," Spradlin said. "I get a much better picture now of what needs to be done, why it needs to be done, and who may be able to help in solving that problem."

Once the problem is precisely defined, organizations can prioritize it against others and assign proper resources to effect a desired outcome for their consumers, shareholders, benefactors, or—in the case of government—constituency. "What is it, why are we doing it, what is it going to impact, what levers does it touch, why have things failed in the past?" Spradlin said. "Then at the next stage, what audiences are we trying to target? And then with those audiences, you can define what those incentives will be, and based on those incentives, you finalize the competition design. Now I can roll that program out."

One prize does not fit all. Thus, competition designers must carefully consider what will induce the desired audience to engage, understanding whether to appeal to intrinsic or extrinsic motivations. In the case of a public-good problem, such as slowing malaria in Sub-Saharan Africa, Spradlin found the dollar amount to sometimes be a "disincentive," with participants wanting to work on a problem that matters, focusing on how many they can help and perhaps, secondarily, on their own opportunity for fame and credit. So he recommended many foundations minimize money and maximize exposure—spending resources on inviting the world's participation and celebrating those who succeed.

In most commercial challenges, however, Spradlin found that extrinsic motivators tend to take precedence, and "people want to get paid," either in the currency of a cash prize or in the "opportunity for highlighting what you do in front of a crowd that could include venture capitalists that may fund your ideas as a startup." After all, the participant is choosing not to engage in some other activity to allocate time to this one, and is aware of the possibility that someone else may profit from their solution. "You need to know, deep down, that you won't feel foolish for this a year from now, so I sure hope the upside is worth it," Spradlin said.

Spradlin places many governmental challenges in the middle of the motivational spectrum, between those presented by nonprofit and commercial entities: "If you are trying to drive a technical solution to a big problem for the Environmental Protection Agency, very often the problem itself won't carry the same kind of public draw that a challenge for clean water in the third world would draw. Therefore, you sort of blend the motivations. We often recommend to those organizations a healthy prize amount and a reasonably healthy amount of money to be spent on driving awareness of the challenge and its impact for the public good, for public health, or for air quality . . . To do both."

Spradlin applauded the federal government's fundamental "changing of the environment," helping to enable prizes and competitions as problem-solving multipliers; he called the reauthorization of the America COMPETES Act that authorized them "a monumental step forward."

"I think government is taking it very seriously, moving extremely quickly to sort of catch up to what has been available in the private sector," Spradlin said late in 2012, adding that he had observed the federal government posing the correct questions and running the necessary pilots. "What I've seen happen in the last two, or two-and-a-half years, I would have guessed would have taken ten."

While he spoke of government's experimentation with prizes as still in its nascent stages, with looming questions about policy application, he was convinced these approaches were embedded enough to outlast any Presidential administration: "I don't think either party has a vested interest in rolling back programs that can drive better government, more democratic involvement, and better and low-cost solutions."

It would be odd for any person or entity to object to what the Air Force accomplished in 2011, with Spradlin's assistance.

The Departments of Homeland Security and Defense had shared a common interest in addressing the issue of uncooperative vehicles—to reduce the risk to anyone here or abroad who might be endangered by a vehicle that violates a checkpoint or is fleeing an urban combat zone, or might be endangered by the use of presently available lethal tools designed to stop it. The Department of Homeland Security (DHS), in 2005, had initially turned to a typical government procedure. Through its Small Business Innovation Research Program (SBIR), DHS issued a request for proposals on the topic "uncooperative vehicle stopping using non-lethal methods," and awarded a contract eventually worth $850,000 to the Arizona-based Engineering Science Analysis Corporation.[15] That investment produced the SQUID, which entangled the wheels without harming the vehicle. But the SQUID, produced in 2009, had limitations: it needed to be prepositioned and then triggered into action at exactly the right time as the vehicle runs over it.

In 2011, the Air Force took off in a different direction, partnering with InnoCentive for the Vehicle Stopper challenge.[16] "Quite wisely, the government opened up this challenge to new and novel ideas from anyone and anywhere in the world," Spradlin said. The $25,000 prize attracted 1,071 initial competitors, 119 of which submitted detailed proposals. The winner was a sexagenarian from Peru, Dante Barbis. The retired mechanical engineer chose to implement currently available technology in an unconventional manner.

"Imagine taking a remote-control go-cart and making it launchable, so it can be shot very quickly from a vehicle at high speed and then controlled," Spradlin said, with estimates of that speed at 130 miles per hour within three seconds of launch. "Now imagine this thing has an air bag on top of it, so we shoot it underneath the fleeing vehicle; we guide it right there, the airbag deploys. The fleeing vehicle then loses traction, spins, and comes to a stop, and then those in pursuit can surround and take control of that situation. A brilliant idea. Does it meet the generally logical needs of existing, dependable technology that can be deployed? Check. Relatively low cost? Check. Deployable in a variety of situations? Check. Highly effective? Check."

At press time, the project was still in testing, but undeniably promising. Spradlin called it a "win-win-win across the board," for the civilian population, for the military, for anyone involved in the process.

"Just a wonderful example of the potential here," Spradlin said. "You compare this kind of program to what might have been a fully funded, long-term government program to come up with new nonlethal approaches to manage a situation like this, and it's hard to imagine that not being a program in the tens or hundreds of millions of dollars. This has all the properties you want. Fast, quick to market, these are the kinds of things that can change the economics of innovation and drive very quick solutions."

You might wonder from where the government-challenge competitors, and solutions, might come.

You might not think to look inside a Sizzler steakhouse. But that's where Victor Garcia, an immigrant from Mexico, was working while pursuing an engineering career. At the time, he was taking classes in computer-aided drafting at ITT Technical Institute in California, but he wasn't satisfied. Since he was a child, he had dreamed of becoming an inventor. Then, while waiting tables, he saw a commercial about a technical center that was designing muscle cars.

"I was like, 'That's cool!'" he recalled.

It was cool enough to alter his direction. He pursued a bachelor of science in transportation design from the Art Center College of Design in Pasadena, then spent two years after graduation working with BMW in Newbury Park on all sorts of vehicles, including semitrucks, until landing in Texas as a part-time designer for Peterbilt Motors. There, in the Lone Star State, Garcia and his pregnant wife were waiting for the birth of their first child. They did so with excitement, but also apprehension. Without health insurance, Garcia was concerned about the costs of caring for a newborn. That's when a different sort of challenge, a DARPA challenge, caught Garcia's eye.

Acutely aware of the out-of-control costs and lengthy time lags inherent to acquisitions, the Department of Defense had set an ambitious goal: reducing the time it takes to design and develop weapons systems by 80 percent, while significantly cutting expense. To catalyze that effort, DARPA called for the design of an Experimental Crowd-Derived Combat-Support Vehicle or XC2V. It promised a modest $7,500 top prize, and promoted the contest through Local Motors, an open source automotive manufacturing enterprise with a community of 25,000 hobbyist innovators, from enthusiasts to engineers to fabricators.

"Immediately, my mind starts running," Garcia said. "I grew up with GI Joes. I still have a ton and I collect them. I'm a big military buff, World War II, Civil War. It just intrigued me to do a military vehicle. And since it was funded by the government, DARPA, it seemed very real to me. I didn't know exactly what it would look like, but I had a ton of ideas, so I had to jump on it."

He had to, and not simply due to his desire to support his wife and unborn son. He had to, because he believed he had it *in* him. He believed he could win, even though the project was outside the scope of his usual work, even though many may have deemed someone with his background a sizable underdog, and even though he only had four weeks to complete what amounted to an immense undertaking. Buoyed by a supportive wife and boss, Garcia spent every available extra hour, late into the night, on sketches, illustration, and research. Too short on time to perfect the illustration, he felt good about the potential of the unique shape he submitted in March 2011. "I knew I would be in the top 10," Garcia said. "But to hear the CEO of Local Motors say, 'You are the winner—' I was a little emotional calling my wife to say that I did it. I knew it was a huge thing for my family, to be able to cover my son. That was a huge weight off my back. And then, by June 21, he was born."

Three days later, Victor met President Obama in Pittsburgh, for the unveiling of his creation: the XC2V FLYPMode. "I was very, very happy," Garcia said. So was DARPA, learning plenty through the exercise about the power of social media for future R&D projects. And so was Local Motors, which earned a new client in Peterbilt. After a promotion to senior designer at Peterbilt, Garcia convinced the company to engage in its own private sector open innovation endeavor, inviting the Local Motors community to compete for a $10,000 prize, for the design of a fuel-efficient Class 8 sleeper cab tractor truck. And when Jay Rogers, CEO of Local Motors, spoke with Peterbilt, he was told, "They did 40 man years' worth of work in four weeks."

Garcia sees his unlikely story as representing a potential "paradigm shift" in America's approach to major issues, including those related to the ways the nation protects its people, at home and abroad. For the conception and implementation of critical government projects, why must sluggish and expensive be the norm? Why should the idea hunt be limited to the same tired terrain, inhabited by the same so-called experts, directed toward the same established, expensive contractors? Why not venture into the wilderness, tapping into talent that others might have missed, talent itching to be taken seriously?

"Given a chance, there's a voice that can be heard," Garcia said. "I think this is an opportunity for somebody like me, who nobody would consider, to have a chance. Just give them the right criteria. We do have the resources. Sometimes we get caught up in the whole political thing, but it doesn't have to be like that. Let's not wait 10 years. Let's make a change."

Dr. Farzad Mostashari wasn't willing to wait even 10 weeks before making his mark on the situation he inherited in 2011, as Deputy Director of the Office of the National Coordinator (ONC) for Health IT in the Department of Health and Human Services (HHS). The ONC had originated in response to President Bush's bold statement in 2004 that every American would have access to a personal health record by 2014. Yet, due in part to a modest annual budget of $60 million, the agency's achievements trailed that pace, with only 25 percent of eligible physicians and

15 percent of acute care hospitals adopting electronic health records as of 2010. Recall, as introduced in Chapter 6, that the agency had received a one-time $2 billion cash injection in 2009 as part of the Health Information Technology for Economic and Clinical Health (HITECH) Act in the stimulus bill, to be spent over the next few years on the creation of a nationwide interoperable health information network.[17] Then, a year later, the Patient Protection and Affordable Care Act further validated the HITECH Act by recognizing health IT as a critical enabler in health care delivery reform.

Even with all those enabling ingredients in place, Dr. Mostashari recognized that the agency needed to evolve from its legacy culture. That had emphasized process, largely measuring its success based on the amount of grants given to states, rather than on what the money actually produced. "We had to turn that around to say, no, no, no, if the country fails, we have failed," he said. "And it's not enough to have done things with the right form, we care about the outcomes. We had to give people the courage to do things differently. Our identity at ONC was to become government entrepreneurs, and that's everybody from our grant management staff to our project officers. The core is, how can we see tomorrow as better than today? We're not going to keep doing things the way we've been doing them, and we're going to look for opportunities for those disruptive innovations."

That meant turning to cloud technologies to speedily support the expansion of their mission; putting a premium on accountability; and setting seemingly impossible goals, because in Dr. Mostashari's mind, "When you know it is an impossible goal, then risk taking becomes less risky." That also meant turning to different procedures, in concert with procurement, in order to achieve existing and ongoing objectives.

"You can either do a grant and you have no control, or you can do contracts, and then you're paying through the nose, and there's no incentive for them to really deliver cheaper or better, and you only get one shot at it—you do the wrong selection of who you are going to work with, you're screwed," Dr. Mostashari said. "Prizes and awards seemed like a great way to get out of that box of the typical government procurement options."

Nor would it be a one-time trick. ONC would become the first agency to fully operationalize the prize authority that, a few months earlier, had been granted by the reauthorization of the America COMPETES Act. Mostashari's agenda was twofold: speedily surface a series of solutions while creating a culture of community problem solving. His first major foray, the Investing in Innovations (i2) Initiative, included the allocation of nearly $5 million to fund prize purses, and was supplemented by administrative support from private sources.[18] As a primary partner, Dr. Mostashari wisely chose Health 2.0 LLC, an event planner that, since 2007, has been hosting conferences, code-a-thons, and challenges in the consumer health space. In October 2009, I addressed that organization's annual conference and was overwhelmed by the size and passion of the audience: more than 500 developers, entrepreneurs, and health care professionals who had also brought their own ideas for lowering costs while improving quality through better wellness and prevention services. Those ideas, unlimited in terms of imagination, were limited in their financial potential by the predominant payment system in health care: fee for service.

As of this writing, ONC has sponsored more than 25 challenges tied to the use of information technology, with goals as varied as ulcer prevention, quality of life improvement for cancer survivors, and better reporting of medical errors. One representative example was the One in a Million Hearts Challenge, designed to complement HHS's broader Million Hearts campaign to prevent one million heart attacks and strokes within five years.[19] The winners were named in March 2012, with THUMPr taking the $50,000 grand prize—it was a web-based application through which users entered personal health profiles, then received unique recommendations for specific, actionable steps related to the ABCS (Aspirin, Blood Pressure, Cholesterol, Smoking Cessation) that would represent a healthy heart plan. The $20,000 runner-up, mHealthCoach, was submitted by South Asian immigrant Aamer Ghaffar.[20] It was built on top of his startup's $25,000 first prize winner in the Walgreens Health Guide Challenge, which took HHS data feeds, compiling the 20 most common questions related to cardiovascular patients, and providing a search engine for simple use by health guides Walgreens was employing to assist customers. For the HHS challenge, mHealthCoach leveraged social media sites Twitter and YouTube to supplement education with organization and enjoyment, allowing the user to integrate doctor's appointments and gym sessions with a Yahoo or Google calendar, play games that demonstrate what happens to blood as it encounters exercise versus cigarettes, or even use maps to invite friends to fitness groups at nearby parks.

Ghaffar spoke of enjoying a sizable publicity and credibility boost from each challenge but reaping the greater overall reward from the public sector competition, even though the prize was $5,000 less. That's because the two-way dialogue with HHS and ONC—as compared to the private sector sponsors—continued after the conclusion of that challenge. "They recognize that the next hurdle of innovation is the lack of deployment or feasibility trials," Ghaffar said, explaining that the availability of such testing environments—the sort government has the power and impetus to provide—can make the difference for small enterprises limited in their financial resources and connections to power.

Later, Ghaffer would compete for other challenges, finishing second in an important one in the private sector, the Patient Engagement Blue Button Challenge sponsored by the Advisory Board Company.[21] That was the latest in a long line of competitions related to the still-developing Blue Button movement, as private and public sponsors attempted to make consumers, even the technology-averse, more comfortable serving as the central hubs for their own health care information, and more responsible for sharing it. The Advisory Board stepped up to the sponsorship challenge based on the belief that the market was best suited to create simpler, more accessible, and appealing products—ones that would compel patients to make the downloadable Blue Button file a core component of their health care routines.

On the private sector side, the 2010 Health 2.0 Blue Button Developer Challenge produced a rather impressive winner. Michael Jackson (no relation to the international celebrity) didn't have the money for college while growing up in Baltimore. So he worked as a power plant operator and enlisted as a Coast Guard reservist to earn money for college; then he earned an MBA and took several technology jobs before ultimately joining Adobe, the gold standard of graphic design software companies, in March 2010.[22] The challenge, sponsored by the Markle and Robert Wood Johnson Foundations, gave Jackson a chance to, as he put it, "prove myself to Adobe, and prove what Adobe could do for the industry." His cross-functional team worked for 60 days to finish a prototype, creatively converting the Blue Button's raw dump of text into a more attractive and useful package, including features that allow the user to easily, visually identify trends or spikes in health measures such as blood sugar levels. After winning, Jackson got a shout-out from the CEO, Shantanu Narayen, at the company's government conference and, even better, a promotion.

In search of a similarly uplifting outcome, Dr. Mostashari teamed with Health 2.0 in 2011 to present the Blue Button Mash Up Challenge, calling for competitors to create a broadly available application that blended Blue Button data with other data sources.[23] Humetrix, a software innovator with a 15-year history, won the contest with its submission iBlueButton, which integrated eight different federal government data sources, all while taking the complicated coding and unwieldly length out of up to three years of Medicare claims history. The result? After logging on to the application, a patient—or the patient's authorized caregiver—can tap a blue button to quickly download his or her Medicare record, and scroll down an organized, detailed list of diagnoses, medications, prescribing doctors (with contact information), allergies, hospital visits and stays, procedures, lab work, and even family history. With an extra click, the patient can receive additional contextual information, such as the potential side effects of current or considered medications, or preventative services, all drawn from those public databases. Then the patient can "push" his or her medical record to a provider who has downloaded a related app on a mobile device. After the medical professional accepts the transfer, they can review the record together, one bound to be more accurate than what the patient would recall from memory. And they can make more informed, collaborative decisions.

The Humetrix story, and the dozens of others that surfaced on account of Dr. Mostashari's emphasis on prizes, further inspired him to institutionalize the approach, so that it would be sustained long after his tenure. He did so through the Federal Health Information Technology Strategic Plan, published in September 2011.

The prize tool for government innovators is gathering momentum, especially in the area of IT software development, which has been riddled with cost overruns. As noted earlier, Veterans Affairs had embodied the losing culture of government IT acquisition, with the nasty habit of contracting first—based on the fancy prose of some written proposal—without viewing a working prototype. Among the most egregious examples: a nearly decade-long, ultimately doomed, $127 million effort to help veterans schedule appointments with doctors, hospitals, and nursing care facilities online.

An audit report from The Government Accountability Office stated the situation plainly in 2011: "Unable to implement any of the planned capabilities. The application software project was hindered by weaknesses in several key management disciplines, including acquisition planning, requirements analysis, testing, progress reporting, risk management, and oversight."

By then, Roger Baker—after assuming the role of VA CIO in 2009—had already overseen a thorough review of that and two dozen other underperforming major IT projects. He had suspended the scheduling project to stop the bleed, but knew that veterans still needed the service. With an assist from VA CTO Peter Levin, Baker launched the VA Medical Scheduling Contest—which we mentioned earlier. The challenge, with a total $3 million prize purse, fit snugly into Dwayne Spradlin's characterization of ideal competition construction: a clearly defined problem with a logical connection to existing technologies that could be deployed at relatively low cost, and one that may not have surfaced through traditional models of government procurement.

Across the country, millions of well-meaning public servants, feeling restrained by bureaucracy, limited in authority, and shackled by shrinking budgets, can still lead in the prize movement. Take Tom Baden. As a teenager and into his 20s, he was a singer and strummer in rock bands, playing Black Sabbath and Led Zeppelin covers and even sharing a stage with Yanni.[24] Three decades later, as the Chief Information Officer at the Department of Human Services in Minnesota, he sought to make some noise inside state government by modernizing its historically siloed data systems.

After learning of the White House Office of Management and Budget's $45 million Partnership Fund for Program Integrity Innovation, a fund to support innovations that reduced waste, fraud, and abuse, Baden began to assemble a coalition of states that shared a common interest in solving these problems, ultimately securing the support of Louisiana, Oregon, and Utah.[25] He would scope a small enough project with sufficient impact to move forward—standardizing the registration process for doctors and hospitals when qualifying for Medicaid services. This targets the first of three stages during which states can intervene to thwart fake providers who cost them an estimated $11 billion in improper payments each year (the other stages being just before the claim is paid and after a claim is paid and deemed fraudulent).[26] After winning the grant funding, Baden still needed to coordinate the project across the states, and he found a crowdsourcing vehicle called TopCoder—a highly competitive community for software development and digital creation, and one that had an existing agreement with a federal government "center of excellence" on prizes based at NASA. "What that did was take the complication out, which really accelerated the whole process," Baden said.

Working with the Centers for Medicare & Medicaid Services (CMS) and TopCoder, and facing significant skepticism, Baden's team set the objective for the project: the creation of a screening tool to run background checks as well as identity, licensing, and financial verifications on newly enrolled providers. It followed the TopCoder formula of breaking down the project into smaller incremental parts, in this case 132 of them starting with conceptualization, with a prize for each piece ranging from $500 to $5,000 and "bug hunts" to reward hole pokers with small prizes to, as Baden put it, "Keep you honest every step of the way and drive up the quality of the product."

Through his commonsense approach, Baden drove up the quality of government without doing the same to the quantity of dollars—as of this writing, his project is still on course to successful completion.

"The thing I like about TopCoder is that you only pay for the products that you like," Baden said. "If you run a contest and there's no winners, then you're not paying anybody."

While it is natural for prize sponsors of all stripes to welcome the way these crowdsourcing models keep costs down, by compensating only a select, successful number of participants, this model is not necessarily a favorite of all professional societies.[27] For instance, the American Institute of Graphic Arts (AIGA) has argued that such speculative work can devalue the design process, specifically the importance of feedback and experimentation to produce quality product; and that it can devalue the designers, diminishing the true economic value of their work.[28] Designers have even created websites, such as nospec.com, to educate the public about the perils of spec work and to discourage their colleagues from performing it. And, in June 2011, more than 1,200 people signed a petition objecting to the Department of Interior's $1,750 competition on crowdspring.com for a new logo for placement on clothing, one that complemented—but did not replace—the department's existing seal.[29]

While recognizing people's right to reasonably disagree about the methods through which prize competitions are administered, and even to choose not to participate in this process, I believe there will always be a pool of talent motivated more by the mission than the reward. Government is tapping into that spirit, by broadening the range of competition topics—beyond its larger budgetary responsibilities such as defense and health care—to include those intended to foster equality, justice, and social welfare. That's precisely how members of President Obama's cabinet have utilized competitions to address key, often-unfunded priorities—expanding government scope without an equivalent, unwanted increase in size and cost.

Start with equality. Hilda Solis, the Labor Secretary, took inspiration for her open innovation challenge from the 2012 State of the Union, in which President Obama declared that to create "an economy built to last," America needed to "encourage the talent and ingenuity of every person in this country. That means women should earn equal pay for equal work."[30] He had attempted to address this issue with the first bill that he signed in 2009, the Lilly Ledbetter Fair Pay Act, which allowed for a longer time horizon for suing retroactively for pay discrimination. A follow-through attempt, the Paycheck Fairness Act, a preventative step designed to protect employees who share salary information at work from retaliation by an employer, died in Congress.

Solis assembled public and private salary data from sources including the Bureau of Labor Statistics and Salary.com, as well as cases brought through the Equal Employment Opportunity Commission (EEOC) for the purposes of supporting her Equal Pay Apps Challenge.[31] She also convinced Professor Linda Babcock at Carnegie Mellon University to share her negotiating tips for others to incorporate into new tools. A team of graduate students at Carnegie Mellon's Heinz College, led by Rachel Koch, won one of the grand prizes with the Close The Wage Gap app, which offered more personalized advice, in an application that included a negotiation cheat sheet for women. Laquitta Martell-DeMarchant was an especially inspirational grand-prize winner. Her childhood had been shaped by watching her two grandmothers raise families without husbands, a hardship that forced their children to work in the cotton fields of Louisiana to raise extra money. She came to believe that if more women could achieve equal pay, it would eliminate some of the burden. Her iPhone- and iPad-accessible application, Aequitas, includes the ability to compare compensation by ethnicity, and she has used the prize perks—including a scholarship toward an eight-week immersive coding skills training program—to build her company, FuzionApps. She is even planning a Spanish-language version. The President invited Koch and Martell-DeMarchant to the White House in June 2013, to commemorate the 50th anniversary of the Equal Pay Act, explaining his administration's desire to "help workers get the information they need to figure out if they're underpaid.

And thanks to innovators like Rachel and Laquitta, who are up here, we can now say, 'There's an app for that.'"

Thanks in part to Michelle Obama, there are now Apps for Healthy Kids too. That was a contest I conceived with two Cabinet Secretaries, Tom Vilsack of Agriculture and Kathleen Sebelius of Health and Human Services, in March 2010. This was what Dwayne Spradlin would classify as a participation challenge, one most concerned about generating the most possible awareness for an issue; to do that, we tapped into the First Lady's passion and celebrity. The prizes, funded by the public and private sectors, were modest, totaling $60,000 for a dozen winners, whose diversity and commitment would speak to our success. Their winning submissions ran the gamut from an online tool (Pick Chow!) aimed at childhood obesity to Trainer, a game in which players create creatures, moving them around an illustrated map to satisfy their dietary and fitness needs while exercising alongside with a web cam. The winners' backgrounds and motives were varied, too: parents concerned about caring for a sick child, a student class at the University of Southern California, and even entrepreneurs who had quit jobs to start businesses based on what they had created.

Sometimes, a challenge aimed at advancing social good can even lead to the birth of a new industry.

In 2009, Energy Secretary Steven Chu announced that his department's Vehicle Technologies Program would expand its relationship with the active Progressive Insurance Automotive X PRIZE competition by providing a $5.5 million grant for technical assistance.[32] The competition was consistent with the program's redeeming mission, to develop vehicle technologies and alternative fuels that would reduce greenhouse gas emissions, lessen America's dependence on foreign oil, and help the U.S. transportation industry remain competitive.

The prize itself was substantial, a total of $10 million raised privately, available to three teams—with $5 million to the winner—for the construction of safe cars that could achieve at least 100 MPGe (or the equivalents) in a real-world driving environment. To win the high-level prize for the mainstream class, a car needed to have four wheels, seat at least four passengers, and have a range of at least 200 miles. In this case, unlike the Apps for Healthy Kids challenge, the money mattered.

Oliver Kuttner had first become interested in competitions when he was 10 years old, winning a physics prize that had been sponsored by a defense contractor and airplane company. This one had a significantly greater payoff. "If it wasn't for the prize, we wouldn't have really looked at it," said Kuttner, a Virginia commercial real estate developer; race driver; and automobile dealer, collector, and builder.[33] "When we studied it, we realized the conventional wisdom just wasn't right, and there were real misconceptions. One was that if you do an electric car, you have a chance to win, otherwise you don't."

With other competitors already several laps ahead, Kuttner had a need for speed. He swiftly assembled a team called Edison2, which set up in an abandoned textile factory in proximity to machine shops in Lynchburg. Kuttner leaned on the team's experience in the racing world to produce results quickly and to recognize that weight and safety weren't mutually exclusive. At 830 pounds, its four-passenger Very Light Car wasn't much heavier than the average motorcycle. "When the car showed up, everyone laughed at it," Kuttner said. "Then they figured out they couldn't get within halfway of us on the consumption end."

For an initial $2.7 million outlay, including some assistance from investors, Edison2 not only captured the $5 million prize, but put itself on an inside track to pioneering the ultra-lightweight car industry. By the spring of 2012, it had spent an additional $8 million to continue developing and redesigning the vehicle in an attempt to bring the safest, most effective lightweight car to the mainstream market.

"If a large car company decided to do this, I can guarantee they would not be where we are if they spent 10 times as much," Kuttner said.

He got a tailwind in 2012, when the federal government raised corporate average fuel economy standards, putting pressure on car manufacturers to innovate in order to achieve a near doubling of standards to 55 MPG by 2025.[34] Word had spread of Kuttner's initial—if, by his own admission, incomplete—achievement. So calls started coming in, with inquiries about the incorporation of some of his technology into other companies' existing product lines, or even about the possibility of bringing to market some version of the Very Light Car itself. And, in 2013, he introduced an electric-powered version that he intended to take to market.

Some social justice challenges hit closer to the heart.

Such was the case for me, a father of two daughters, when I spent my 39th birthday alongside members of the President's cabinet, for a meeting that Vice President Biden had convened to address sexual assault and dating violence against high school and college-aged women. Biden had long championed this issue, aware of the alarming statistics that nearly one in five college women will be victimized by sexual assault, and one in 10 teens will be hurt by someone they are dating. We set out not only to help prevent such attacks, by giving women improved tools to safely and discreetly communicate distress but also to help women better connect to resources in the aftermath of an assault. Biden and Secretary Sebelius launched Apps Against Abuse, challenging developers to create applications that make women less vulnerable.[35]

Nancy Schwartzman learned of the challenge from a Twitter follower who had seen her 2009 documentary film, *The Line*, which featured footage of her confrontation with the acquaintance who had raped her. Schwartzman's Twitter contact suggested that she compete as a means of complementing the film, which was screening on college campuses. She deemed that silly. "I'm a filmmaker," she thought. "I don't know how to make an app."

That was July. In late August, she e-mailed her colleague Deb Levine in California who had done text (SMS) work related to safe sex and HIV for youths, and they agreed to blend that technical expertise with Levine's access to young people. Schwartzman knew, from all her outreach, that college students tended to stay inside their bubbles and networks, eschewing assistance from off-campus services, including law enforcement. She also knew students would only use an application that spoke their language and acknowledged their lifestyles, which meant she needed to solicit their input, make it simple, and avoid any judgmental features. College students party off campus. They often drink, and sometimes lose their bearings. The point wasn't to stop such activities, but to make students as safe as possible in any situation. Nor did she want the application to appear threatening, with an alarm or a danger icon, because—as she was advised by a domestic violence survivor during a crowdsourcing stop at the University of Wisconsin-La Crosse—that might alert and anger a snooping, abusive partner.

Working with a designer that Schwartzman had used for her film work and an engineer to write the code, the team worked up to the competition deadline. Her team worked pro bono, Schwartzman characterizing the exercise as "a perfect coming together of people who want to make a difference." Their concept was Circle of 6, a casual, social, gender-neutral application that appears as an attractive, but still inconspicuous, icon on a smartphone, one that allows users to choose six trusted friends for their circle—and then, by tapping the phone twice, send a preprogrammed SMS alert message with an exact location or request an interrupting phone call. It also allows users to call two preprogrammed national hotlines or a local emergency number of their choice.

On November 1, 2011, Vice President Biden announced that Circle of 6 was a cowinner of the Apps Against Abuse Challenge, calling it "a new line of defense" for young people against violence in their lives. That validation, and the subsequent interest and excitement, convinced the Circle of 6 team to go beyond the competition, and get the product in as many hands as possible. Even with a small grant from the Robert Wood Johnson Foundation, a small investment from Motorola Mobility, and a rousing reception at the CTIA Wireless Convention, they found financial resources scarce. True to her documentary filmmaking background, Schwartzman kept scrapping. She managed to get a tiny mention in *Cosmopolitan* magazine, which led to thousands of downloads before the product's official launch.

Schwartzman has received testimonials from female college students around the nation—including one at Cornell who had been fearful due to reports of a guy groping girls around the dark, vast campus; and another at Duke who now feels more comfortable studying late at the library. She's heard from women who use the call-me function to excuse themselves from creepy dates, from young professionals in cities who use the GPS capability to get picked up in unfamiliar neighborhoods. She's heard from massage therapists and house cleaners who use it just to let people know where they're working. Schwartzman heard from families who put their grandparents on Circle of 6 so they know the latter's whereabouts, which she thinks is "really adorable," and parents who do the same for their teenage children when the latter start driving ("so there's no question that they'll come get their kids anytime, anyplace").

"It's becoming a care network for each other," Schwartzman said.

Not just in America either. While presenting at the United Nations, Schwartzman fielded requests for translations to countless languages.

"The GPS is international, we have two hotlines built in, and one is customizable," she said. "If you are in Canada, New

Zealand, Australia, India, England, or Germany, these are all the places we've heard that are using the app."

The global impact became clearest to Schwartzman in 2012. After the brutal gang rape of a 23-year-old physiotherapy intern in New Delhi, India, Schwartzman began to notice a spike in downloads from that region, from a few hundred to several thousand, making it the second-largest market for the app behind the United States.[36] To assist those users, she launched a New Delhi version in April 2013, one translated into Hindi and able to provide local hotlines and resources. She even enlisted a Bollywood superstar, John Abraham, as a celebrity endorser.

In the fall of 2013, Circle of 6 crossed a milestone: 100,000 downloads. And Schwartzman wasn't stopping, working on a version for Mexico City officials. Through Tech 4 Good LLC, she is working with her team to make the app a commercial enterprise.

All of the above represented progress in problem solving, by thinking in ways big and small, but mostly smart. That was the aspirational vision that President Obama had articulated, after he first bridged the few blocks between the White House and the National Academy of Sciences in April 2009. President Obama used that stage to call for a fresh approach toward confronting America's most confounding quandaries. He invoked one of his greatest predecessors, the one who used the Civil War as an opportunity to innovate, not stagnate. "Lincoln refused to accept that our nation's sole purpose was mere survival," President Obama said. "He created this academy, founded the land grant colleges, and began the work of the transcontinental railroad, believing that we must add—and I quote—'the fuel of interest to the fire of genius in the discovery . . . of new and useful things.' This is America's story. Even in the hardest times, against the toughest odds, we've never given in to pessimism; we've never surrendered our fates to chance; we have endured; we have worked hard; we sought out new frontiers."

Today, we need to explore new frontiers not only in terms of the problems we try to solve but in the manner in which we attempt to solve them. Collectively and creatively. Much more is possible, if the government makes the populace part of the process, so the greatest number of people can assemble and share their ideas and gifts for the greater good.

As Obama put it, "I think all of you understand it will take far more than the work of government. It will take all of us. It will take all of you."

Tom Kalil certainly understood that, as he continued taking steps to scale and cement prize policy throughout the government, including his February 2012 recruitment of the chief operating officer of The X PRIZE Foundation, Cristin Dorgelo, to join the administration. Together, they would champion the already-bustling Challenge.gov platform. Over the first three years since its start in 2010, that platform hosted roughly 200 competitions that were sponsored by more than 40 federal agencies—with those agencies receiving design and execution support from the new NASA Center of Excellence for Collaborative Innovation. The Challenge.gov program itself won Harvard's prestigious Ash Center Innovations in Government Award in 2014.[37]

But this isn't just about milestones already achieved and accolades already earned. The real power of prize policy is where it can take us.

"You change people's views of what is possible," Kalil said. "If I said to you a couple of years ago, California is going to pass legislation to create a legal framework for self-driving cars, you might have looked at me like I was crazy, right?"

That, however, is what's happening. Aiming to get soldiers out of harm's way, DARPA issued a series of Grand Challenges starting in 2004, with a Grand Challenge defined by Kalil as, "Ambitious yet achievable goals that capture the public's imagination and that require innovation and breakthroughs in science and technology to achieve."[38]

This one called for the replacement of one-third of America's ground fleet with autonomous vehicles by 2015. In the first trials, none of the robot vehicles completed the 150-mile route alongside Interstate 15 from Barstow, California, to the Nevada border. In 2005, DARPA ran a do-over, on an even more winding, mountainous, turn-heavy course. Twenty-two of the 23 entered vehicles went farther than any of the vehicles the years before, and five completed the course, paced by Professor Sebastian Thrun's Stanford Racing Team and its Stanley vehicle. Google later hired the Stanford talent to further demonstrate the vehicle's safety, and the company's subsequent breakthroughs compelled California Governor Jerry Brown to sign SB 1298 into law in October 2012, allowing for testing of Google's self-driving cars on the road, with a human passenger along as a safety measure.[39] Cadillac, a division of General Motors, has predicted it will be manufacturing fully autonomous cars by the end of the decade.

Imagine that. Or software that replicates the personalized approach of a premier tutor. Or green buildings that produce all the energy they consume. Or increasing access to health care for pregnant women in the developing world by at least 50 percent. Or making solar cells as cheap as paint.[40] Those were among the lofty long-term ambitions that the President outlined in his Strategy for American Innovation.[41] That report inspired an interim measure, the SunShot initative to make solar cells as cheap as coal by 2020. That Grand Challenge inspired a prize competition, the $10 million Race to the Rooftops challenge, with an even more tightly defined goal. The windfall prize goes to the first team to install solar panels across 5,000 rooftop systems, at $1 per watt—as measured by the nonhardware costs of permitting, interconnection, and inspection.

When that prize is awarded, we'll all win.

Chapter 8

Lean (Government) Startups

George Patton had already gone above and beyond for his country by the breakout of the Second World War. In World War I, he had commanded the United States tank school in France and earned full colonel status, the Distinguished Service Medal for excellence in performing duties of high responsibility, and the Distinguished Service Cross for exceptional bravery in combat—bravery that included taking a bullet through the thigh while advancing on the enemy.

In the two decades following America's victory, Patton continued rising through the U.S. Army ranks, even as the nation resumed a peacetime posture. In the summer of 1939, with Adolf Hitler's Germany already acting as an aggressor in Europe, and Asia falling into turmoil, Patton was called to serve as a tank brigade commander in the Second Armored Division, based in Fort Benning, Georgia. There had been advancements in technology in the intermittent years, but those were not reflected in the fleet Patton found at Fort Benning. Due to military underinvestment after World War I, 85 percent of the machinery in the Army's arsenals was over 10 years old, this at a time of rapid technological change. And some parts were just plain missing. A *Life* magazine article reported in 1942 that "once, on his own responsibility,

Patton bought some quickly-needed equipment direct from Sears, Roebuck." Yes, on his own time, and dime.[1]

Obviously, ordering from Sears, Roebuck wasn't an ideal approach to preparing for the full-scale war that appeared well on its way. In his fireside chat on May 26, 1940, titled "On National Defense," President Franklin D. Roosevelt assured the nation that its military was steeling and reshaping itself for conflict, leaning "on the latest that the brains on science can conceive" when it came to weaponry and tactics.[2] Unlike other nations, America would not manage nationalized industries and centrally plan production; rather, the government would search for the best ways to work with its private domestic partners.

While he acknowledged in the speech that private industry, not government, would need to manufacture the majority of "the implements of war," he emphasized that government stood ready to provide investment capital for new plants and plant expansions, employee hiring, and any other capacity-building activities to meet the wildly ambitious production goals the military had set. But the government would also need the private sector's assistance, especially in a coordination capacity, since few government employees had the requisite experience and expertise, whether in product and service creation or in mass production techniques. So he enlisted private sector experts to align with the government, and entrusted them to take the coordination lead, for a common cause.

"Patriotic Americans of proven merit and of unquestioned ability in their special fields are coming to Washington to help the Government with their training, their experience and their capability," Roosevelt said. "It is our purpose not only to speed up production but to increase the total facilities of the nation in such a way that they can be further enlarged to meet emergencies of the future."

President Roosevelt's call for outside assistance had a precedent—in World War I, President Woodrow Wilson recruited industry leaders as "dollar-a-year men," named as such because, by U.S. law, government employees need some compensation to bind their contract.[3] And, as in World War I, many of the nation's most accomplished and prominent people, from a variety of fields, reported for government duty, undeterred by the pittance paid. By the end of World War II, there would be more than 300 business leaders in the program, under the supervision of Sears Chairman Donald M. Nelson, who had succeeded GM President William S. Knudsen. Seventy percent of those participants were experienced manufacturers, many of them with a research and development background, and their ability to apply newer mass production techniques and supply chain management manifested itself in a dramatic increase in manufacturing output. For the government, they served a translation function, a communication bridge between the public and private sectors, between military planners and industrial producers.

Take aluminum, one of the staples of modern warfare, used extensively in aviation. In 1939, the country produced no more than 350 million pounds, only one-quarter of Defense Department projections for the necessary amount in the coming years, and almost entirely from Alcoa Corporation. Nelson's team of dollar-a-year men, including Alcoa's Arthur Bunker, worked with the Defense Plant Corporation, under considerable scrutiny from the press and public due to the monopolistic nature of his company. Still, it was hard for anyone to argue with the results. In the spring of 1944, the Truman committee investigating the war program revealed that, in 1943, the supply of aluminum had grown to 2.79 billion pounds, such a significant surplus (620 million pounds) that it recommended releasing some to manufacturers of civilian articles. The committee commended Alcoa for "the prompt and effective manner in which it expanded at its own expense its annual production from 350 million pounds to more than 850 million pounds, as well as the expedition with which it constructed the Government-owned aluminum and alumina facilities."[4] The committee also concluded that "plants built by Alcoa for the Defense Plant Corp. are equally or more efficient than those owned by Alcoa itself." Also, for all the concern about Alcoa acting as a monopoly, the war program actually created competition. Other suppliers, including Reynolds Metals—which had urged increases in aluminum production capacity—gained strength as a result of the effort.

World War II was a victory for America and the allies well beyond its borders. But, while we recall many of the heroes and battles fought in faraway lands, the domestic lessons are often lost, such as the good that came from civility and collaboration between those from the private and public sectors and those from different political parties. Here was Roosevelt, considered the classic liberal and a proponent of expansive government, ceding coordination responsibilities to largely conservative business leaders. And here were those business leaders, many skeptical of government, serving it in its time of greatest need. At a press conference on April 15, 1941, Roosevelt joked about the preponderance of Republicans on the dollar-a-year list.[5] He said he asked Knudsen why there weren't more Democrats and was told: "There's no Democrat rich enough to take a job at a dollar a year."

Presidential administrations since Roosevelt may not have confronted world wars, but all have faced varied and vexing challenges, domestic and abroad, that forced them to recognize the need to venture outside their comfortable circles of party loyalists, campaign volunteers, and policy advisers to tap into the expertise of those not already working in government. They have gone to great lengths to frame government work as honorable and appealing, with rewards beyond the financial, in order to attract the interest of premier talent among the general populace.

This came into play in the 1960s, when President John F. Kennedy instructed his brother-in-law Sargent Shriver to head a Talent Hunt Committee for filling Cabinet spots and other key positions in his administration.[6] Shriver started by securing a list of first-team academics from a Harvard professor, but he didn't want to rely on one person's recommendations. He sought a diversity of opinions and candidates. He told a staffer, Harris Wofford (a future U.S. Senator from Pennsylvania), "We're going to comb the universities and professions, the civil rights movement, business, labor, foundations, and everywhere, to find the brightest and best possible."

Once he identified those people, he needed to sell government to them. That may have been a bit easier in those days, as even Shriver acknowledged at a JFK legacy seminar a quarter-century later.[7] At the dawn of the Kennedy administration, government was not, as he put it, widely perceived as the "capital of an evil empire of bureaucrats and dunces and incompetents." Plus, Shriver could sell the opportunity to associate with a charismatic President. That allowed for selectivity, and they filled more than 200 positions, many with people who shared the administration's optimistic, almost idealistic vision. As Shriver later recalled, "If you believed in America's destiny, the efficiency of democracy, this was truly a glorious time to be alive." In his inaugural address, President Kennedy famously bellowed, "Ask not what your country can do for you—ask what you can do for your country." The underlying corollary, when it came to his administration's evaluation of potential employees, was that a person needed to be good enough for government, not the other way around.

Times and attitudes changed over the course of the next four decades, with scandals, incompetence, and media-amplified polarization dragging down government's prestige and popularity, but the election of President Obama—on a platform of Hope and Change—signaled a fresh opportunity for government to polish its reputation. As candidate Obama said at the ServiceNation Presidential Forum at Columbia University during the 2008 campaign, "Part of my job, I think, as president, is to make government cool again."[8] That had to start somewhere, and Valerie Jarrett, the cochairperson of the transition team, started here: "I think we're open to innovative ideas for new ways of government doing business."[9] That was appealing enough to convince entrepreneurs to invoke the spirit of the dollar-a-year men, and leave more lucrative private sector opportunities behind for a role in Washington. In turn, the administration could be selective, populating government with those who had demonstrated an ability to use the latest technology to strengthen or further an enterprise, whether a startup, a new product, or a social cause.

President Obama started with his own White House, recruiting Internet-savvy entrepreneurs to serve as Chief Technology Officer (me), Chief Performance Officer (Jeff Zients), Chief Information Officer (Vivek Kundra), and Director for Social Innovation (Sonal Shah), among other senior positions. And he directed his Cabinet to do the same, including the previously mentioned CTOs at HHS (Todd Park) and the VA (Peter Levin). More than 50 other entrepreneurs would fill senior roles, reporting directly to department and agency heads, and tasked with applying technology and innovation to advance that agency's mission. The White House supported these policy entrepreneurs in two ways: one, by providing them "air cover," or a Presidential license to innovate; and two, by convening them on a monthly basis via an Innovation Cohort, to exchange their best practices so they could scale across the government.

The participants brought a wide range of experience. Jim Shelton, the cofounder of the school management company LearnNow and the educational manager for the Bill & Melinda Gates

Foundation, joined the Department of Education to design the Investing in Innovation competitive grant program. That vehicle would provide seed capital for promising ideas and provide scaling capital for those, like Diplomas Now (DN), already proven viable.[10] DN developed a predictive model to flag children at a high risk of dropping out as early as sixth grade—based on the ABCs of Attendance records, Behavior, and Course failure in math—and pair them with nonprofit social service groups to monitor and improve their situations. DN received a $15 million validation grant to scale the program across the 2,000 schools that account for a majority of high school dropouts, partnering with those schools to develop and execute customized strategic plans for students. Those interventions have already significantly cut the number of students failing math.

Maura O'Neill, who had started companies in electricity efficiency, customer information systems, e-commerce, and digital education, joined the U.S. Agency for International Development.[11] There, she founded Development Innovation Ventures with a similar, staggered model to Shelton's program for education, allocating more funding to the best defined, developed, and tested projects. One was Mere Gao Power, a startup that uses microgrid technologies to replace kerosene with cleaner, renewable energy; early results, across 1,000 rural village homes in India, showed more than a 50 percent weekly reduction in costs, and earned the company the White House spotlight in a June 2013 We the Geeks Google Hangout.[12]

Alec Ross, who had cofounded the global nonprofit One Economy to close the digital divide for the poor, joined the State Department under Secretary Hillary Clinton, to lead her 21st Century Statecraft initiative, designed to take advantage of this "Internet Moment" in foreign policy.[13] His team intervened to delay Twitter's planned network maintenance in June 2009, to keep the social media platform open to Iranians during their uprising, allowing them to communicate with each other and the rest of the world. He also championed the administration's text messaging initiatives during international disasters, with the effort following the Haiti earthquake contributing to more than $32 million in donations.

The entrepreneurs who joined the government brought more than their respective skill sets. Many also brought a different way of working, one with its roots in Silicon Valley, and its fertile field of technology startup companies. Eric Ries, an entrepreneur, adviser, and author who had moved to that area in 2001, called that philosophy and methodology "lean startup."

When I first met Ries on my first official trip to Silicon Valley as the nation's CTO in the summer of 2009, he had little experience with established organizations, and had given little thought to applying his lean startup principles to government. In defining a startup as "a human institution designed to create something new, under conditions of extreme uncertainty," he had always left the identity of that institution open-ended, whether for-profit or nonprofit, private or public sector. Still, over time, even he was surprised by the proliferation of the principles and how they were applied by many "in situations that I considered to be quite strange." Those tinkerers included division managers at major companies, foundation directors, policy makers—and, well, me. Eventually, Ries would come to understand this hunger for a new approach, especially in areas in which the traditional ways of working were proving insufficient or even obsolete.

"People talk about the twentieth century being the management century, and I really think that's true," Ries said. "We've become so good at general management, you think about the global supply chain to keep us all alive, you think about the government programs that have lasted decades and really provided for the welfare of a large number of people, that's a real accomplishment to be celebrated. But those tools are really based in planning and forecasting, which makes it work well under conditions of nice, stable environments. Nothing changes too fast. So those tools are not really the best for situations of disruptive innovation, technological turmoil and change—the new paradigms."

He believes his lean startup strategies are better suited to handle uncertainty by leaders in all walks of life: "What we want to do is grow a management discipline that can be just as good as general management has been in the twentieth century, but with some tools that are more appropriate for the twenty-first."

What we wanted, in the wake of Wall Street reform and the 2010 passage of the Dodd-Frank Act, was a new agency that stood up for the American consumer in the increasingly cloudy and confusing financial marketplace, protecting citizens from predatory lending by financial service companies. President Obama tapped Elizabeth Warren to help establish and organize the agency, which would be called the Consumer Financial Protection Bureau (CFPB). She requested the assistance of my deputy, Eugene Huang, himself a successful tech entrepreneur, in modeling the agency more after nimble Internet startups than plodding government bureaucracies—leveraging technology, data, and innovation to maximize efficiency and impact. In August 2010, Huang and I attended a small dinner in Silicon Valley, where technology leaders offered suggestions about how the CFPB should operate. Ries later recalled his advice in *The Lean Startup*, his 2011 book: "Treat the CFPB as an experiment, identify the elements of the plan that are assumptions rather than facts, and figure out ways to test them." For instance, one of the elements of the CFPB was a call center to field consumer complaints about credit card companies, mortgage brokers, and other financial services. To establish staffing levels and budget authority, Congress needed to assume a certain level of call volume, but those assumptions were really just guesses, with no way to accurately account not only for how many citizens were victims of fraud, but how many would actually pick up the phone to inform the government. Instead, Ries suggested a more targeted approach that might avoid understaffing and the risk of caller frustration, while also avoiding overstaffing and the corresponding waste of man hours and tax dollars. His impromptu suggestion of a minimum viable product would consist of creating a simple mobile app, saturating one neighborhood with flyers, asking anyone with financial issues to call a simple hotline number on the Twilio.com cloud-based communications platform, and then extrapolating the number of actual callers to what might occur with expansion to the larger population.

"That microexperiment would be cheap, and it's better than market research, because you're not asking what you would do or putting out a survey," Ries said. "It's actually an experiment where people reveal their behavior through their actions. And if they don't agree with you about what topics they want to talk to you about, they're right, not you."

With Huang acting as an advocate, CFPB adapted Ries' experimental, incremental approach in a slightly different way, by initially rolling out the call center (and web) complaint service for credit card issues only, so that it could be used as a test bed and training ground for other financial services issues, such as those related to student loans, vehicle loans, mortgages, and debt collection. But it played an even greater role in an initiative mandated by the Dodd-Frank Act, one aimed at removing complexity and confusion from the mortgage process. As Warren said: "With a clear simple form, consumers can better answer two basic questions. Can I afford this mortgage, and can I get a better deal someplace else?"[14]

The agency engaged those who would use the new forms—consumers, lenders, mortgage brokers, and settlement agents—through a website called Know Before You Owe, posting two prototype loan estimates for review and input.[15] Then it took the testing on a nationwide tour, meeting with small businesses, adding elements, and posting the revised products for further feedback. In sifting through more than 25,000 comments over 10 months, the agency was able to hear, and then heed, requests for clearer language and cleaner design, to make cost comparisons easier. In February 2012, President Obama held up the latest incarnation of the redesigned mortgage application form at a Falls Church, Virginia, community center, hailing it as a key component of the "Homeowners Bill of Rights."[16] He recalled how he and Michelle, two trained lawyers, had struggled with the complexity of the documents required for buying their first home, and the President argued that a new form where "terms are clear" and "fees are transparent" would keep consumers from getting "cheated."[17] In later months, he would speak on the campaign trail of the ways that Know Before You Owe was expanding to college financial aid letters—the Student Loan Fact Sheet—and credit card agreements, all aimed at allowing borrowers to make the most informed choices.

The CFPB officially got the lean startup seal of approval during one of Ries' trips to Washington as an informal adviser. As he sat in the bureau's offices, the environment reminded him of Silicon Valley, in the manner that people worked and spoke, obsessed with experimentation and rapid iteration. He was amazed by the integration of his philosophy in other agencies as well, even by those employees who didn't know his name—people who had come from entrepreneurial backgrounds or longtime government employees whose entrepreneurial instincts had been awoken. He saw these seeds growing up healthy in what many assumed to be impossibly hostile soil.

"I was really skeptical," Ries said. "I didn't believe it when people would tell me that government is innovative. But there are honest-to-god real-life entrepreneurs working in the federal government."

We had seen the Ries philosophy, experimental and incremental, planting itself in what he would call "a green field opportunity," an agency starting from scratch. But what about more established agencies and departments, those defined by entrenched bureaucracy? In those legacy institutions, there's often a *way* to do things, because it's the way they have always been done, even if that way isn't particularly efficient and hasn't always worked out well. It was easier to turn something on, than to turn it around.

Two agencies would represent this truer test of the latter around, because they had a reputation for constraining the innovation economy: the Food and Drug Administration (FDA) and the United States Citizenship and Immigration Services (USCIS). That's why we targeted those two agencies with our Entrepreneurs in Residence (EIR) program, which married external and internal talent, and asked them to apply lean startup principles to a clearly-defined mission over a six to nine month period.

The administration did not discriminate based on attitudes toward government. Otherwise, Dean Kamen never would have become one of the 20 people chosen for the EIR program in the FDA. The inventor of the Segway and numerous medical device products had been among the most vocal critics of the painstaking approval process for new medical devices, claiming that the continuation of business as usual would result in more innovation occurring outside the country.

"When you actually diagnose the process—and this is classic general management—the thing that made it slow didn't make it more safe, it's just because everyone is risk averse and afraid of failure," said Ries, who addressed the team early in its efforts. "It goes slow because no one is taking responsibility for a process that is really bad and creates silos between people that are really dumb. These are supply chain and manufacturing ideas that have been [incorporated] into general management that worked really well in olden times."

It wasn't working for Kamen. At the TEDMED 2011 conference, he mocked the FDA's intransigence in green-lighting an advanced prosthetic arm he had designed for veterans who had lost limbs in combat.[18] His acerbic commentary illustrated the serious rift between the regulatory agency and the innovators under its watch and, in reality, thumb.

Fully aware of this division, and determined to engage rather than enrage experts in the field, Dr. Peggy Hamburg set out to redefine the relationship. The agency sent out a signal for Kamen and 19 other leaders of industry, academia, venture capital, and research—including embolectomy catheter inventor Dr. Thomas Fogarty and retired Medtronic CEO William Hawkins—to work with the best and brightest in the FDA's Center for Devices and Radiological Health.[19] They were tasked with designing a better process for regulators to evaluate the risks and benefits of approving medical devices, a process that was more mindful of the innovator's perspective and could get patients faster access to safe, state-of-the-art products. The team targeted one ailment, end-stage renal disease (ESRD), which afflicts more than half a million Americans, and for which patients have few options other than dialysis or kidney transplant.[20] The team then zeroed in on specific parts of the process that were counterproductive.

"What if we had the same examiner who reviewed the initial application also review the follow-up application?" Ries asked. "That examiner wouldn't have to get up to speed—brand new—every time the new application came in. That's pretty common sense, an obvious thing to do. But just having a commonsense idea is not enough. You've got to have a team that can pilot it, test it, and see if it will work. So the key parts are a cross functional team with a limited mandate, six months not just to write a report or come up with new ideas but to implement the new solution, iterate it, prove that it works."

In April 2012, the FDA announced that three ESRD technologies had emerged from a competitive pool of 32 and would get the opportunity to earn regulatory approval through the new pathway. In announcing the selections, the Center for Devices and Radiological Health's director, Dr. Jeff Shuren, highlighted the overwhelming response, arguing that it "demonstrates that there is a desire from developers of innovative technologies for earlier and more collaborative agency interaction."[21]

To initiate its EIR program, USCIS would also turn to an agitator. Brad Feld, an early-stage investor and prolific blogger, had become exasperated when officers of two promising startups under his watch were forced to return to their home countries because they couldn't secure visas. He shared their story on a blog, attracting the attention of other entrepreneurs, including Ries, who couldn't understand why there was no visa category for an entrepreneur with American investors and employees. In lieu of that category, many entrepreneurs were at the mercy of visa examiners who didn't understand how they operated. At the point of visa application, many startups had not hired many employees or generated much revenue. This confused traditional visa examiners, who would then ask odd and irrelevant questions, often before a denial. To give just one example, it's been years since AOL required a compact disc to use its service. And yet, visa examiners were demanding proof of a warehouse, where software startups would store their CD inventory for shipping to customers.

As Feld's idea of a "startup visa" became intertwined with, and paralyzed by, the broader debate on comprehensive immigration reform, the USCIS, with White House support, sought to accomplish something administratively within the existing law. It instituted an EIR program, to organize and educate a specialty unit of immigration officers to handle entrepreneur and startup nonimmigrant visa cases.[22] The project also called for educating entrepreneurs about the available options, one of which they may have overlooked. For instance, the O-1 visa, which was reserved "for those with extraordinary ability," had proven a successful channel for actors, athletes, musicians, directors, scientists, artists, businessmen, engineers, and others who could provide ample evidence of their unique and impressive abilities, attributes, awards, and accolades. It had even created some controversy, when visa evaluators took the term "model" to an extreme, awarding a visa to one of Hugh Hefner's ex-girlfriends, a Playboy centerfold from Canada named Shera Berchard.[23] If she was confident enough to assert and explain her "extraordinary ability," why weren't entrepreneurs?

Like the team at the FDA, the EIR team enlisted entrepreneurs familiar with the obstacles, including SoftLayer senior executive Paul Ford, to work alongside the USCIS personnel committed to removing or clearing them. "You get fresh thinking, you get a very low-cost way of trying to impact the situation because the people doing this are committed to try to find what's not working and propose solutions, rather than take a partisan or political or hierarchical or structural view to the environment," Feld said. "They're short-timers, so they're committed for a period of time to come do something, but they're not here for career advancement, so they are going to speak their mind."

Feld also believed that the presence of Ford and other outside entrepreneurs made the participants feel more comfortable to speak freely than if they had been working with government officials alone. In the spring of 2012, the team began building a prototype of an alternative application process for entrepreneurs and by fall had achieved a significant breakthrough: the launch of the Entrepreneurship Pathways web portal, designed to close the information gap between USCIS and those in the entrepreneurial community, by letting them know which visa may be most appropriate—including the O-1—for their situation.[24] While the results of this exercise were not empirically conclusive at the time of an interview for this book, Feld did offer his anecdotal assessment "that there's an increased number of people who I know have been able to get into the country and get valid visas who are entrepreneurs. I've definitely heard a decrease in the negative."

One case study was unquestionably positive. Fabien Beckers was born in France, where he, as a physicist, tried unsuccessfully to build a company for seven years.[25] Convinced of grander opportunity in America, he enrolled at Stanford University, graduated with a master's in business and, with a partner, started Morpheus Medical Inc. to build cloud-based software for noninvasive diagnosis of cardiac defects in babies. His work visa, however, was set to expire on December 13, 2012, and, in attempting to extend his stay, he was denied an H1-B visa because he did not have an employer.

"It was hell," he said.

With other options exhausted, he applied for the O-1 visa that the Entrepreneurship Pathways portal had included as one of the viable possibilities for someone with his "extraordinary ability." One week prior to his deportation date, and likely aided by the education that visa examiners had received, he was approved. With Beckers' status assured for at least the next three years, investors felt comfortable contributing to his cause, and he quickly secured nearly $2 million and hired four employees.

"It's really, really amazing," Beckers said. "We're so happy now."

Yet he was not satisfied. He became a visible proponent of the passage of the aforementioned startup visa, hoping to make it easier for others than it had been for him to contribute something meaningful in, and for, America.

Todd Park wasn't satisfied either, even after inroads that the Entrepreneurs in Residence had made at the FDA and USCIS.

He had been the pioneer of the open data movement from his post as CTO of Health and Human Services, prior to becoming my successor as the nation's Chief Technology Officer on March 9, 2012.[26] That promotion positioned him to expand upon our attempts to alter the culture of the entire federal government. He would build toward the future by drawing from the past: the White House Fellows program that had endured since President Lyndon B. Johnson established it in 1964 to give promising Americans a chance to work inside government for a year. Park would give that time-honored program a more modern spin, integrating Eric Ries' lean startup principles of lightning speed and limited scope.

In May 2012, Park proposed a Presidential Innovation Fellows program to bring together external and internal innovators to work for six months on what he deemed "game-changing projects."[27] With President Obama's support, and leadership from John Berry at the Office of Personnel Management, Park selected 18 fellows from more than 700 applicants, to work on five projects. I have covered two (scaling Open Data and increasing the awareness of Blue Button personal health records) extensively in this book. The others were MyGov, to streamline communication between government and citizens by organizing the more than 1,200 government websites around people's needs rather than around the bureaucracy; RFP-EZ, to create an easy online marketplace to better connect government and private sector technology firms during the request for proposal (RFP) process, allowing government to buy better technology at less expense; and the 20% Initiative, which aimed to transition international development assistance from cash to electronic payments to reduce fraud and theft and lower administrative costs.

Park didn't force the projects, or the fellows, on the agencies. He wanted willing, eager partners who saw a need for outside assistance.[28] He required that those agencies compete for the right to house—and pay for—the fellows, by submitting proposals and explaining how they would enable and empower the new personnel. He got the fellows going quickly, so quickly that it stunned even Ries; by the swearing-in ceremony, after only a few days together, some had already hit their first milestones. "The speed of it is so refreshing," Ries said. "It's refreshing for those of us who are frustrated with government, but it's even more refreshing for the people in government. A lot of those people want to go faster; they want to be innovative, they want to do a good job. There's this caricature of them that they're lifetime bureaucrats who don't care. That's not *true*. I'm sure there are some of those people, but the ones I've met get excited about trying to serve their country."

Ries credited Park for showing respect to those people, by not giving the newcomers too much license at their expense, and creating resistance or resentment.

"That would be a catastrophic failure, if we go get a bunch of people from the outside and we drop them like aliens on the lawn of the government, and they sort of tell the government what to do," Park said. "That has been tried before, and that project would be flaming wreckage."

Instead, Park used a Ries-inspired technique to assist the entrepreneurs in government who may have felt stifled by a general management environment: he gave them more like-minded help and, through a supportive structure, gave everyone permission to experiment and fail.

"What we said instead was 'What are you trying to do? What kinds of capabilities and skills do you want to bring in from the outside to help you? OK, let's form a team that has your best people on it, and bring in people from the outside that have the skills you want, and then have that new team execute in a lean startup mode to change the game, do more than either could do separately, and deliver successfully against that mission,'" Park said. "That recipe is working incredibly well."

At times, it required adding a pinch of spice to the mix: entrepreneurs who, like Dean Kamen, may be somewhat skeptical of government. Clay Johnson hadn't even voted prior to the 2004 Presidential election, when his mother's breast cancer, and the corresponding hike in health care costs, led him to become the lead programmer of Democratic candidate Howard Dean's website. After his subsequent technology firm, Blue State Digital, designed websites for the Democratic National Committee and then-Senator Barack Obama, he became the director of the nonprofit Sunlight Labs. In that capacity, he collaborated with the government on Data.gov, including the Apps for America contest that produced the aforementioned upgrades to the *Federal Register* website. Over the years, he came to conclude that government reform required more than just the noble goal of transparency.

"When you are dealing with government, there is always this question in the back of your head, Is this corruption or is this incompetence or is this inertia?" Johnson said. "And it could be one of those three things that is frustrating you inside of government. More than likely, most of the time, it's not corruption, it's not incompetence; it's usually inertia, and inertia is just as much of a corrosive influence on the business of government as money or malfeasance."

After leaving Sunlight Labs, he captured his frustration with the current political discourse in a book called *The Information Diet*, arguing that the public, taking a cue from its leaders, was arguing about the wrong things. "What the Republicans say is 'We need to cut programs' and the Democrats say, 'Well, we need to raise revenues,'" Johnson said. "And it doesn't make any sense. It's as though America is a fat guy on the couch. And the Republicans are saying, 'We've got to get him off the couch, the best way for him to get off the couch is for him to lose weight, the best way for him to lose weight is to cut off his legs.' The Democrats are saying, 'No, no, to get him off the couch, he needs more energy, and the best way for him to get more energy is for him to eat more,' which is also not going to get him off the couch. We need to have conversations about how to get government to run better and work better."

After completing the book, Johnson would receive another opportunity to actively participate in that conversation—to, as acquaintances challenged him, "do something about all of those things you've been complaining about." One of those things had been the government's procurement process, which had frustrated him again during a failed bid to provide website development services for Recovery.gov. He concluded that the government's arcane restrictions and overreaching requirements caused it unnecessary expense, as it consistently paid more than the private sector for similar technology services. The White House agreed, which is why it made RFP-EZ one of the five initial Presidential Innovation Fellow projects, assigning Johnson, GovHub cofounder Adam Becker, and innovation designer Ed Wood to the Small Business Administration.

The team approached the project in lean startup fashion, with the intention of speeding up the interminable RFP process so that the product, service, or technology requested wasn't out of date by the time it was received. It also sought to make the process less overwhelming to small-business bidders, who sometimes gave up because they didn't speak the language of government, and less intimidating to program officers and contracting officers, who are sometimes scared to even post work for bidding because they don't have time to do the necessary diligence on bulky proposals.

The RFP-EZ team identified one of the root causes of the problem: agencies had been asked to outline their needs in overly complex and clunky statements of work (SOWs), often from scratch or with little guidance, and in a language that neither they nor many vendors really understood. The result was fewer bidders, many incurring costs to interpret the statement and passing on those costs in higher prices. So, as its first deliverable, the team launched the SOW Composer, a way of creating simpler forms patterned after what the Internal Revenue Service has done with the 1040EZ for a subset of its filers.[29] The SOW Composer is a template repository of simplified stock content for statements of work, all ready to be repurposed. The tool not only allows authorized government contracting officers to choose exactly what they want in the statements of work, by checking boxes and filling in blanks, it also offers tips on how to make sure the content developed is easily located and understood by small businesses. The tool eliminates repetition and leaves space for users to add their own requirements.

Then the team, in an open source manner, developed other tools, such as BidMaker, which helps small businesses create their bids; the Marketplace, where small businesses sort through opportunities and make their bids; and BidMonitor, which helps contracting officers swiftly sort through those bids, search databases with background about the bidding company, match the bid up to the statement of work, and use a drop-down menu ("price too high" or "irrelevant proposal") to explain why they dismissed or awarded the bid.

In its initial pilot, RFP-EZ posted five website development and database contract requests on its new platform, four of them simultaneously posted on the traditional portal, FedBizOpps.gov.[30] The bids received on the new RFP-EZ platform attracted 270 businesses that had never competed for government work. Not surprisingly, the bids were 30 percent lower on average.

Following his fellowship, Johnson returned to the private sector, but didn't turn his back on the open government movement; with a seed grant from the Knight Foundation, he and Becker started a company called the Department of Better Technology to create a number of products, including Screendoor, based on the RFP-EZ software and designed "to make the process of procurement less painful—both for government and for business."[31]

Johnson emerged from his government experience believing that the culture must change more, to reward innovation over compliance. He strongly advocates educating all government employees—especially newcomers—about the importance of innovation through open government and open data. He actually found some senior staffers to be more open to such alternative policies, perhaps because junior staffers are concerned about doing anything that might undermine their ascents.

"But we'll get there," Johnson said.

The White House turned to a civic pioneer, Jen Pahlka, to lead the Presidential Innovation Fellows program to the next level in 2013, its second year.[32] Pahlka had made her name through Code for America, an endeavor that demands considerable exploration here, because it embodies so many of the concepts in this book: people pulling together to solve problems; working with government rather than against it; using nontraditional lean startup methods; and getting out of the traditional boxes and arguments to enrich the lives of others, as well as their own—often in unexpected ways.

I first met Pahlka when she was working for TechWeb. We were at a 2009 conference meant to foster greater collaboration between government professionals and their traditional contractors—which had been on one side—and a new breed of social media entrepreneurs in the Beltway area that potentially could offer added functionality and lesser cost. At the time, she viewed these relationships optimistically, expressing her belief that if these parties simply became more aware of each other, they would share information in a way that would benefit everyone. (There were others who took a more jaundiced view of these relationships. Vivek Kundra would represent that perspective in a *New York Times* op-ed he wrote after leaving his position as the nation's CIO.[33] In making a case for companies that operate with newer technologies like cloud computing, he called out an "I.T. cartel" of powerful private contractors that make government dependent on "inefficient software and hardware that is expensive to acquire and to maintain.")

By our next meeting, at the Gov 2.0 Expo in May 2010, Pahlka had decided to blend her optimism with activism, still believing the government was capable of smarter acquisition and usage of technology, but no longer willing to wait for that to occur on its own. She invited me to join private sector technology leaders—including Tim O'Reilly, Facebook founder Mark Zuckerberg, and Twitter founder Biz Stone—in a public service video to recruit for her inaugural class of Code for America fellows.[34] She aimed to attract the most promising people in the technology field; to fan them out to cities (initially eight); and pair them with able, underutilized public servants to address localized issues. The video was called "What If," and its participants posed questions like this: "What if some of the most talented designers and technologists in the country applied those talents to building web apps that work for cities and for citizens?"

After 362 people applied for the 2011 fellowship, she chose 20 with a mix of skill sets, but all with track records of results. The passion to serve was assumed—after all, the annual stipend was a modest $35,000, plus health care benefits and some travel expenses. Pahlka viewed the program as a Peace Corps for technologists, one requiring a finite commitment of 11 months. The time constraint applied healthy pressure to accomplish something significant before the music stopped and a new crop of fellows, with their own perspectives and projects, came along to replace them. As an Eric Ries disciple, Pahlka adhered to the lean startup philosophy by emphasizing speed at every stage. "Let's put something up that will teach us something about the problem, instead of spending two years defining it, then three years prototyping, and by the time you're ready to address the problem, it's just out of date," she said.

The specific problems differed depending on the city, yet Pahlka came to view many in a common context: as persisting or worsening due to a disconnect between government and its people and, in turn, serving to deepen that disconnect. Pahlka analogized government to a smart phone: government costs far more than such a device, through the collection of taxes, and yet if it doesn't provide the features and services promised, there's no remedy. There's no receipt or warranty to use to get it fixed or replaced. There's no satisfaction, at least until the next election. And even then, there's little confidence among the consumers—the citizens—much will be different. Above all, Pahlka saw a desperate need to repair that relationship, and restore some of that confidence, so citizens feel compelled to contribute rather than just complain, lending a hand as well as a voice.

"What I realized is it's not about transparency to hold government accountable, it's about transparency to sell the value of government to citizens, and to sell citizens that they are able to be involved in this process," Pahlka said. "In the absence of the access to that information, citizens are going to assume that the government isn't going to do anything. That's the basic building block of this enormous distrust between citizens and government that is killing our country. If we are able to create interfaces that are simple, beautiful, and easy to use and open the door, you start to have people caring about government and wanting to support it, instead of hating it and wanting to take it down."

Pahlka ran into some resistance, because cities aren't monolithic institutions, and some officials are invested in the status quo, concerned about any change that might somehow decrease their value or simply scared of new technology they assume to be overly complex. Still, she said that pushback was "much less than you would think," and credits that to a model that calls for cities to self-identify some need for change, and to making the technology as understandable as possible to city officials.

"Let them own it as their agenda, let them find their own way that they can express it in their community, and then tell that story," Pahlka said. "Then you're sort of creating all these allies. Does that always work? No. You've still got people who want to see the current system persist—the current way of doing things—because they're waiting for retirement. But I would say in general, public servants in the United States are far and away one of biggest undervalued resources in our country. Treat them as such. 'You're the key to this. You went into public service to serve the public. This is a way you can do that better.' Tap into what got them into the field in the first place. And I think it actually goes pretty well."

Pahlka observed that, after working with Code for America, some government officials take different approaches to problems, more "consistent with government as a platform—different skill sets that they're hiring for, different positions they may create, very often different policies, especially around data. It can mean a whole host of things that can signal true institutional change. We're really building a network of local government leaders and community agents to care about this agenda and can support each other and work with each other. We want to tell those stories and spread those kind of outcomes as well, not just the applications but the organizational and institutional changes."

During the first two years of Code for America, the encouraging stories occurred all over the map, with one even off the U.S. mainland. The team sent to Honolulu, Hawaii, in 2012 encountered a common deficiency in city government, unacceptable at this stage of the Internet era: an unwieldly, exasperating website, one that sent residents down rabbit holes of useless text, outdated information, and broken links. This also stressed city staffers, forced to field flurries of angry calls from those who couldn't find content buried deep on that site. Recognizing the folly in attempting to rewrite an entire website in a few months, a former Yahoo employee named Sheba Najmi and the other fellows borrowed an interface from gov.UK, checked the search logs of honolulu.gov to find the 10 most common questions ("how do I get a new driver's license?"), and provided a search box that linked to the appropriate answers and forms. The team also recognized that 10 answers would not suffice so, in partnership with the city, it called a civic Write-a-Thon. That meant inviting officials and citizens to rise early on a Saturday to spend three hours in a government office to, in Najmi's words, "rewrite government." Nearly 60 people participated, posing questions and writing more than 120 total response "articles" in simple jargonless language, as if explaining to a neighbor. Many of those made it to the Honolulu Answers site, such as a page providing the prescription for a local dilemma: "What do I do about wild roosters?"[35]

Pahlka saw more value in this inclusive, collaborative, incremental solution than in the fellows rewriting the website on their own. "They've got the community now involved in it, and wanting to make it better all the time," she said. "You start to create social norms, to say, yes, government is something we do together. I don't just pay taxes and vote, I am an active participant helping to make our community work. That's really, in the end, what we're going for. That's the real outcome of government as a platform beyond first-class notions of transparency and efficiency and participation."

What does this engagement look like? Sometimes, it looks low tech, such as a Santa Cruz man painting photos of bicycles on lockers so riders would know the lockers were meant for them. Sometimes, it means citizens looking for hydrants or tsunami sirens or storm drains to "adopt"—entering their information on an application, clicking on a map, and then checking to make sure the key service is working properly in an era of strapped city budgets. "Money's tight, and no one is checking these sirens anymore," Pahlka said. "The city's not going to do it. Who does it? You do."

The engagement also looks like what started happening in Philadelphia, when citizens were given new ways to influence the city's plans for the future. The city had invited in-person feedback one evening per month to influence elements of its 2035 plan. Predictably, that once-a-month schedule generated negligible and unbalanced interest, not representative of the populace: many single mothers, for instance, couldn't regularly spare two hours at some meeting. Code for America's fellows leveraged technology to bring the questions to the people, posing them on posters in strategic locations such as transit stops: asking riders, for instance, to text to a "yes" or "no" number, indicating whether they would like to see a line extended. For city planners with a simple log-in, this is a means of cheaply, quickly, accurately soliciting and compiling citizens' opinions. "You can get hundreds and hundreds of people answering one question, instead of 20 people answering all of their questions," Pahlka said. That application, like many in the Code for America portfolio, is being scaled, or studied for scaling, in several other cities.

Finally, the engagement looks like what's happening in New Orleans, and a story—BlightStatus—that is especially emblematic of Pahlka's vision, and the tenets of this book.

Seven years after Hurricane Katrina, one of America's most unique and culturally vibrant cities was still holding on to a much more dubious distinction: ranking among America's three most blighted, fraught with foreclosures, and abandoned, crumbling edifices.[36] City officials were acutely aware of the problem, and many, including the new mayor, Mitch Landrieu, were intent on addressing it. He had made post-Katrina demolition and restoration a priority of his administration, even establishing monthly BlightSTAT meetings, through which the city could give its citizens a macro sense of how many houses were being repaired or demolished, with a goal of reducing the city's blight count by 10,000 by 2014. But, on the whole, the city still wasn't capably communicating to its citizens what it was attempting to accomplish.

"So to the people of New Orleans, it's just a mess," Pahlka said. "You come home one day, and something's been demolished, and you had no idea that was going to happen, you had no input into it, you weren't able to signal that, in fact, a different property on your block was really a problem. And you cannot really find out what's going on through that process."

As 2012 Code for America fellows, Eddie Tejeda, Amir Reavis-Bey, Alex Pandel, and Serena Wales would be responsible for abating those frustrations. They had attended different colleges, before pursuing different careers in different corners of the country: Tejeda, a software engineer in the civic technology space; Pandel, a graphic designer with a degree in studio art and work featured in magazines; Reavis-Bey, a technologist for Wall Street investment banking firms; and Wales, a web developer working with museums, nonprofits, and corporations.[37] They shared only a strong interest in service, beating out roughly 550 others to earn four of the 26 spots in Code for America's 2012 class. They spent four weeks working together in San Francisco, receiving crash courses in municipal government, civic technology, and design. Then the quartet shipped off to New Orleans, a city two had never previously visited, to bond in close quarters. There, they took the pulse of the people, outside and inside government, hearing how blight was affecting neighborhoods, interactions, and lives and learning what citizens were doing and what they wanted done. They encountered frustration in every corner and on all sides, whether from overwhelmed government staffers, underappreciated community leaders, or beaten-down citizens, frustration that had virtually paralyzed conversation and progress. And they began to understand how much this issue mattered, and the desperate need to close the information divide.

There was the woman from the Bunny Friend Neighborhood Association Inc., who spent several hours every night monitoring and chronicling the conditions of properties. She was so appreciative of the fellows listening, understanding, and attempting to assist that she hugged them. "You've got people who have lived there for their whole lives; they are fighting to make their communities work, they are fighting to be able to create the kind of communities they want to live in," Pahlka said. "And they cannot be partners to the city government in that fight if they don't have the access to some basic information and in a way that they can understand that information. They had just felt shut out. After years of being shut out, the door is now open. To someone who cares very deeply about fixing their neighborhood, that's an emotional moment for them. To be told, we're now going to collaborate with you on what happens to these blighted houses on your block, instead of just doing it *to* you, they feel validated, they feel hopeful, and they feel like they are now in a dialogue with the set of services that people are providing them."

There was the woman from Mid-City who kept photographs, printouts, letters, and complaints and consequences, largely unsatisfactory. Tejeda recalled her being "really tense" and even "angry at times," as she frantically flipped through a gargantuan, archaic, offline contraption. "It made me realize, 'Wow, this is how she stores information, in this binder, and here she is, stressed out, trying to find some piece of information,'" Tejeda said. "And a lot of this information, when we talked to people at City Hall, existed already, and it was in digital form."

The Code for America team sought to free these activists from unnecessarily pounding the pavement, pens in hand, to uncover what officials already knew, to allow them to invest their energy in helping to push properties through the blight process. The team also wanted to create conditions for a more constructive conversation, giving citizens and city staff the means to access the most specific and accurate information, and allowing them to recast their relationship as collaborators rather than adversaries—more common ground and common sense, less wasted time. They wanted to empower citizens to click on a specific property, point it out at one of those BlightSTAT meetings, and ask why a scheduled inspection hadn't occurred, instead of making some generalized accusation. "These questions are actually a lot easier for the city officials to answer," Tejeda said. "They can say, 'Oh, that guy was sick that day so he couldn't make it.' In terms of the relationship, it's much easier for citizens to communicate with city officials. Instead of frustration, yelling at each other, demanding things."

This is where technology came in.

"The main point is all of this information already existed in city hall," Pandel said. "We thought that clearly the format the information is in, in the city, is not working for citizens."

The team presented several basic concepts to the stakeholders at city hall, learning what was legal, feasible, and most critical. Then, back in the Bay Area, it reunited with fellow fellows, brainstorming with them about their projects while getting feedback on the blight work. The team returned to New Orleans to start testing a minimum viable product, one that would leverage open government, pulling from more than a dozen data sets to give citizens greater knowledge of the city's activities related to properties already reported. Less than five months later, the team officially launched the BlightStatus site at the monthly BlightSTAT meeting. It took five minutes to demonstrate how the application worked: how citizens could enter an address and receive a current status report of "Inspection" or "Notification" or "Hearing" or "Judgment" or "Foreclosure" or "Demolition," how they could sort by case status, and how they could scroll through the map. The team knew its application could be useful to citizens (clean format), staffers (less reliant on other departments, better able to answer questions), and planners (conceiving strategies to reduce citywide blight). Still, the response surprised them. "I remember when we got to the map page—that sort of showed all of the properties that currently had in 'open case'—people literally gasped and started to applaud, because I think they realized, 'Oh, so now I can basically have a BlightSTAT meeting in my home anytime,'" Pandel said. "They get the statistics now in real time, at their fingertips, instead of having to wait for the city to manually compile a report and hold this public meeting. So it was really very cool. It felt very rewarding."

The meetings continued in the city and still served a purpose, especially for those without Internet access. But the fellows had used technology to give the citizens more options, not through big government, but through making a big problem seem a bit smaller, more personal, more manageable.

"People cared overall about the overarching climate of how blight was being tackled in the city, but they want to know what's happening on their block, they want to know what's happening on the street around the corner, the properties that affect them directly," Reavis-Bey said. "So people were superexcited all over the place. People were interrupting the meeting, saying, 'Oh wow, I am looking right now, and I can see that this property was inspected, this property is in a hearing.' People were just really, really thrilled; it was as if the lights had been turned on."

That experience lit a flame for Tejeda, Reavis-Bey, and Pandel that they weren't prepared to blow out when their fellowships ended. They sought to make the progress sustainable. "It shouldn't happen that a project goes well, and people like it, and then it just dies because there's no one there to support it," Tejeda said. "This felt too important. It was New Orleans only, but hopefully we can expand it out to different cities that have similar needs. This is not an area where there are a lot of people who want to build tools for communities, and this is an important space, where you can have a real impact in fixing cities and helping people be involved in their government. If we can continue to work in this space, and people see the potential in this product—I wanted to make sure that we could."

So they passed over opportunities with established technology companies, staying in New Orleans and signing up for Pahlka's incubator program, which allowed some teams to continue their work while benefiting from the access to advisers and structure already in place. They came into this phase with contacts, confidence, and ambition, perfecting their pitch that, as Pandel put it, "there's space for innovative software with a user-centered approach, using the lean startup method, that can actually better meet the needs of cities and cost them less," and that it made more sense for a city to hire them to improve its communication with citizens than pay a major corporation to attempt to replicate their work.

During an interview in late 2012, Pandel related that "when we've been expressing the (relatively low) cost of this, people have been kind of surprised; they don't know what to make of us. 'Wait a second, this is a software system that provides value to me, and I don't have to go through procurement for it. I don't understand.' So we really think there's room in the civic space for projects like this."

Tejeda spoke of the potential to be "trailblazers."

"We get to be the first to try and disrupt this space at a fraction of the cost. We can possibly build a relatively big, successful company, and what we're doing is displacing these big, gigantic dinosaurs that are just not providing the kind of value that they should to cities at the cost that they charge," he said. "So I think we are all relatively optimistic as far as the space. There are legal challenges, as far as procurement, but this is what we are going to be working on now. But that's the gamble of this opportunity, not whether the market is big enough."

The gamble would continue paying off in 2013, when the team began incorporating permitting and licensing data to its application, moved back to Northern California, changed its name from Blight-Status to Civic Insight, began working closely with the city of Palo Alto, entered the $3.2 million Knight News Challenge on Open Gov along with 800 others, and was named one of eight winners.[38] That came with a $220,000 Knight Foundation investment grant.

"So we have legs for a little while longer," Tejeda said during the summer of 2013. "We can talk to other cities."

Code for America, in concert with Civic Insight, is smoothing the path for adoption by other cities, with the former creating a Code Enforcement Housing Data standard and the latter working to create an API that would connect to it.

"There's a lot of momentum," Pandel added.

"They get to go from cogs in the wheel to creating something long term that they are a founder of," Pahlka said. "It's not just doing good, it's a narrative of success."

It's an open innovation bonanza, featuring elements of open data, standards, and challenge competitions, all put to great use by entrepreneurial talent that government encouraged to assist.

Meanwhile, Pahlka continued writing her own narrative of success. Upon taking the one-year leave from Code for America to work as Todd Park's deputy, she oversaw the expansion of the Presidential Innovation Fellows program in its second year, from 18 to 43 fellows, and from five to 10 projects, some of them second phases of first-year projects (such as Open Data; Blue Button; RFP-EZ; and MyUSA, the next iteration of MyGov) and some (in the areas of disaster response, VA modernization, and federal agency accounting) representing new technological spins on long-standing issues.[39] She also brought in the U.S. General Services Administration (GSA) to assist in scaling prototype solutions to multiple agencies. Her intention, after institutionalizing lean startup and collaborative principles inside the federal government? To bring the lessons back to Code for America as new fuel for the virtuous cycle.

So the narrative of open innovation will continue. It is a hopeful story of people coming together—through handoffs and handshakes —to create the "wiser, frugal government" that Thomas Jefferson envisioned: one that is more transparent, participatory, and collaborative; one that is defined not by its size but by its smarts.[40] One that, believe it or not, can work.

Postscript

You may not have heard much about any of this. Not the gatherings of influential voices from different sides working in good faith to seek common ground, such as the December 2010 CEO summit at the Blair House. Not the actions taken in the aftermath of those gatherings to meaningfully address some of the structural and regulatory issues constraining our nation's economic growth, such as the National Wireless Initiative and the JOBS Act. Not the progress made in open government over the course of President Obama's tenure, with federal agencies experimenting in ways big and small: from the Department of Health and Human Services giving life to a new industry of private sector health information applications to the Department of Defense reaching beyond the usual Beltway bandits to a former Sizzler waiter for the design of a combat support vehicle.

You may not have heard much about the Washington to which I bore witness, one that was so much more collaborative than is customarily portrayed, especially when the camera lights were off, and ideological groups weren't raising a ruckus.

In the hardcover edition of this book, I made the case that the public was in the dark largely because the media wasn't especially interested or informed. Major media outlets are conditioned to focus on now rather than next, strife rather than substance, conflict rather than cooperation, and most of all, caricatures rather than context. This is especially true when they confront voices and topics that don't conform to the typical ideological constraints.

To illustrate this in the postscript for the hardcover edition of this book, I focused on Eric Ries's experiences. Outside of the public eye, he had seen excitement spread for the application of his "lean startup" principles in government, from the local (including Mayor's Innovation Fellows in San Francisco and the Office of New Urban Mechanics in Boston) to federal levels, as evidenced by the Presidential Innovation Fellows. "They all have their unique spin on it, but the core principles are very much alike," Ries said. Yet Ries had still struggled to find the right spin to make all of this meaningful and palatable for the national media machine; he was shouted down and cut off on cable news shows, by hosts and guests only capable or willing to debate tired old dichotomies like taxes and spending, small and big, left and right. He believed the public would appreciate and embrace fresh approaches, if they only knew more about them. Instead, he characterized the overall level of awareness as "zero."

"It's hard for the traditional political media to report on, because they are so locked onto 'he said, she said' and polarized reporting, that this doesn't fit the category," Ries said. "It's pro-growth *and* pro-government. They're like, 'What!? How do you write that article?' When I try to talk to the traditional political press, they don't know what I'm talking about. Every story, they've already written a million times. They're just changing the names."

The media's unsophisticated, incomplete approach to issue analysis undoubtedly contributed to the nastiness of the debate about Healthcare.gov. You surely heard *plenty* about that Obama administration initiative initially, when it began as an unequivocal technical disaster, neatly fitting the narrative of government incompetence, this time in the areas of policy and technology.

Naturally, you have probably heard much less about it since, now that it has begun to serve as an example of the good that government can do when technology is correctly applied.

First, it's instructive to review what initially went so awry. The administration's policy was intended to protect the American people by barring insurance companies from discriminating against prospective patients due to their medical histories. The site itself was intended to help them easily find the right plan, in line with income, circumstances, and newly enacted tax credits, so selection would be no more stressful than buying an airline ticket.

That didn't mean the construction of the site would be easy, and it wasn't, with the Department of Health and Human Services encountering many challenges. Some, such as outdated and restrictive IT procurement rules, were of government's own making, while others—such as state officials imposing political agendas—were beyond its control.

Let's start with procurement. As I have covered in earlier chapters, much of the $80 billion spent on government IT goods and services is purchased through broken contracting vehicles. Such was the case again in August 2011, when career staffers at the Centers for Medicare & Medicaid Services (CMS) put out a purchase order request for the construction of the new Healthcare.gov system. They did so through a 2007 "Indefinite Delivery, Indefinite Quantity" (IDIQ) contract, one that had been established before Barack Obama was ever a candidate for president, let alone presiding over his signature legislation.[1] This contracting vehicle constrained the Affordable Care Act's choice of technology developer to an established a pool of just 16 vendors, all of which had more experience accommodating government bids than building complex Internet-scale e-commerce sites.[2]

I suspect this approach was taken largely due to time constraints; it would be virtually impossible in today's federal acquisition culture to post an open call for bids, since that would require detailed initial requirements, careful selection of a vendor, and a request for completed work within a couple of years. Even if the vendor were chosen quickly, the increasingly common phenomenon of losing vendors filing protests likely would lead to unmanageable delays for the agency, as the Department of Defense noted in a 2007 memorandum.[3]

What about the shortcomings in governance? I devoted much attention in the original postscript to the corrosive political climate and the way it manifested itself in states with leadership unfriendly to the Obama administration—rather than implementing the exchanges as envisioned by the law, they often took actions that made failure more likely. One example: Oklahoma. In October 2010, U.S. Department of Health and Human Services (HHS) announced a competition between states, encouraging them to build their own sites. The Sooner State responded with a vision not only for meeting the baseline requirements, but also for upgrading the delivery, via the Internet, of many other social services. As a result, in February 2011, the state received the highest dollar award ($54.6 million) among seven "Early Innovator" winners. But in March, the newly elected governor, Mary Fallin, rejected the grant, returned the money, and killed the project. In August, her colleague, Kansas Governor Sam Brownback, similarly returned his state's $31.5 million share of the grant funds. Ultimately, 36 states chose to be entirely reliant on the federal government's version of Healthcare.gov, an odd stance considering how many of those states' decision makers typically touted states' rights.

So, certainly, political governance was a problem. Still, since the publication of the hardcover edition of this book, we have learned much more about the failures in *technical* governance as well. Simply, the original Healthcare.gov implementation team failed to take seemingly obvious steps in delivering a consumer-facing website. It was necessary, in order to get the enrollment campaign back on course, to get back to basics by establishing a clearer chain of command, all while bringing some fresh eyes to the project.

In mid-October, with the site more troubled than had been originally understood, my successor, Todd Park, initiated a "Tech Surge," recruiting a team of technical experts more capable of fully evaluating its issues, and charged them with getting the site functioning smoothly for the majority of users by November 30. Those recruits had backgrounds in site reliability, software development, user experience design, and other common areas of expertise found in technology companies around the world. They weren't asked to solve the unsolvable but merely to identify and fix relatively obvious issues.[4]

Without much difficulty, they identified problems big and small. For starters, the operations center lacked visibility into the performance of the website so, following the old adage "You can't manage what you can't measure," the rescue team installed site monitoring, which began systematically improving response times.

Additionally, the original team's plan adopted an old-school development methodology, with complex "waterfall" charts detailing very specific milestones and expectations on the way to the final target. It left little room for adjustment to accommodate the modern realities of software development, which tends to happen at its own pace, and after many unforeseen occurrences (from software bugs to evolving user requests and requirements), a more agile approach was called for.

Finally, and perhaps most troublesome, the personnel hadn't been managed correctly, with teams of technology workers operating in separate silos and without clear direction on where to prioritize resources. That lack of coordination stalled progress when one team was working on something without an understanding of how it would affect, or be affected, by what another team was doing.

Jeff Zients, who had served as the inaugural U.S. chief performance officer and was tapped to lead the National Economic Council in early 2014, was put in charge of the rescue team. And while he devoted some attention to the first two problems, he was most focused on the third: improper usage of personnel. He organized the equivalent of a daily management scrum: a standing meeting where everyone had the chance to update the group on progress, or point out areas in need of attention. By maintaining a comprehensive "punch list," the rescue team knew what needed to be done and had the resources necessary to address those tasks one by one.[5]

Yet as President Obama later pointed out in a July 2015 cover story for *Fast Company*, it wasn't enough to rescue one, albeit important, broken site. He saw the Healthcare.gov crisis as proof that no matter how far the administration had come in using technology to address issues, there was still some way to go, and it required even more of his attention. The blessing in disguise was that, now, other policy makers, the press, and the public might pay more attention too. As he told *Fast Company*, "With all the crises we were dealing with—the economy collapsing, the auto industry on the verge of collapse, winding down wars—this did not get the kind of laser-focused attention until Healthcare.gov, which was a well-documented disaster, but ended up anyways being the catalyst for us saying, 'Okay, we have to completely revamp how we do things.'"[6]

Where better to start than in the preparation for Healthcare.gov's second enrollment cycle. Park had barely caught his breath after helping to stabilize the site when he dispatched half a dozen engineers to essentially start from scratch. He emphasized the same "lean startup" principles that you have read about in detail in this book, and that he—inspired by the work of a private sector web designer named Ed Mullen—had deployed in building the first digital service of the Affordable Care Act back in the summer of 2010: the healthcare plan finder tool. That tool launched as a "minimum viable product" within ninety days, featuring a comprehensive list of all available insurance plans and their respective benefits as well as additional information—such as how frequently each plan denied coverage to applicants on account of preexisting conditions and added surcharges based on a patient's medical flags. Within a few months, the site increased users' searching power by adding pricing data and, by March 2012, standardized the access to that data via a new "Plan Finder API," which powers sites including U.S. News & World Report's Health Insurance Finder among others fully operational today.[7]

So now, fast forward to the point at which Park and his team had "rescued" Healthcare.gov, with a handful of those team members sticking around to prepare for the second enrollment cycle. A small group of newcomers joined too. Together, they worked on what would be known as "Marketplace Lite."

They started by putting more of a premium on the consumer shopping experience. They assumed the persona of an insurance shopper, sitting in the same seat as millions of Americans working their way through the site, and were troubled to find that it could take as many as 20 minutes, clicking through 76 screens, to complete the session.[8]

This needed to be simplified, especially since, in the first enrollment cycle, nearly 25 percent of signups came through mobile devices. That platform would clearly benefit from a cleaner intake process. So, first, for the mobile shoppers, the Marketplace Lite team reduced the number of screens required for setting up an account and signing in from five down to two. Simultaneously, it set out to reduce the number of screens for everyone, especially for those who clearly didn't need so many—the majority of shoppers had uncomplicated health histories. By redesigning the workflow, the team reduced the number of screens from as many as 76 down to 16, and the "worst case" completion time from 20 to 9 minutes.

This streamlining undoubtedly played a role in mobile shoppers sticking with the insurance purchase process through its conclusion; the conversion rate, from visitors to purchasers, rose by 30 percent in the second year.[9]

In addition to improving the consumer experience, the part that people would see, they also worked on the back end systems by using more modern technologies—easier, faster, cheaper—than had been applied in the previous version and in government in general.

Ever find yourself on a string of emails with lots of people sharing files? Ever struggle to find the most current version? There's an app to assist in each of those circumstances. It's called HipChat, a simple collaboration tool to make sure everyone is on the same page, widely used in the private sector. The Lite team decided to try it too.

Does your company IT department tell you to wait six months to order a secure computer server that would make your department more productive? Wouldn't you welcome the chance to rent one in minutes from the Amazon Web Services (AWS) cloud? The Marketplace Lite team fought for, and won, the right to use it, in order to fix one of the buggiest aspects of the site: the log-in screens. Originally, the log-in system had been built on custom servers meant to meet the government's specifications at a cost of roughly $250 million. They also required $70 million in annual maintenance, and for what? They were operational only 91 percent of the time (two hours of downtime daily), and accounted for 70 percent of the site's errors. The Marketplace Lite team, using the government-certified version of the AWS cloud, built a "scalable log-in system" for a modest $4 million, with an annual maintenance cost of less than $1 million.

This technological transformation of the site had a significant effect on transaction success rates, from 55 percent in the first year to 85 percent in the second year. Plus, response times typically taking five seconds or more were down to hundredths of seconds, and there were fewer clicks required to get to the finish.

The Marketplace Lite team's accomplishments demonstrated again, and even more dramatically, that altering the approach to government IT could have a demonstrable benefit. The president took notice, seeking to scale up these lessons by directing the key players of the Healthcare.gov rescue to launch the U.S. Digital Service in August 2014. Atop the list: Mikey Dickerson, a former Google site reliability engineer who agreed to lead the new expert agency within the White House. Its mission was "to improve and simplify the digital experience that people and businesses have with their government."[10]

With the Healthcare.gov turnaround accomplished, my successor, Todd Park, stepped away from his CTO post and was replaced by Megan Smith, an MIT engineering alumnus who had served as the head of Google X, the experimental lab responsible for such moonshots as Google Glass and self-driving cars.[11] Park moved back home to Silicon Valley, but continued to serve Smith and the White House as the "tech recruiter in chief," working with elite executives Reid Hoffman of LinkedIn, John Doerr of Kleiner Perkins, and others to challenge other technology talent to assist ongoing and emerging efforts in Washington. He didn't want them to wait, either, for when they might be between startup jobs. Rather, as he colorfully stated at one Bay Area recruiting event, he wanted them to do it, "Right. The. (Bleep). Now."[12]

Smith sought, through these efforts, to raise the government's "TQ," or technical quotient, meaning that engineers would always have a seat at the table when major technology-related decisions are made, ensuring that implementation plans are vetted with the same rigor as economic or political analyses.[13] As evidence of the success of these recruiting drives, consider the case of DJ Patil, someone whom Park has described as "the Michael Jordan of data scientists," and who, along with Jeff Hammerbacher of Cloudera, is credited with coining the term "data science." He had little reason to move his young family from Silicon Valley, where he had recently sold a startup and previously been chief data scientist at LinkedIn.[14] Like many throughout our economy, he had a desire to serve the greater good. During my tenure as CTO, it took the form of advice when we sought ideas on how to put market data to work to advance the mission of the new Consumer Financial Protection Bureau.

But now Park could make a more direct appeal with something more enticing: the opportunity to serve as the first U.S. chief data scientist in the White House Office of Science and Technology Policy with a broad mandate to influence society using skills Patil had developed throughout his private sector career. That offer proved impossible for Patil to resist, especially after President Obama personally and repeatedly courted him and his wife. It wouldn't take long for him to lead on a broad range of initiatives. These would include empowering patients and providers to develop individualized care based on genomics and health data through the Precision Medicine Initiative; increasing the supply of data science talent to grow the economy, especially from underrepresented communities; and working toward balancing the scales of justice, at a time when many increasingly perceived a double standard based on race.

That latter subject was especially complex and controversial in light of tragic deaths in Missouri, Ohio, New York, and elsewhere, resulting from police encounters with unarmed African-Americans. For many Americans not familiar with the scale of the problem, it was shocking to see video evidence of the fatal use of force on such victims as Eric Garner, killed on Staten Island after being stopped for the allegedly illegal sale of cigarettes, and twelve-year-old Tamir Rice, who was shot by police in Cleveland while playing with a toy gun. For many, these incidents served as a call to action, whether on social media or on the streets, as the "Black Lives Matter" movement formed and grew.

For the families affected and for society at large, it was a time of discovery, and not a pleasant one. Mostly, we learned about the limitations of our system to address its own shortcomings.

We fiercely debated whether officer Darren Wilson should have been held accountable for Michael Brown's death in Ferguson, only to learn in the lead-up to the grand jury that accountability is rarely achieved. We didn't know that since 2011, less than 3 percent of the 18,000 state and local police agencies voluntarily reported fatal shootings by their officers to the FBI.[15]

We were stunned that towns like Ferguson relied so heavily on court fines for seemingly innocuous crimes to operate its budget, with the burden falling far more heavily on poor minorities. We were aghast at the sight of military-style trucks and armor rolling into the streets of Ferguson to frighten otherwise peaceful protesters, only to learn that such equipment routinely makes its way from the Defense Department to localities with little community dialogue little concern about whether these so-called upgrades might convey a sense of an occupying force.

These emotionally charged topics may seem to stray from many of the policy and technological discussions in *Innovative State*. And yet, they don't, not at all, because the most persistent, pervasive, seemingly intractable problems call for the most creative thinking. And President Obama made the connection himself, in May 2015, when he delivered a passionate speech in Camden, New Jersey, devoted to restoring trust in our criminal justice system.

Why Camden? Because it had been "trapped in a downward spiral" prior to redirecting its police force towards community engagement.[16] Now the President viewed the city as a "symbol of promise for the nation . . . [where] police and residents are building trust." Violent crime fell 24 percent and 911 response times dropped from one hour to five minutes.

To further that progress, the President announced a Police Data Initiative in collaboration with the Arnold Foundation to help cities like Camden "use data to strengthen their work and hold themselves accountable by sharing it with the public." For Camden specifically, it would mean access to a tech team to help modernize the municipality's 41 different data systems to "make sure data is used effectively" to identify trouble spots in the system, as well as officers who might need additional training and assistance.

As New Jersey Senator Cory Booker, coauthor of the proposed Police Reporting of Information, Data, and Evidence Act of 2015, noted, "It's hard to have a substantive debate, focused on specific solutions, without a foundation of accurate data."[17]

In the weeks and months since the president's announcement of the Open Police Data Initiative, Patil and his team have worked with 26 local police agencies to release 40 datasets in machine-readable form, including 14 years of officer-involved shooting data from Austin, Texas.[18] In addition, DJ's team has encouraged civic participation to restore public trust.

Take Michael Harrison, the New Orleans police chief, who wrote his first line of code at a three-day coding event organized by the nonprofit Operation Spark for the New Orleans Police Department. High school students learning how to code for the first time built an application over two days on top of 911 call records in order to visualize where requests for help originated during larger events like Mardi Gras.[19]

Those efforts paved the way for several groundbreaking projects. The *Guardian* has painstakingly re-created a national database of publicly reported shootings, not from government records, but from journalists at the source. The Huffington Post has published an account of the usage of DOD equipment, accelerating and edifying the discussion about how much we want our local police militarized. The Burlington Vermont Police Department returned night vision goggles after a review concluded that those items didn't materially contribute to public safety.[20]

The Police Data Initiative is actually just one of several dozen new open government commitments that President Obama initiated in the latter half of his second term. They include a College Scorecard database of cost and outcomes, the Open311 standard to make government service delivery requests more transparent, and a Workforce Data Initiative to spur innovation in various pathways to employment.[21]

Leading the activity surge? The team serving in the Office of the Chief Technology Officer, an office that continues to evolve into a leadership vehicle for "delivering innovative government with and for the people."[22] Megan Smith has doubled down on many of the ideas we've detailed throughout *Innovative State*, and has added several new ones that blend skilled talent, a creative culture, and underlying technology advancements to foster more rapid transformation of the public sector.

She's formalized an Innovation Toolkit that government agencies can call upon with greater ease. This includes flexible hiring authorities to onboard the necessary talent without the typical delays; blueprints for agency "innovation labs" that test, validate, and eventually scale ideas that would otherwise sit idle in a risk averse culture; franchise models for agencies to build their own world-class digital services teams based on the core features operationalized by the U.S. Digital Services division; and tiered funding models for programs that work based on evidence.

This latest Toolkit, along with its offshoots in operation in governments within the U.S. and across the globe, is evidence that the movement continues to strengthen. As this postscript went to press, there were 69 countries participating via the Open Government Partnership program, responsible for more than 2,500 open government commitments developed in consultation with civil society.[23]

Since the initial publication of this book, I've continued to engage in this movement, mostly as a catalyst within the private sector to get the country closer to the full vision of an innovative state. I've frequently been asked, whether in America or abroad, about the application of its core principles. The reception has been heartening; there is a real desire not only for change, but also for an altered approach toward achieving it.

Yet, on occasion, I've encountered some folks, even some really smart folks, who still aren't convinced. This was evident during my interaction with Larry Summers, former Harvard University president and my colleague when he was serving President Obama as chairman of the National Economic Council.

In February of 2015, at the "Future of Work in the Age of the Machine" Hamilton Project Forum,[24] MIT professors Andrew McAfee and Erik Brynjolfsson shared a bullish outlook on economic growth in what they termed the upcoming "second machine age"—an era expected to be even more bountiful with consumer benefits, whether pushing a button to summon a self-driving cab or calling upon an Amazon Prime drone to deliver food within a few minutes.

Summers and I served on the response panel, debating whether this new era will diverge from prior technology-fueled robust economic periods in one key area: job creation. How can we avoid leaving many citizens behind? I suggested we apply these same machine-learning technologies to reduce friction in the labor market itself and make it easier to connect talent with opportunity, so that the workforce can grow to meet the demand for new skills born of all the modernization.

To Summers, however, this emphasis was "largely whistling past the graveyard," and "an evasion." He cited MIT professor

Esther Duflo's findings that job placement assistance in France failed to boost net employment in markets with existing high unemployment. In other words, it simply helped some people at the expense of others who might have otherwise filled those jobs, essentially, a zero-sum game.[25]

Instead, Summers espoused a combination of traditional fiscal stimulus policies to boost aggregate demand at a time when the cost of public borrowing is virtually free on account of near-zero interest rates, and a reduction in barriers to further business investment, among other interventions.[26] Not surprisingly, these ideas, which he had previously expressed, sparked enthusiasm among economists on the left for their roots in Keynesian policies, and were challenged by those on the right who prefer "supply-side" principles of limited government intervention and more tax cuts.[27]

In a deeply divided political climate, it is difficult to imagine much will come of either of these two economic interventions—more government spending or more tax cuts—that have been at odds for decades. So let's return to my suggestion that we work on innovative solutions to make the labor markets work better for everyone. Is Summers correct that such ideas are an "evasion"?

Time will tell, but from my seat, tackling the inefficiencies in the labor market by thoughtfully applying new technologies actually represents an opportunity for another of those handshakes and handoffs we've outlined throughout the book. A handshake between the left and the right, in the form of opening more labor market data to the public. And then, a handoff to entrepreneurs and innovators, giving them the responsibility of unlocking the full value of human capital in the same way our economy has historically—and successfully done—with investment capital.

A June 2015 study by McKinsey Global Institute, "Connecting Talent with Opportunity in the Digital Age," estimates that these resulting innovations, categorized as online talent platforms, could raise global GDP by up to $2.7 trillion, or 2 percent, which would translate to 72 million new full-time-equivalent jobs.[28]

In the United States, our workforce system is organized by a patchwork of federally funded, state-governed, and locally administered programs. Safety net programs like unemployment compensation provide temporary relief while the higher education system is meant to provide access to the necessary skills training programs to ensure workers can compete in an increasingly dynamic global economy.

Operating alongside the public workforce system are employer-sponsored programs to fill critical vacancies, nonprofit stakeholders to offer a wide variety of training and support services, and a growing digital ecosystem of professional networks personalizing recommendations for job seekers and employers.

Realizing the 2 percent GDP growth opportunity will require unprecedented collaboration. As McKinsey noted, "Much of this data is being captured by individual platform operators, but taking this capability to the next level may require a consortium of such companies or cooperation with the national statistical agencies that currently track labor market data and outcomes."

What would such new capability mean for workers?

Imagine a future in which you receive daily notification of the one new opportunity tailor-made for your unique talents, with compensation that will boost your economic mobility. A future in which you can get instant information about the demand for your skills in a particular market, or about the gap between your knowledge base and specific job requirements—along with a prioritized list of training programs that could help you meet those requirements in days, weeks, or months, rather than years.

We're taking a few early steps towards this future in Virginia.

In August 2014, Governor Terry McAuliffe issued a "New Virginia Economy Workforce Initiative" via executive order that created the Commonwealth Consortium for Advanced Research and Statistics to "provide real-time data about human capital, regional skills gaps, local and state wage data, university research and talent, and availability of local and state workforce programs."[29]

As a gubernatorial appointee on the Council on Virginia's Future responsible for guiding program implementation, I intend to apply each play in the playbook as we've described throughout this book:

Building on the President's Workforce Data Initiative, we can publish data on outcomes for training programs and higher education institutions so workers can make smarter decisions for their lifetime learning.

In collaboration with the private sector, we can encourage employers to adopt an industry standard for online job postings to make it easier to understand what skills are in demand—at the firm level, or in their communities.

By shifting the payment formula from rewarding enrollment to rewarding outcomes, we can incentivize the use of such data for personalizing workforce program recommendations for each job seeker.

Employing a "lean startup" approach for improving digital employment services, we can enable job seekers, via talent management platforms such as LinkedIn or Monster.com, to take full advantage of the benefits to which they are entitled.

The net result of all of this would be a more productive workforce development system, one that ultimately makes citizens less dependent on the government. It's another example of the government serving as a conduit rather than a constrainer, empowering the private sector to provide better recommendations for every decision in your life.[30]

So you will be hearing more about this. Much more. And I, for one, can't wait to see what the next book will say.

Acknowledgments

Innovative State, like so many of the achievements it spotlights, was a collaborative effort. It required the assistance of friends and associates from way back, and countless others I've met along the way.

My journey began with a generous gift from an old college roommate, Ethan J. Skolnick. A popular sports journalist, Ethan offered his time and talents to both immerse himself in the growing open government innovation movement and to share its most inspiring stories in a more accessible way. I am so grateful for his friendship and would suggest that if you found *Innovative State* a useful read, it is largely on account of Ethan's writing. That, and the enriching work of our agent, Carol Mann, her hyper-connected colleague, Laura Yorke, our publisher, Morgan Entrekin, and his brilliant colleague at Grove Atlantic, Jamison Stoltz.

For much of the historical context, I turned to two distinguished thinkers and authors. One, Ken Baer, had shined light on a great deal of this work from his perch at the Office of Management and Budget, and had previously covered the growing reinventing government movement, including Elaine Kamarck and James Pinkerton, in his thoughtful book, *Reinventing Democrats.* The other, Dr. Michael Lind, had forgotten more in a few minutes than I had ever known in terms of the history of America's growth and prosperity. I am deeply grateful for his generous contributions related to America's impressive track record in public sector innovation, and enthusiastically recommend a reading of his *Land of Promise: An Economic History of the United States*.

While Ethan, Ken, and Michael were instrumental in shaping the material herein, the heartbeat of *Innovative State* was provided by those who are engaged in the day-to-day work of making our country more innovative and collaborative. We were blessed that so many eagerly cooperated with us. I consider many of these passionate public servants to be part of my extended family. I'm especially thankful for my successor, Todd Park, and for my dearest friend, Vivek Kundra, who has been alongside from the start of Governor Tim Kaine's administration. Both represent the best of the best, when it comes to open government innovators.

They are among those who have had an immeasurable influence on me. That list is quite long.

For inspiration, no one trumps President Obama, whose riveting speech at the 2004 Democratic Convention stirred my already active passion for public service, and whose vision for harnessing the full power and potential of technology, data, and innovation to both grow the economy and solve problems gave life to this fledgling movement. Thank you for entrusting me with the opportunity to put that vision into action. And I know I wouldn't have had the opportunity to serve you if it hadn't been for the support of my two mentors—former Virginia Governors Mark Warner and Tim Kaine. They embody all that is good in public service and for the great people of the Commonwealth, and we are blessed that both currently serve us in the U.S. Senate.

There are so many others, some of whom we introduce in *Innovative State*. Start inside the White House: former Chief of Staff Rahm Emanuel and his highly effective deputy, Mona Sutphen; Our sponsor in the West Wing, Valerie Jarrett; Peter Orszag and his fellow OMBers—my former boss at the Advisory Board

Company, Jeff Zients, and our intellectual godfather, Cass Sunstein; our open government global ambassador, Samantha Power; the original policy entrepreneur, Tom Kalil; the smartest man I've ever known, John Holdren; my partners on all matters innovation, Phil Weiser (with support from his bosses, Larry Summers, Gene Sperling, and Jason Furman), Sonal Shah, Terrell McSweeney, and Austan Goolsbee; and the man who made WAVES, Norm Eisen. Our small but scrappy CTO team deserves the lion's share of credit in translating ideas to action. That roll call includes Beth Noveck (the reigning queen of open government–land!), Andrew McLaughlin, Scott Deutchman, Danny Weitzner, Chris Vein, Tom Power, Eugene Huang, Nick Sinai, Steve Ondra, Brian Forde, and Tristen Pegram.

We amassed an exciting band of brothers and sisters across the government, from federal to state to local, and we have shared many of their exploits throughout this book. Thank you, first and foremost, to Julius Genachowski who generously extended his hand to welcome me in the Obama community. Thank you, George Arnold, Doug Fridsma, Pat Gallagher, Pat Hoffman, Peter Levin, Farzad Mostashari, Jen Pahlka, Jim Shelton, and Tom Baden. I wish to especially thank the gurus who generously offered both personal guidance and global leadership on this approach to problem solving. From my childhood, I'd heard of the legendary Sam Pitroda and would later pinch myself when given the chance to partner with him on the U.S.-India Open Government Dialogue. During my graduate school years, I was fortunate to befriend Dr. John Halamka, who has mentored me on every step toward IT-enabled reform. And, over my decade plus association with the Advisory Board Company, I was equally blessed with the opportunity to learn corporate values under David Bradley's leadership, an entrepreneur with a rich soul and caring heart.

Though *Innovative State* is written on my experiences in the public sector, it is shaped by the leading voices in the private sector advocating and implementing open innovation to bring new ideas to life. The movement owes a great deal of gratitude for the time and energy invested by our hero, Tim O'Reilly, whose phrase "government as a platform" embodies the essence of our approach. Additionally, thought leaders Henry Chesbrough, Eric Ries, Mitch Kapor, Brad Feld, Peter Diamandis, and Bruce Brown contributed greatly to our policy work, and all are quoted in this text.

Further, on this front, I would be remiss if I didn't close with my deepest thanks to the thousands of entrepreneurs and innovators who deployed a bit of their cognitive surplus (hat tip, Clay Shirky) to demonstrate our capacity to solve big problems. Thank you to leaders from a variety of backgrounds, like Jon Bon Jovi and Karen Austin, who used their platforms to foster improvement in areas as diverse as access to homeless services and energy savings for families. Thank you to David Kenny, Dwayne Spradlin, Jay Rogers, Mark Emblidge, and so many others for building platforms that connect them to opportunities. Thank you to all of those moving this movement forward: Dave Augustine (and his Federal Register partners, Bob Burbach and Andrew Carpenter), Fabien Beckers, Brian Chiglinsky, Chuck Drake, Gail Embt, Victor Garcia, Aamer Ghaffar, David Hart, Michael Jackson, Waldo Jaquith, Clay Johnson, Mike Krieger, Oliver Kuttner, Arien Malec, Amir Reavis-Bey (and his Blight teammates Alex Pandel and Eddie Tejeda), Karen Rheuban, Nancy Schwartzman, David Van Sickle, and Tony Webster.

I save my favorite thank you for last.

Thank you to my family—to my parents for instilling in me a sense of what's possible in this great country, and to my beautiful and incredibly supportive wife, Rohini, and our two daughters for, well, everything. I love you with all of my heart. I am thankful that the intensity of the past several years has eased a bit so we can spend more time together. As my oldest childhood friend reminds me, it's time to feed the ducks.

Notes

Prologue

1. *Face the Nation*, transcript, CBSNews.com, October 13, 2013, cbsnews.com/8301-3460_162-57607292/face-the-nation-transcripts-october-13-2013-schumer-mccain-ayotte-huelskamp/?pageNum=2.

2. https://www.whitehouse.gov/the_press_office/TransparencyandOpenGovernment

3. https://www.whitehouse.gov/the-press-office/president-obama-welcomes-ceos-white-house-forum-modernizing-government

4. http://www.c-span.org/video/?291323-3/forum-modernizing-government

5. Medicare Access and CHIP Reauthorization Act of 2015

Chapter 1

1. "Publication 100—The United States Postal Service—An American History 1775–2006: The Pony Express," USPS.com, last modified November 2012, about.usps.com/publications/pub100/pub100_013.htm.

2. Leroy R. Hafen, *The Overland Mail, 1849–1869: Promoter of Settlement Precursor of Railroads*, p. 166.

3. Michael Lind, *Land of Promise: An Economic History of the United States,* Harper Reprint edition (April 9, 2013) amazon.com/Land-Promise-Economic-History-United/dp/0061834815/ref=cm_cr_pr_product_top.

4. Michael Lind, *Land of Promise: An Economic History of the United States* (New York: Harper, 2013).

5. Cynthia Monaco, "The Difficult Birth of the Typewriter," *American Heritage's Invention & Technology* 4, no. 1 (Spring/Summer 1988), 50.57.231.74/IT/content/difficult-birth-typewriter-1?page=6.

6. "The Federal Civil Service and the Death of President James A. Garfield," *The Garfield Observer*, last modified September 21, 2012, garfieldnps.wordpress.com/2012/09/21/the-federal-civil-service-and-the-death-of-president-james-a-garfield.

7. Abbrevations for Securities and Exchange Commission, Federal Communications Commission, Civil Aeronautics Board, National Labor Relations Board, National Recovery Administration, Works Progress Administration, Civilian Conservation Corps.

8. "Distrust, Discontent, Anger and Partisan Rancor: The People and Their Government," Pew Research Center for the People & the Press, last modified April 18, 2010, people-press.org/2010/04/18/section-1-trust-in-government-1958-2010.

9. Seymour Martin Lipset and William Schneider, "The Decline of Confidence in American Institutions," *Political Science Quarterly* 98, no. 3 (Autumn 1983): 379–402, planethan.com/drupal/sites/default/files/The%20Decline%20of%20Confidence%20in%20American%20Institutions%20%20By%20Lipset%20Seymour%20Martin%20and%20Schneider%20William%20Political%20Science%20Quarterly%20Fall83%20Vol%2098%20Issue%203%20p379.p.

10. The National Commission on Excellence in Education, "A Nation at Risk: The Imperative for Educational Reform, A Report to the Nation and the Secretary of Education," United States Department of Education, April 1983, scribd.com/doc/49151492/A-Nation-at-Risk.

11. Ben J. Wattenberg, *Values Matter Most* (New York: Free Press, 2007) 22.

12. Sally R. Sherman, "Public Attitudes Toward Social Security,"

Social Security Bulletin 52, no.12 (December 1989), ssa.gov/policy/docs/ssb/v52n12/v52n12p2.pdf.

13. D. Andrew Austin and Mindy R. Levit, "Mandatory Spending Since 1962," Congressional Research Service, March 23, 2012, fas.org/sgp/crs/misc/RL33074.pdf.

14. "Public Trust in Government: 1958–2013," Pew Research Center for the People & the Press, October 18, 2013, people-press.org/2013/10/18/trust-in-government-interactive/. And William A. Galston and Elaine C. Kamarck, "Change You Can Believe in Starts with a Government You Can Trust," Third Way, thirdway.org/publications/133.

15. See Kenneth S. Baer, "The Spirit of '78, Stayin' Alive," *Washington Post*, July 13, 2008, articles.washingtonpost.com/2008-07-13/opinions/36901048_1_tax-rates-tax-increases-property-taxes. On the larger, worldwide movement toward markets, see: Daniel Yergin and Joseph Stanislaw, *The Commanding Heights: The Battle for the World Economy* (New York: Touchstone, 1998).

16. Ronald Reagan, Inaugural Address, January 20, 1981, reagan.utexas.edu/archives/speeches/1981/12081a.htm.

17. For a summary of the Grace Commisison, see Milton Friedman, "Why Government Is the Problem," Wriston Lecture, Manhattan Institute, 1991, manhattan-institute.org/html/wl1991.htm.

18. On Pinkerton and the New Paradigm, see Mickey Kaus, "Paradigm's Loss," *The New Republic* 27 (July 1992): 16–22.

19. Richard Darman quotes per nytimes.com/1990/11/17/us/darman-says-bush-is-exploring-shift-in-benefits.html?pagewanted=2&src=pm and nytimes.com/1993/02/28/magazine/how-jack-kemp-lost-the-war-on-poverty.html?pagewanted=all&src=pm.

20. Jim Pinkerton, *What Comes Next: The End of Big Government—and the New Paradigm Ahead* (New York: Hyperion, 1995), amazon.com/What-Comes-Next-Government-Paradigm/dp/0786861053.

21. John Tamny, "What Parkinson's Law Says About Federal Spending," RealClearMarkets.com, last modified March 29, 2013, realclearmarkets.com/articles/2011/03/29/what_parkinsons_law_says_about_federal_spending_98934.html.

22. Elaine C.Kamarck, *The End of Government As We Know It: Making Public Policy Work* (Boulder, CO: Lynne Rienner Publishers, 2007).

23. Mickey Kaus, *End of Equality* (New York: Basic Books, 1993)

24. Peter F. Drucker, *Innovation and Entrepreneurship* (New York: Harper 1985).

25. David Osborne and Ted Gaebler, *Reinventing Government: How the Entrepreneurial Spirit Is Transforming the Private Sector* (New York: Plume, 1993), 17.

26. On the impetus for reform and the REGO movement, see Elaine C. Kamarck, *The End of Government As We Know It: Making Public Policy Work* (Boulder, CO: Lynne Rienner Publishers, 2007); David Osborne and Ted Gaebler, *Reinventing Government: How the Entrepreneurial Spirit Is Transforming the Public Sector* (New York: Penguin, 1992); Morley Winograd and Dudley Buffa, *Taking Control: Politics in the Information Age* (New York: Henry Holt 1996).

27. On the rise of the New Democrats, see Kenneth S. Baer, *Reinventing Democrats: The Politics of Liberalism from Reagan to Clinton* (Lawrence, KS: University Press of Kansas, 2000).

28. Bill Clinton and Al Gore, *Putting People First: How We Can All Change America* (New York: Times Books, 1992).

29. Quoted in James Pinkerton, *What Comes Next: The End of Big Government—and the New Paradigm Ahead* (New York: Hyperion, 1995), 82.

30. For an early assessment of REGO, see Donald F. Kettl, *Reinventing Government: A Fifth-Year Report Card*. Washington, D.C.: Brookings Institution, September 1998.

31. James Fairhall, "The Case for the $435 Hammer," The Free Library, January, 1, 1987, thefreelibrary.com/The case for the $435 hammer.-a04619906.

32. Paul Light, "Fact Sheet on the New True Size of Government," the Brookings Institution, September 5, 2003, brookings.edu/~/media/research/files/articles/2003/9/05politics%20light/light20030905.pdf.

33. For details on REGO's accomplishments, see Al Gore, *The Best Kept Secrets in Government: How the Clinton Administration is Reinventing How Washington Works.* (New York: Random House, 1996).

34. See President George W. Bush's budget, "A Blueprint for New Beginnings," (FY 2002): 179, gpo.gov/fdsys/pkg/BUDGET-2002-BLUEPRINT/pdf/BUDGET-2002-BLUEPRINT.pdf.

35. Christie Dickson, "Christie Dickson's SAVE Award Story," WhiteHouse.gov, last modified December 17, 2009, whitehouse.gov/blog/2009/12/17/christie-dicksons-save-award-story.

36. George Washington, "Circular to the States, 8 June 1783," *Writings* 26: 484–89.

Chapter 2

1. Immigration and Nationality Act of 1965, a.k.a. the Hart-Cellar Act, H.R. 2580; Pub. L. No. 89–236, 79 Stat. 911 (1965), library.uwb.edu/guides/usimmigration/1965_immigration_and_nationality_act.html.

2. Martin Tolchin, "Retreat in Congress; The Catastrophic-Care Debacle—A special report.; How the New Medicare Law Fell on Hard Times in a Hurry," *New York Times*, last modified October 10, 1989, nytimes.com/1989/10/09/us/retreat-congress-catastrophic-care-debacle-special-report-new-medicare-law-fell.html.

3. K. Desmond, J. Gabel, and T. Rice, "The Medicare Catastrophic Coverage Act: A Post-Mortem," *Health Affairs* 9, no. 3 (1990): 75–87, content.healthaffairs.org/content/9/3/75.full.pdf.

4. "1993: The Graphical WWW is Born with the Release of NCSA Mosaic," CED in the History of Media, cedmagic.com/history/mosaic-1993.html.

5. "A Technical History of the ARPANET," Think: Technical Histories of Network Protocols, last modified January 29, 2010, cs.utexas.edu/users/chris/think/ARPANET.

6. "With Tears in His Eyes, He Recalls Nehru's 'Tryst with Destiny' Speech," *Hindustan Times,* last modified August 15, 2010, hindustantimes.com/India-news/NewDelhi/With-tears-in-eyes-he-recalls-Nehru-s-tryst-with-destiny-speech/Article1-587065.aspx.

Chapter 3

1. "Governor Kaine Announces Partnership with Google to Improve Citizen Access to Digital Government," Library of Virginia, Governor Timothy Kaine Administration Collection, last modified June 23, 2009, wayback.archive-it.org/263/20091025151045/https://governor.virginia.gov/MediaRelations/NewsReleases/viewRelease.cfm?id=400&printpage=Yes.

2. "2007 Session of the General Assembly: Science and Technology Legislative Update," the Virginia Joint Commission on Technology and Science, dls.virginia.gov/commission/Materials/Tech%20Legislation%20Update%202007.pdf.

3. "Cloud," Cio.gov, last modified 2013, cio.gov/building-a-21st-century-government/cloud.

4. Matthew S. Olson, *Stall Points: Most Companies Stop Growing —Yours Doesn't Have To* (New Haven, CT: Yale University Press, 2009), amazon.com/Stall-Points-Companies-Growing-Yours-Doesnt/dp/0300158513.

5. "The Last Kodak Moment?," *The Economist*, January 14, 2012, economist.com/node/21542796.

6. "Addressing the Education, Skill, and Workforce Needs of Adults without a High School Diploma or Equivalent: Report of the Virginia Adult Learning Panel, Report to the Governor, September 2008, leg2.state.va.us/dls/h&sdocs.nsf/By+Year/RD4162008/$file/RD416.pdf.

7. PluggedIn VA, last modified October 31, 2013, pluggedinva.com.

8. "Virginia STAR—Index," Virginia Star, 2013, vastar.schoolfusion.us.

9. "Government Funding and Service Relationships," *Council on Virginia's Future*, no 7 (August 2011), future.virginia.gov/docs/IssueInsights/Insight%207-GovtFundingandServiceRelationships-Web.pdf.

10. "Reproductive Health: Preterm Birth," Centers for Disease Control and Prevention, last modified October 30, 2013, cdc.gov/reproductivehealth/maternalinfanthealth/pretermbirth.htm.

11. Productivity Investment Fund, last modified 2011, pif.virginia.gov/programs.shtml.

Chapter 4

1. David Leonhardt, "Obamanomics," *New York Times Magazine*, August 20, 2008, nytimes.com/2008/08/24/magazine/24Obamanomics-t.html?pagewanted=all&_r=0.

2. "Obama's Speech on the Economy," *New York Times*, last modified January 8, 2009, nytimes.com/2009/01/08/us/politics/08text-obama.html?pagewanted=all&_r=0.

3. "Track the Money: Recipient Projects," Recovery.gov, last modified October 30, 2013, recovery.gov/Transparency/RecipientReportedData/Pages/RecipientReportedDataMap.aspx.

4. Mary Le Carnevale, "White House Launches Recovery.gov to Track Stimulus Spending," *Wall Street Journal*, February 17, 2009, blogs.wsj.com/washwire/2009/02/17/white-house-launches-recoverygov-to-track-stimulus-spending.

5. "President Obama Discusses Efforts to Reform Spending, Government Waste; Names Chief Performance Officer and Chief Technology Officer," WhiteHouse.gov, transcript of the President's weekly address, April 18, 2009, last modified April 18, 2009, whitehouse.gov/the_press_office/Weekly-Address-President-Obama-Discusses-Efforts-to-Reform-Spending.

6. Tim O'Reilly, "Why Aneesh Chopra Is a Great Choice for

Federal CTO," O'Reilly Radar, April 18, 2009, radar.oreilly.com/2009/04/aneesh-chopra-great-federal-cto.html.

7. *Nominations to the Department of Transportation, the Executive Office of the President, and the Department of Commerce Hearing, Before the Senate Committee on Commerce, Science, and Transportation,* 111th Cong. (May 19, 2009), gpo.gov/fdsys/pkg/CHRG-111shrg54288/html/CHRG-111shrg54288.htm.

8. "Stumble Safely," Apps for Democracy: Community Edition, last modified November, 12, 2008, appsfordemocracy.org/stumble-safely.

9. "Crowdsourcing," m-w.com, merriam-webster.com/dictionary/crowdsourcing.

10. Beth Noveck, "Open Government Directive, Phase III: Drafting," WhiteHouse.gov, June 22, 2009, whitehouse.gov/blog/Open-Government-Directive-Phase-III-Drafting.

11. See whitehouse.gov/innovation.

12. "Remarks by the President on Innovation and Sustainable Growth," WhiteHouse.gov, September 21, 2009, whitehouse.gov/the_press_office/Remarks-by-the-President-on-Innovation-and-Sustainable-Growth-at-Hudson-Valley-Community-College.

13. "Remarks by the President at the Opening Session of the Forum on Modernizing Government," WhiteHouse.gov, January 14, 2010, whitehouse.gov/the-press-office/remarks-president-opening-session-forum-modernizing-government.

14. Kate Andersen Brower and Julianna Goldman, "Obama Says 'Progress' Made in CEO Meeting on Fueling Economy," Bloomberg.com, December 16, 2010, bloomberg.com/news/2010-12-15/obama-says-progress-was-made-in-meeting-on-economy-with-chief-executives.html.

15. "Remarks by the President at the Signing of the America Invents Act," WhiteHouse.gov, September 16, 2011, whitehouse.gov/the-press-office/2011/09/16/remarks-president-signing-america-invents-act.

16. "Remarks by the President at JOBS Act Bill Signing," White

House.gov, April 5, 2012, whitehouse.gov/the-press-office/2012/04/05/remarks-president-jobs-act-bill-signing.

17. Jesse Lee, "The President on the National Wireless Initiative: 'We're Going to Have to Up Our Game, Marquette,'" WhiteHouse.gov, February 10, 2011, whitehouse.gov/blog/2011/02/10/president-national-wireless-initiative-we-re-going-have-our-game-marquette.

18. "Designing a Digital Future: Federally Funded Research and Development in Networking and Information Technology," President's Council of Advisors on Science and Technology, December 2010, whitehouse.gov/sites/default/files/microsites/ostp/pcast-nitrd-report-2010.pdf.

19. "Obama Administration Unveils 'Big Data' Initiative: Announces $200 Million in New R&D Investments," Office of Science and Technology Policy, March 29, 2012, whitehouse.gov/sites/default/files/microsites/ostp/big_data_press_release_final_2.pdf.

20. "Fact Sheet: Big Data Across the Federal Government," Office of Science and Technology Policy, March 29, 2012, whitehouse.gov/sites/default/files/microsites/ostp/big_data_fact_sheet_final.pdf.

21. Aneesh Chopra, "Memorandum for the Science and Technology Council Committee on Technology: Open Innovator's Toolkit," WhiteHouse.gov, February 8, 2012, whitehouse.gov/sites/default/files/microsites/ostp/openinnovatortoolkit_nstcmemo.pdf.

22. Larry Huston and Nabil Sakkab, "P&G's New Innovation Model," Harvard Business School, last modified March 30, 2006, hbswk.hbs.edu/archive/5258.html.

23. Beth Stackpole, "P&G Offers Free Simulation Software to SMB Manufacturers," *Design News*, last modified July 6, 2011, designnews.com/document.asp?doc_id=230931.

24. "Partnering with the World to Create Greater Value," P&G.com, pg.com/en_US/downloads/innovation/C_D_factsheet.pdf.

25. Carl Marinucci, "Tech Leaders Upbeat about Jobs as Debt Drama Ends," SFGate, August 2, 2011, sfgate.com/bayarea/article/

Tech-leaders-upbeat-about-jobs-as-debt-drama-ends-2336748 .php.

26. "New TechNet Sponsored Study: Nearly 500,000 'App Economy' Jobs in the United States," TechNet.org, February 7, 2012, technet .org/new-technet-sponsored-study-nearly-500000-app-economy-jobs-in-united-states-february-7-2012.

27. Friedrich A. Hayek, "The Use of Knowledge in Society," Library of Economics and Liberty, 1945: econlib.org/library/Essays/hykKnw1 .html.

28. "The Meeting at Harvard on a Health Information Technology Platform: Executive Summaries," September 29, 2009, smartplatforms.org/wp-content/uploads/2012/10/HMS-HIT-Platform-final-v110909-1.pdf.

29. "Open Data: Unlocking Innovation & Performance with Liquid Information," McKinsey Global Institute October 2013.

30. Aneesh Chopra, "Memorandum for the Science and Technology Council Committee on Technology: Open Innovator's Toolkit," WhiteHouse.gov, February 8, 2012, whitehouse.gov/sites/default/files/microsites/ostp/openinnovatortoolkit_nstcmemo.pdf.

31. Thomas Jefferson, "First Inaugural Address," Bartleby.com, bartleby.com/124/pres16.html.

Chapter 5

1. "Weather Observations," Monticello, monticello.org/site/research-and-collections/weather-observations.

2. The passages on the history of weather derive from several sources, including: "Evolution of the National Weather Service," NOAA's National Weather Service, last modified April 19, 2013, nws.noaa .gov/pa/history/timeline.php; "History of the National Weather Service," NOAA's National Weather Service, last modified January 25, 2012, nws.noaa.gov/pa/history/index.php; "A History of Observing the Weather," NOAA.gov, last modified May 31, 2007, celebrating200years .noaa.gov/foundations/weather_obs/#earlyyear.

3. Frank Millikan, "Joseph Henry's Grand Meteorological Crusade," *Weatherwise* 50 (October–November 1997): 14–18, siarchives.si.edu/history/jhp/joseph03.htm.

4. Lisa Rein, "Civil War Gave Birth to Much of Modern Federal Government," *Washington Post,* October 7, 2011, articles.washingtonpost.com/2011-10-07/lifestyle/35279330_1_federal-government-civil-war-federal-employees.

5. "About DOJ," The United States Department of Justice, last modified March 2012, justice.gov/about/about.html.

6. "Benjamin Harrison: First Annual Message, December 3, 1889," Gerhard Peters and John T. Woolley, eds., the American Presidency Project Online, presidency.ucsb.edu/ws/?pid=29530.

7. "Fair Weather: Effective Partnerships in Weather and Climate Services," Committee on Partnerships in Weather and Climate Services and Committee on Geophysical and Environmental Data, National Research Council, 2003, nap.edu/openbook.php?record_id=10610&page=57.

8. Holly Doremus, "Time to Make NOAA Official," Legal-Planet, January 29, 2010, legalplanet.wordpress.com/2010/01/29/time-to-make-noaa-official.

9. Frank Konkel, "NOAA's Budget Boost Could Help Weather Satellite Program," FCW.com, April 11, 2013, fcw.com/articles/2013/04/11/noaa-budget.aspx.

10. "About Us," CompuWeather.com, 2013, compuweather.com/about-us.

11. The passage relating to NOAA's private sector policies derive from the following: National Weather Service, Policy on Industrial Meteorology, *National Weather Service Operations Manual* (78–24, Part A, Chapter 55, 1978) 1–3; "Policy on Partnerships in the Provision of Environmental Information," NOAA.gov, noaa.gov/partnershippolicy/; Bill Kearny, "Fair Weather: Public vs. Private Forecasting," *The National Academies In Focus* 3, no. 1 (Winter–Spring 2003), infocusmagazine.org/3.1/env_weather.html; Committee on

Partnerships in Weather and Climate Services et al., *Fair Weather: Effective Partnership in Weather and Climate Services,* Appendix B (Washington, DC: The National Academies Press, 2003), nap.edu/openbook.php?record_id=10610&page=121.

12. "National Digital Forecast Database (NDFD) Simple Object Access Protocol (SOAP) Web Service," graphical.weather.gov, last modified October 4, 2011, graphical.weather.gov/xml.

Jeremy Zawodny, "XML Weather Data Available," Jeremy Zawodny's Blog, December 6, 2004, jeremy.zawodny.com/blog/archives/003201.html.

David Bollier, "Open Source Weather," On the Commons, December 9, 2004, onthecommons.org/open-source-weather.

13. Richard Mandel and Erik Noyes, "Beyond the NWS: Inside the Thriving Private Weather Forecasting Industry," Weatherwise.org, 2010, weatherwise.org/Archives/Back%20Issues/2013/January-February%202013/beyond-nws-full.html.

14. "The Weather Channel Apps Rank in Top 10 for iPad, iPhone," Weather.com, May 3, 2013, weather.com/news/twc-apps-ipad-iphone-20130503.

15. Sam Roberts, "New Figure for 2010 Census: $1.6 Billion Under Budget," *New York Times*, August 10, 2010, nytimes.com/2010/08/11/us/politics/11census.html.

16. Michael Lind, *Land of Promise: An Economic History of the United States* (New York: Harper, 2013).

17. Michael R. Lemov, *People's Warrior: John Moss and the Fight for Freedom of Information and Consumer Rights* (Madison, NJ: Fairleigh Dickinson University Press, 2011), amazon.com/Peoples-Warrior-Freedom-Information-Consumer/dp/161147471X.

18. "History of FOIA," Electronic Frontier Foundation, eff.org/issues/transparency/history-of-foia.

19. "Open Government Directive: Evaluating HHS Progress," United States Department of Health and Human Services, hhs.gov/open/plan/actions.html.

20. Aneesh Chopra, "The Race to the Top for Openness and Innovation: Announcing Agency Open Government Plan Leading Practices," WhiteHouse.gov, August 12, 2010, whitehouse.gov/blog/2010/08/12/race-top-openness-and-innovation-announcing-agency-open-government-plan-leading-prac.

21. Roni Zeiger, "Making U.S. Community Health Data Accessible and Useful," *Google Public Policy Blog*, last modified June 2, 2010, googlepublicpolicy.blogspot.com/2010/06/making-us-community-health-data.html.

22. More information relating to the use of open health data can be found at "Health Data Initiative Starter Kit," HealthData.gov, last modified January 5, 2012, healthdata.gov/health-data-initiative-starter-kit; Mike Painter, "Lightning Strikes Datapalooza," Robert Wood Johnson Foundation, June 5, 2012, rwjf.org/en/blogs/pioneering-ideas/2012/06/lightning_strikesda.html.

23. David Maris, "Bon Jovi's Next Hit Could Be an App for the Homeless," Forbes.com, June 6, 2012, forbes.com/sites/davidmaris/2012/ 06/06/bon-jovi-rocks-health-datapalooza.

24. Dylan Scott, "2012 Health Datapalooza Takes Pulse of Open Data Movement," *Governing*, June 6, 2012, governing.com/news/technology/gov-2012-health-datapalooza-takes-pulse-of-open-data-movement.html.

25. Kathleen Sebelius and Todd Park, "Entrepreneurs and Innovators Rock 3rd Annual Health Datapalooza," WhiteHouse.gov,June 18,2012.whitehouse.gov/blog/2012/06/18/entrepreneurs-and-innovators-rock-3rd-annual-health-datapalooza.

26. Scott Pace, et al., "Appendix B: GPS History, Chronology, and Budgets," *The Global Positioning System: Assessing National Policies*, last modified September 28, 2012, cs.cmu.edu/~sensing-sensors/readings/GPS_History-MR614.appb.pdf.

27. Material for the section on GPS derives from multiple sources, including: Catherine Alexandrow, "The Story of GPS," *DARPA: 50 Years of Bridging the Gap* (U.S. Department of

Defense and Faircount Media Group, Tampa, FL, 2008), darpa.mil/WorkArea/DownloadAsset.aspx?id=2565; Thomas B. McCaskill, "Overview," GPS Inventor, gpsinventor.com/; Office of Science and Technology Policy, "Fact Sheet: U.S. Global Positioning System Policy," March 29, 1996, clinton4.nara.gov/textonly/WH/EOP/OSTP/html/gps-factsheet.html; Office of Science and Technology Policy, "President Clinton: Improving the Civilian Global Positioning System (GPS)," May 1, 2000, clinton4.nara.gov/WH/EOP/OSTP/html/0053_4.html; Office of Science and Technology Policy, "Fact Sheet: U.S. Global Positioning System Policy," March 29, 1996, clinton4.nara.gov/textonly/WH/EOP/OSTP/html/gps-factsheet.html.

28. Information on the economic aspects of GPS derives from the following sources: "Fiscal Year 2013 Program Funding," GPS.gov, last modified May 22, 2013, gps.gov/policy/funding/2013/; Nam D. Pham, PhD, "The Economic Benefits of Commercial GPS Use in the U.S. and the Costs of Potential Disruption," NDPConsulting.com, June 2011, saveourgps.org/pdf/GPS-Report-June-22-2011.pdf.

29. "David Van Sickle," WhiteHouse.gov, whitehouse.gov/champions/technology-and-innovation/david-van-sickle.

30. "Health Expenditure, Total (% of GDP)," The World Bank, last modified 2013, data.worldbank.org/indicator/SH.XPD.TOTL.ZS.

31. "An Innovative Device to Detect Patterns of Asthma and Improve Treatment," Robert Wood Johnson Foundation, July 6, 2011, rwjf.org/content/rwjf/en/about-rwjf/newsroom/newsroom-content/2011/07/an-innovative-device-to-detect-patterns-of-asthma-and-improve-tr.html.

32. Rip Empson, "Asthmapolis Wants to Hack the Inhaler and Help 26 Million Americans Better Track and Manage Their Asthma," TechCrunch.com, techcrunch.com/2013/04/05/asthmapolis-wants-to-hack-the-inhaler-and-help-26-million-americans-better-track-and-manage-their-asthma.

33. Material for Champions of Change is derived from Aneesh Chopra, "Open Government to Solve Problems: Meet Champions of the Open Innovation Movement," WhiteHouse.gov, August 2, 2011, whitehouse.gov/blog/2011/08/02/open-government-solve-problems-meet-champions-open-innovation-movement; "White House Champions of Change—Open Innovators Event," Kids Play Guide, June 15, 2011, kidsplayguide.com/mommapsblog/2011/06/white-house-champions-of-change-open-innovators-event/; "Champions of Change: Winning the Future Across America," WhiteHouse.gov, whitehouse.gov/champions.

34. "White House Champions of Change—Open Innovators Event," Kids Play Guide, June 15, 2011, kidsplayguide.com/mommapsblog/2011/06/white-house-champions-of-change-open-innovators-event.

35. Material for the section on the *Federal Register* was supplemented by the following sources: Christine Pierpoint, "Federal Register 2.0 Is The Real Deal," *Welchman Pierpoint*, July 29, 2010, welchmanpierpoint.com/blog/federal-register-20-real-deal; "About Us, or Our Pursuit of Free Data," Critical Juncture, criticaljuncture.org/about-us.html; Paul Blumenthal, "Apps for America 2 Winners," Sunlight Foundation, September 10, 2009, sunlightfoundation.com/blog/2009/09/10/apps-for-america-2-winners/; Tom Lee, "Meet the New Federal Register," Sunlight Foundation, July 26, 2010, sunlightlabs.com/blog/2010/meet-the-new-federal-register.

36. "Resolution Celebrating the 75th Anniversary of the Federal Register Act," American Association of Law Libraries, July 8, 2010, aallnet.org/main-menu/Leadership-Governance/resolutions/resolution-registeract.html.

37. "Transcript of Obama's Remarks to the U.N. General Assembly," *Wall Street Journal,* September 23, 2010, blogs.wsj.com/washwire/2010/09/23/transcript-of-obamas-remarks-to-the-un-general-assembly.

38. "Remarks by the President at Open Government and Technology Exposition," the White House, November 7, 2010, whitehouse.gov/the-press-office/2010/11/07/remarks-president-open-government-and-technology-exposition.

39. "Medicare Provider Charge Data," CMS.gov, last modified October 29, 2013, cms.gov/Research-Statistics-Data-and-Systems/Statistics-Trends-and-Reports/Medicare-Provider-Charge-Data/index.html.

40. Information on San Francisco's open data efforts was derived from the following sources: "Open Gov: San Francisco Strengthens Open Data Commitment," sfgov.org, last modified October 15, 2012, www5.sfgov.org/sf_news/2012/10/open-gov-san-francisco-strengthens-commitment-to-open-data.html; Luke Fretwell, "San Francisco's Open Data Directive," govfresh.com, December 20, 2009, govfresh.com/2009/12/san-franciscos-open-data-directive.

41. Jeff Blagdon, "Facebook's 'Billion Dollar' Instagram Acquisition to Actually Cost $715 Million," the Verge, October 24, 2012, theverge.com/2012/10/24/3551872/facebook-instagram-acquisition-715-million.

42. "Memorandum for the Heads of Executive Departments and Agencies: Open Data Policy—Managing Information as an Asset," Office of Management and Budget, May 9, 2013, m.whitehouse.gov/sites/default/files/omb/memoranda/2013/m-13-13.pdf.

Chapter 6

1. Bruce Goldfarb, "The 1904 Fire and the Baltimore Standard," Welcome to Baltimore, Hon! September 20, 2010, welcometobaltimorehon.com/the-1904-fire-and-the-baltimore-standard.

2. Information for the section on VHS and DVD technology was derived from the following sources: Jin Chyung, "New Rules for Setting Standards in Today's Hi-Tech Market: Lessons Learned from the VHS-Betamax War," October 8, 2008, besser.tsoa.nyu.edu/impact/f96/Projects/jchyung/; Robert Chapin, "History of DVD,"

miqrogroove, September 24, 1999, miqrogroove.com/writing/history-of-dvd.

3. Barry Ritholtz, "DVD Sales Boom, 2004 a Record Year," The Big Picture, February 9, 2005, ritholtz.com/blog/2005/02/dvd-sales-boom-2004-a-record-year.

4. Rexmond Canning Cochrane, "Measures for Progress: A History of the National Bureau of Standards," no. 275 (1966) National Bureau of Standards, U.S. Department of Commerce, nist.gov/nvl/upload/MP275_06_Chapter_I-__AT_THE_TURN_OF_THE_CENTURY.pdf.

5. "American Chemical Society National Historic Chemical Landmarks," National Institute of Standards and Technology, acs.org/content/acs/en/education/whatischemistry/landmarks/nist.html.

6. "Case Studies in American Innovation: A New Look at Government Involvement in Technological Development," the Breakthrough Institute, April 2009, thebreakthrough.org/blog/Case%20Studies%20in%20American%20Innovation.pdf.

7. Information on Herbert Hoover and the Associative State was derived from the following sources: David Hart, "Herbert Hoover's Last Laugh: The Enduring Significance of the 'Associative State' in the U.S.," March 17, 1998, davidhart.gmu.edu/pdfs/publications/articles_essays_reports/JPH%201998%20-%20web%20version.pdf; "Herbert Hoover, Economic Mastermind," Library of Congress, lcweb2.loc.gov:8081/ammem/amrlhtml/inhoover.html; "National History Day Topics 2011–12: Elimination of Waste—Reforming American Industry in the 1920s," Herbert Hoover Presidential Library and Museum, hoover.archives.gov/education/nhd/historydayEliminationWaste.html.

8. Ethel H. Triebel, "The Department of Commerce Under Herbert Hoover 1921–1928" (master's thesis, Loyola University, Chicago, 1939), ecommons.luc.edu/luc_theses/407.

9. David Hart, *Forged Consensus: Science, Technology, and Economic Policy in the United States 1921–1953* (Princeton, NJ: Princeton University Press, 1998), 44, books.google.com/books? id=EqUuv

Udrs_MC&pg=PA44&dq=forged+consensus+hoover+secretary+commerce+waste&hl=en&sa=X&ei=fv-oUczmC4WpiQLHhYDYBQ&ved=0CDAQ6AEwAA#v=onepage&q=forged%20consensus%20hoover%20secretary%20commerce%20waste&f=false.

10. Council on Competitiveness, 2013, compete.org.

11. "Advance: Benchmarking Industrial Use of High Performance Computing for Innovation," Council on Competitiveness, 2008, compete.org/images/uploads/File/PDF%20Files/HPC_ADVANCE_FINAL0508(1).pdf.

12. "Overview," NDEMC.org, 2013, ndemc.org/index.php/details.

13. Information for the Jeco Plastics story was derived from the following sources: "Jeco Plastics Project with NDEMC," YouTube.com, December 7, 2011, youtube.com/watch?v=a7SdKJiRKk4; "NDEMC Helps Jeco to Exceed Growth and Financial Expectations," Council on Competitiveness, 2012, compete.org/images/uploads/File/PDF%20Files/NDEMC_Jeco_01.pdf.

14. Ronald E. Giachetti, "A Standard Manufacturing Information Model to Support Design for Manufacturing in Virtual Enterprises," *Journal of Intelligent Manufacturing* 10, no. 1 (1999): 49–60, mel.nist.gov/msidlibrary/doc/standard_sms.pdf.

15. "Digital Manufacturing and Design Innovation (DMDI) Institute," Manufacturing.gov, manufacturing.gov/docs/DMDI_overview.pdf.

16. "Remarks by the President at Applied Materials, Inc.—Austin, TX," The White House, May 9, 2013, whitehouse.gov/the-press-office/2013/05/09/remarks-president-applied-materials-inc-austin-tx.

17. James F. Schooley, *Responding to National Needs: The National Bureau of Standards Becomes the National Institutes of Standards and Technology,* U.S. Department of Commerce (Washington, DC, 2000), nist.gov/nvl/upload/Responding_to_National_Needs-SP955-FULL.pdf.

18. "Reauthorization of COMPETES Act Brings Changes to

NIST," NIST.gov, January 5, 2011, nist.gov/director/competes_010511.cfm.

19. "Memorandum for the Heads of Executive Departments and Agencies: Principles for Federal Engagement in Standards Activities to Address National Priorities," WhiteHouse.gov, January 17, 2012, whitehouse.gov/sites/default/files/omb/memoranda/2012/m-12-08_1.pdf.

20. "Electrification History 1—Early Years," Greatest Engineering Achievements of the 20th Century, National Academy of Engineering, 2013, greatachievements.org/?id=2988.

21. Fact Sheet: President Obama's Blueprint for a Clean and Secure Energy Future," WhiteHouse.gov, March 15, 2013, whitehouse.gov/the-press-office/2013/03/15/fact-sheet-president-obama-s-blueprint-clean-and-secure-energy-future.

22. Information for the section on the smart grid was supplemented by the following sources: "Fact Sheet: The President's Plan for a 21st Century Electric Grid," WhiteHouse.gov, June 13, 2011, whitehouse.gov/sites/default/files/microsites/ostp/smart-grid-fact-sheet-6-13-2011.pdf; "What Is the Smart Grid?," SmartGrid.gov, smartgrid.gov/the_smart_grid#smart_grid; "The Recovery Act: Transforming the American Economy Through Innovation," WhiteHouse.gov, August 2010, whitehouse.gov/sites/default/files/uploads/Recovery_Act_Innovation.pdf; "A Policy Framework for the 21st Century Grid: Enabling Our Secure Energy Future," WhiteHouse.gov, June 2011, whitehouse.gov/sites/default/files/microsites/ostp/nstc-smart-grid-june2011.pdf.

23. "Fact Sheet: Utility Rate Decoupling," Alliance to Save Energy, October 24, 2013, ase.org/resources/utility-rate-decoupling.

24. "How PG&E Makes Money," PGE.com, 2013, pge.com/myhome/myaccount/rateinfo/howwemakemoney.

25. "REQ.21—Energy Services Provider Interface," North American Energy Standards Board, 2013, naesb.org/ESPI_standards.asp.

26. "Chopra on U.S. Internet-Piracy Bill, Smart Grid,"

BloombergTV, January 18, 2011, bloomberg.com/video/84496446-chopra-on-u-s-internet-piracy-bill-smart-grid.html.

27. Jim Witkin, "Pushing the Green Button for Energy Savings," *Green: A Blog About Energy and the Environment*, *New York Times*, January 20, 2012, green.blogs.nytimes.com/2012/01/20/a-phone-app-for-turning-down-the-thermostat.

28. "$100,000 Apps for Energy Contest Launches Today," *Currents: News and Perspectives from Pacific Gas and Electric*, April 5, 2012, pgecurrents.com/2012/04/05/100000-apps-for-energy-contest-launches-today.

29. Richard Hillestad, et al., "Economics of Health Information Technology: Can Electronic Medical Record Systems Transform Health Care? Potential Health Benefits, Savings, and Costs," *Health Affairs* 24, no. 5 (September 2005): 1103–1117, content .healthaffairs .org/content/24/5/1103.full.

30. Reed Abelson and Julie Creswell, "In Second Look, Few Savings from Digital Health Records," *New York Times*, January 10, 2013, nytimes.com/2013/01/11/business/electronic-records-systems-have-not-reduced-health-costs-report-says.html?_r=2&adxnnl=1&adxnnlx =1369594957-Uia58oJHNaL9cuKZ/diU8w.

31. Todd Park and Peter Basch, "A Historic Opportunity: Wedding Health Information Technology to Care Delivery Innovation and Provider Payment Reform," Center for American Progress, May 2009, americanprogress.org/issues/2009/05/pdf/health_it.pdf.

32. For the broader history of the American health care system and its movement toward value-based payment, the following sources are invaluable: "How Did Healthcare Come about in the United States?" Stay Smart Stay Healthy, 2013, staysmartstayhealthy.com/health_care_history_inthe_united_states; Robert Kocher, MD, "Health Care Reform: Trends Driven by the Evolution of U.S. Health Care Policy," Castlight Health, October 2012, content.castlighthealth.com/rs/castlighthealth/images/Health%20Care%20Reform%20White%20Pap%20October%202012%20Bob%20Kocher.pdf; Victor R. Fuchs,

PhD, "The Gross Domestic Product and Health Care Spending," *The New England Journal of Medicine* 369, no. 2 (July 11, 2013): 107–109, nejm.org/doi/full/10.1056/NEJMp1305298.

33. "Video: Blue Button to Download Your Health Information," Markle.org, September 10, 2012, markle.org/publications/1679-video-blue-button-download-capability.

34. Bob Brewin, "Blue Button Access to Health Records Will Save Lives, Top Techie Says," Nextgov, September 16, 2013, nextgov.com/health/2013/09/blue-button-access-health-records-will-save-lives-top-techie-says/70398/?oref=ng-dropdown.

35. "New Rule Protects Patient Privacy, Secures Health Information," U.S. Department of Health and Human Services, January 17, 2013, hhs.gov/news/press/2013pres/01/20130117b.html.

36. "Directed Exchange Adoption," Office of the National Coordinator for Health Information Technology, last modified September 18, 2013, statehieresources.org/program-measures-dashboard/directed-exchange-user-type.

37. Jeanne Lambrew, "More Than Half of Doctors Now Use Electronic Health Records Thanks to Administration Policies," WhiteHouse.gov, May 24, 2013, whitehouse.gov/blog/2013/05/24/more-half-doctors-now-use-electronic-health-records-thanks-administration-policies.

38. "Blue Button+ Implementation Guide," BlueButton+, February 4, 2013, bluebuttonplus.org.

39. Erin Gifford, "Food Bloggers: What Is Schema.org Mark Up, What Does It Mean to Me?" *ZipList Blog*, March 15, 2012, blog.ziplist.com/schema-recipe-mark-up-for-food-blogs.

40. "Recipe," Schema.org, schema.org/Recipe.

41. Carrie Laureno, "Bringing the Very Best of What We Do to the Veteran Community," *Google Official Blog*, November 11, 2011, googleblog.blogspot.com/2011/11/bringing-very-best-of-what-we-do-to.html.

42. Meghan Murphy, "Lightning Developer Challenge: Build an

App for the White House," *Twilio Blog*, January 17, 2012, twilio .com/blog/2012/01/lightning-developer-challenge-build-an-app-for-the-whitehouse.html.

Chapter 7

1. Information for the ironclads history was derived from several sources, including: Joseph P. Reidy, review of *Civil War Ironclads: The U.S. Navy and Industrial Mobilization*, by William H. Roberts, H-Net Reviews (April 2005), h-net.org/reviews/showrev. php?id=10473.; Michael MacRae, "Battle of the Ironclads: John Ericsson and the USS Monitor," ASME.org, October 2011, asme .org/engineering-topics/ articles/history-of-mechanical-engineering/ battle-ironclads-john-ericsson-uss-monitor; Michael J. Feuer, "Ironclad Solutions," letter to the editor, *New York Times,* August 15, 2011, nytimes.com/2011/08/16/science/16letters-IRONCLADSOLU _LETTERS.html?_r=0; Thomas C. Lassman, "Sources of Weapon Systems Innovation in the Department of Defense: The Role of In-House Research and Development, 1945–2000," Center of Military History, August 15, 2008, history.defense.gov/resources/CMH_51-2-1.pdf.

2. "The Founding of the National Academy of Sciences," The National Academy of Sciences, 2013, nasonline.org/about-nas/150th-anniversary/moments-in-academy-history/founding-of-the-nas.html.

3. "History," National Academy of Sciences, 2013, nasonline .org/about-nas/history.

4. Information on F-35 development was derived from several sources, including Bob Brewin, "F-35 Joint Strike Fighter Not Ready For Combat Until At Least 2019, GAO Says," Nextgov, March 12, 2013, nextgov.com/defense/2013/03/f-35-joint-strike-fighter-not-ready-combat-until-least-2019-gao-says/61832/; Ilana Freedman, "F-22 and F-35: America's Costly Boondoggles Are the Victims of Arrogance and Appeasement," Gerard Direct, March 10, 2013, gerarddirect

.com/2013/03/10/uss-f-35-and-f-22-americas-costly-boondoggles-the-victims-of-arrogance-and-appeasement; Bob Brewin, "The A-Bomb and the F-35 Debacle," Nextgov, March 14, 2013, nextgov.com/defense/whats-brewin/2013/03/-bomb-and-f-35-debacle/61886.

5. "F-35 Joint Strike Fighter: Current Outlook Is Improved, but Long-Term Affordability Is a Major Concern," United States Government Accountability Office, March 2013, gao.gov/assets/660/652948.pdf.

6. "Defence Spending in a Time of Austerity," *The Economist*, August 26, 2010, economist.com/node/16886851.

7. "Biography: John Harrison," Royal Naval Museum Library, 2004, royalnavalmuseum.org/info_sheets_john_harrison.htm.

8. Karim Lakhani and Jill A.Panetta, "The Principles of Distributed Innovation," *Innovations: Technology, Governance, Globalization* 2, no. 3 (summer 2007) research paper, no. 2007-7, the Berkman Center for Internet and Society. Available at SSRN, ssrn.com/abstract=1021034.

9. "Workshop to Assess the Potential Technological Advance through Governmental Sponsored Prizes and Contests," Report of the Steering Committee, National Academy of Engineering, April 30, 1999, nap.edu/openbook.php?record_id=9724&page=37.

10. Alan Boyle, "SpaceShipOne Wins $10 million X Prize," NBCNews.com, October 5, 2004, nbcnews.com/id/6167761/#.UnMPuZSxPrY.

11. "America COMPETES Reauthorization Act," cio.gov/wp-content/uploads/downloads/2012/09/Prize_Authority_in_the_America_COMPETES_Reauthorization_Act.pdf.

12. Information on the Tricorder X PRIZE was supplemented by the following sources: "Qualcomm Tricorder X PRIZE Competition Guidelines," QualcommTricorderXPrize.org, July 1, 2013, qualcommtricorderxprize.org/files/qtxp.org/QTXP_Guidelines_20130701_v18.pdf; Jason Dorrier, "Diamandis: Tricorder X PRIZE Offers $10 Million to Build Star Trek Inspired Health Scanner," Singularity

Hub, February 20, 2013, singularityhub.com/2013/02/20/diamandis-tricorder-x-prize-offers-10-million-to-build-star-trek-inspired-health-scanner.

13. "The Moment of Proof: A Revolution in Oil Spill Recovery," Elastec AmericanMarine, elastec.com/PDF/The%20Moment%20of%20Proof%202MB.pdf.

14. David Zax, "Fast Talk: How this Tattoo Artist Became a Tech Entrepreneur," *Fast Company*, fastcompany.com/1812665/fast-talk-how-tattoo-artist-became-tech-entrepreneurax.

15. "Non Lethal Vehicle Stopping Technology," SBIR.gov, sbir.gov/sbirsearch/detail/158780.

16. Information on the Vehicle Stopper Challenge was supplemented by the following sources: "Vehicle Stopper," InnoCentive, March 2, 2011, gw.innocentive.com/ar/challenge/9932698; "InnoCentive and the Air Force Research Lab Announce Completion of Initial Open Innovation Challenges," InnoCentive, October 17, 2011, innocentive.com/innocentive-and-air-force-research-lab-announce-successful-completion-initial-open-innovation-challe; Michael Cooney, "Air Force awards $25K to Inventor of Insanely Fast Device That Stops Fleeing Cars," NetworkWorld, September 2, 2011, networkworld.com/community/blog/air-force-awards-25k-inventor-insanely-fast-d.

17. "HHS and the Office of the National Coordinator for Health Information Technology Introduce New Investing in Innovations (i2) Initiative," U.S. Department of Health and Human Services, June 8, 2011, hhs.gov/news/press/2011pres/06/20110608a.html.

18. Ibid.

19. "One in a Million Hearts Challenge," Health 2.0 Developer Challenge, health2con.com/devchallenge/one-in-a-million-hearts-challenge.

20. Information on Aamer Ghaffar's submission was supplemented by the following sources: "Health 2.0 and Walgreens Announce the Winner of the Health Guide Challenge," Market Wired, September 26, 2011, marketwire.com/press-release/

health-20-and-walgreens-announce-the-winner-of-the-health-guide-challenge-1565539.htm; "mHealthCoach_One in a Million Hearts Challenge submission," YouTube.com, December 31, 2011, youtube.com/watch?v=CwIdwHnflqc&feature=youtu.be; "One in a Million Hearts Challenge," Health 2.0 Developer Challenge, health2con.com/devchallenge/one-in-a-million-hearts-challenge.

21. "Advancing Interoperability and Health Information Exchange," Office of the National Coordinator for Health Information Technology and Centers for Medicare & Medicaid Services, Department of Health and Human Services, *Federal Register* 78, no. 45 (March 7, 2013), gpo.gov/fdsys/pkg/FR-2013-03-07/html/2013-05266.htm.

22. Rick Borstein, "An Interview with Adobe's Michael Jackson on the Blue Button Initiative," *Adobe Healthcare Blog*, December 1, 2010, blogs.adobe.com/healthcare/2010/12/an-interview-with-adobes-michael-jackson-on-the-blue-button-initiative.html.

23. Information on Blue Button challenges was supplemented by the following sources: "Blue Button Mash Up Challenge: Background," Health 2.0 Developer Challenge, 2011, health2con.com/devchallenge/blue-button-mash-up-challenge/#background; "iBlueButton," Health 2.0 Developer Challenge, health2con.com/devchallenge/files/BlueButton-Mashup-Challenge-iBlueButton-Slide-Deck.pdf; "Testimony of Christopher R. Burrow, MD, Before the Subcommittee on Health and Technology Small Business Committee, U.S. House of Representatives," Hearing on Mobile Medical App Entrepreneurs, Changing the Face of Health Care," June 27, 2013, smallbusiness.house.gov/uploadedfiles/6-27-2013_burrow_testimony.pdf.

24. "Dick Tracy Band," Minniepaulmusic.com, minniepaulmusic.com/?page_id=213.

25. "The Partnership Fund for Program Integrity Innovation," partner4solutions.gov.

26. David Levine, "Medicaid Fraud: Is It Worth States' Time

to Fight it?" *Governing*, May 2013, governing.com/topics/health-human-services/gov-medicaid-fraud-fight-value.html.

27. Mike Isaac, "Why Designers Hate Crowdsourcing," Forbes .com, July 12, 2010, forbes.com/2010/07/09/99designs-spec-graphic-technology-future-design-crowdsourcing.html.

28. "AIGA Position on Spec Work," AIGA, aiga.org/position-spec-work.

29. Information on the Department of Interior's crowdsourcing efforts was derived from the following sources: Mary Koster, "U.S. Department of Interior: Stop the US Department of Interior from Crowdsourcing a Logo," Change.org, change.org/petitions/us-department-of-the-interior-stop-the-us-department-of-interior-from-crowdsourcing-a-logo; "Logo: U.S. Department of the Interior," *CrowdSpring*, June 1, 2011, crowdspring.com/logo-design/project/2296807_logo-us-department-of-the-interior/details.

30. "President Obama's State of the Union Address," *New York Times*, January 24, 2012, nytimes.com/2012/01/25/us/politics/state-of-the-union-2012-transcript.html?pagewanted=all.

31. "Equal Pay Apps Challenge," equalpay.challengepost.com.

32. "$5.5 Million in Funding from U.S. DOE to Further Goals of Competition," X Prize Foundation, November 2, 2009, progressiveautoxprize.org/news-events/press-release/55-million-in-funding-from-us-doe-to-further-goals-of-competition.

33. Stephanie Marie Garcia, "Person of the Year: Bad Boy Turned Brazen Brainiac: Oliver Kuttner," *The Hook*, Thursday 16, 2010, readthehook.com/86633/cover-person-year-bad-boy-turned-brazen-brainiac-oliver-kuttner.

34. "Obama Administration Finalizes Historic 54.5 MPG Fuel Efficiency Standards," August 28, 2012, whitehouse.gov/the-press-office/2012/08/28/obama-administration-finalizes-historic-545-mpg-fuel-efficiency-standard.

35. Information about Apps for Abuses was supplemented by the following sources: "About Vice President Biden's Efforts to End Violence Against Women," WhiteHouse.gov, whitehouse.gov/1is2many/

about; Kathleen Sebelius, "'Apps Against Abuse' Challenge to Help Address Sexual Assault and Dating Violence," WhiteHouse.gov, July 13, 2011, whitehouse.gov/blog/2011/07/13/apps-against-abuse-challenge-help-address-sexual-assault-and-dating-violence; "The Department of Health and Human Services Challenged Developers to Create Apps That Empower Young Adults to Prevent Abuse and Violence," Apps Against Abuse, appsagainstabuse.challenge.gov.

36. Rosie Spinks, "Tap for Safety: Circle of 6 to Stop Rape," dowser.org, April 13, 2013, dowser.org/tap-for-safety-circle-of-six-to-stop-rape.

37. "GSA's Challenge.gov Earns Harvard Innovation Award," Harvard Kennedy School Ash Center for Democratic Governance and Innovation, January 23, 2014, ash.harvard.edu/Home/News-Events/Press-Releases/GSA-s-Challenge.gov-Earns-Harvard-Innovation-Award.

38. "The Grand Challenges of the 21st Century: Prepared Remarks of Tom Kalil at the Information Technology and Innovation Foundation," WhiteHouse.gov, April 12, 2012, whitehouse.gov/sites/default/files/microsites/ostp/grandchallenges-speech-04122012-rev.pdf.

39. Heather Kelly, "Self-driving Cars Now Legal in California," CNN, October 30, 2012, cnn.com/2012/09/25/tech/innovation/self-driving-car-california.

40. Supporting material for the passage on Grand Challenge was derived from the following sources: Cristin Dorgelo and Tom Kalil, "21st Century Grand Challenges," WhiteHouse.gov, April 9, 2012, whitehouse.gov/blog/2012/04/09/21st-century-grand-challenges; "The Grand Challenges of the 21st Century: Prepared Remarks of Tom Kalil at the Information Technology and Innovation Foundation," WhiteHouse.gov, April 12, 2012, whitehouse.gov/sites/default/files/microsites/ostp/grandchallenges-speech-04122012-rev.pdf.

41. "A Strategy for American Innovation: Driving Towards Sustainable Growth and Quality Jobs," WhiteHouse.gov, September

2009, whitehouse.gov/administration/eop/nec/StrategyforAmerican Innovation.

Chapter 8

1. John Field, "Patton of the Armored Force," *Life Magazine*, November 30, 1942, 124, books.google.com/books?id=RkEEAAAAMBAJ&printsec=frontcover&dq=life+magazine+november+30+1942&hl=en&sa=X&ei=ztrqUbboI8794APGqYDoCw&ved=0CC8Q6AEwAA#v=snippet&q=patton%20sears&f=false.

2. Franklin D. Roosevelt, "Fireside Chat 15: On National Defense," The University of Virginia Miller Center, May 26, 1940, millercenter.org/president/speeches/detail/3316.

3. Bruce Frassinelli, "President Wilson's '$1-a-year men' Still Inspire," *Morning Call*, May 1, 2009, articles.mcall.com/2009-05-01/opinion/4365157_1_lee-iacocca-chrysler-corp-stimulus-package.

4. Dale McFeatters, "Civilian Aluminum Items May Be Made Again Soon," *Pittsburgh Press*, March 10, 1944, news.google.com/newspapers?nid=1144&dat=19440310&id=bFIbAAAAIBAJ&sjid=lEwEAAAAIBAJ&pg=1833,4944987.

5. Franklin D. Roosevelt, "Excerpts from the April 15, 1941 Press Conference," the American Presidency Project, presidency.ucsb.edu/ws/?pid=16101.

6. "R. Sargent Shriver," the John F. Kennedy Presidential Library and Museum, jfklibrary.org/JFK/The-Kennedy-Family/R-Sargent-Shriver.aspx.

7. Scott Stossel, *Sarge: The Life and Times of Sargent Shriver* (New York: Other Press, 2011), books.google.com/books?id=K2WR945fz2sC&pg=PT279&lpg=PT279&dq=harris+wofford+%22talent+search%22&source=bl&ots=Rsq5IoLJ6q&sig=9Pa2fbk-0K1Z6BQ0_ZahmqePtoQ&hl=en&sa=X&ei=rdjrUc-9NZS34APk_YC4Aw&ved=0CEkQ6AEwBQ.

8. "Transcript: ServiceNation Presidential Forum at Columbia University," Clips & Comment, September 11, 2008, clipsand

comment.com/2008/09/11/transcript-servicenation-presidential-forum-at-columbia-university.

9. Joe Davidson, "Top Transition Official Explains How to Make Government 'Cool' Again," Federal Diary, *Washington Post*, November 10, 2008, voices.washingtonpost.com/federal-diary/2008/11/top_transition_official_explai.html.

10. Information on James Shelton was derived from the following sources: Edmund Newton, "The Root 100 Close-Up: James Shelton," the Root, December 19, 2011, theroot.com/views/root-100-closeup-james-shelton; "Senior Staff: James H. Shelton III, Assistant Deputy Secretary for Innovation and Improvement – Biography," Ed.gov, last modified June 2, 2009, www2.ed.gov/news/staff/bios/shelton.html; "i3 Projects Look Back on Progress and Lessons Learned," Ed.gov, June 6, 2013, ed.gov/oii-news/i3-projects-look-back-progress-and-lessons-learned.

11. Information on Maura O'Neill was derived from the following sources: Joseph Marks, "Development Agency's Chief Innovator to Step Down," Nextgov, April 3, 2013, nextgov .com/emerging-tech/emerging-tech-blog/2013/04/development-agencys-chief-innovator-step-down/62272/; "Maura O'Neill," *Impatient Optimists: Blog of the Bill & Melinda Gates Foundation*, m.impatientoptimists.org/?url=http%3A%2F%2Fimpatientoptimists.org%2FAuthors%2FO%2FMaura-ONeill.

12. Tom Kalil and Robynn Sturm Steffen, "We the Geeks: Innovation for Global Good," WhiteHouse.gov, June 24, 2013, whitehouse .gov/blog/2013/06/24/we-geeks-innovation-global-good.

13. Alec Ross, "Digitizing America," digitizingamerica.shanti .virginia.edu/sites/shanti.virginia.edu.digitizingamerica/files/Alec%20Ross%20Longform%20Bio.pdf.

14. Jim Puzzanghera, "New Consumer Bureau Proposes Simplified Mortgage Disclosure Forms," *Los Angeles Times*, May 18, 2011, articles.latimes.com/2011/may/18/business/la-fi-mortgage-forms-20110519.

15. "Know Before You Owe," Consumer Financial Protection Bureau, consumerfinance.gov/knowbeforeyouowe/#17.

16. "Integrated Mortgage Disclosures under the Real Estate Settlement Procedures Act (Regulation X) and the Truth In Lending Act (Regulation Z)," Bureau of Consumer Financial Protection, *Federal Register*, 12 CFR Parts 1024 and 1026, files.consumerfinance.gov/f/201207_cfpb_proposed-rule_integrated-mortgage-disclosures.pdf.

17. Lucy Madison, "Obama Unveils Mortgage Refinancing Plan," CBSNews.com, February 1, 2012, cbsnews.com/8301-503544_162-57369731-503544/obama-unveils-mortgage-refinancing-plan.

18. Jay Goldman, "Dean Kamen TEDMED2011: What's on the Horizon for Medical Robotics," *Klick Health*, November 2, 2011, klick.com/health/news/blog/tedmed2011-dean-kamen-whats-on-the-horizon-for-medical-robotics.

19. "Entrepreneurs in Residence Program," FDA.gov, last modified December 13, 2012, fda.gov/AboutFDA/CentersOffices/OfficeofMedicalProductsandTobacco/CDRH/CDRHInnovation/InnovationPathway/ucm286138.htm.

20. "FDA Announces Plans to Pilot End-Stage Kidney Disease Technology in New Program," FDA.gov, April 9, 2012, fda.gov/NewsEvents/Newsroom/PressAnnouncements/ucm299339.htm.

21. Alexander Gaffney, "FDA Opens Innovation Pathway to First Round of Devices," *Regulatory Focus*, April 10, 2012, raps.org/focus-online/news/news-article-view/article/1227/fda-opens-innovation-pathway-to-first-round-of-devices.aspx.

22. Supplemental information on the EIR program in USCIS was derived from the following sources: "Entrepreneurs in Residence (EIR)," U.S. Citizenship and Immigration Services, last modified May 8, 2013, uscis.gov/portal/site/uscis/menuitem.eb1d4c2a3e5b9ac89243c6a7543f6d1a/?vgnextoid=d44eee876cb85310VgnVCM100000082ca60aRCRD&vgnextchannel=d44eee876cb85310VgnVCM100000082ca60aRCRD; "DHS Reforms to Attract and Retain Highly Skilled Immigrants," United States Department of Homeland

Security, January 31,2012, dhs.gov/news/2012/01/31/dhs-reforms-attract-and-retain-highly-skilled-immigrants.

23. Supplemental information on the O-1 Visa was derived from the following sources: Vaughan de Kirby, "Playboy Playmate Receives O-1 Visa, Stirs Controversy," deKirby.net, July 5, 2012, dekirby.net/news/playboy-playmate-receives-o-1-visa-stirs-controversy-20120705.cfm; Sarah McBride, "U.S. 'Genius' Visa Attracts Entrepreneurs and Playmates," Reuters, June 29, 2012, reuters.com/article/2012/06/29/us-usa-visa-extraordinary-idUSBRE85S09A20120629; "USA Immigration Work Permits and Visas," SkillClear, skillclear.co.uk/usa/extraordinary-ability-01.asp.

24. "EIR," U.S. Citizenship and Immigration Services, uscis.gov/portal/site/uscis/eir.whitehouse.gov/blog/2012/11/29/new-front-door-immigrant-entrepreneurs.

25. Supplemental information on Fabien Beckers was derived from the following sources: Emily Maltby, "A New Push for Entrepreneur Visas," *Wall Street Journal*, February 12, 2013, online.wsj.com/article/SB10001424127887324880504578298150540138218.html; "Strategic Immigration Reform: Fabien Beckers, Morpheus Medical," YouTube.com, February 4, 2013, youtube.com/watch?v=PVfBHDkhNus; "Morpheus Medical," AngelList, angel.co/morpheus-medical.

26. Sarah Rich, "U.S. CTO Todd Park: 3 Ingredients for a Private-Sector Mentality in Government," Government Technology, October 4, 2012, govtech.com/pcio/US-CTO-Todd-Park-3-Ingredients-for-a-Private-Sector-Mentality-in-Government-.html.

27. "White House Launches Presidential Innovation Fellows Program," WhiteHouse.gov, August 23, 2012, whitehouse.gov/the-press-office/2012/08/23/white-house-launches-presidential-innovation-fellows-program.

28. "The Presidential Innovation Fellows," WhiteHouse.gov, whitehouse.gov/innovationfellows.

29. Supplemental information on RPF-EZ was derived from the

following sources: "The Presidential Innovation Fellows: RFP-EZ and Innovative Contracting Tools," WhiteHouse.gov, whitehouse.gov/innovationfellows/rfp-ez; Clay Johnson, "Let's Make a Deal," RFP-EZ Marketplace, January 17, 2013, presidential-innovation-fellows.github.com/rfpez-blog.

30. Karen G. Mills and Todd Park, "RFP-EZ Delivers Savings for Taxpayers, New Opportunities for Small Business," WhiteHouse.gov, May 15, 2013, whitehouse.gov/blog/2013/05/15/rfp-ez-delivers-savings-taxpayers-new-opportunities-small-business.

31. "Deliver Innovative Technology Without Breaking the Bank," *Department of Better Tech*, dobt.co/screendoor.

Matt Bevilacqua, " 'Department of Better Technology' Wants to Streamline the Open Government Process," Next City, April 17, 2013, nextcity.org/daily/entry/department-of-better-technology-wants-to-streamline-the-open-government-pro.

32. Adam Mazmanian, "Pahlka Named Deputy Federal CTO," *FCW Insider*, May 30, 2013, fcw.com/blogs/fcw-insider/2013/05/pahlka-deputy-cto.aspx.

33. Vivek Kundra, "Tight Budget? Look to the 'Cloud,' " *New York Times*, August 30, 2011, nytimes.com/2011/08/31/opinion/tight-budget-look-to-the-cloud.html?_r=0.

34. "Code for America PSA: 'What If,' " Vimeo.com, July 15, 2010, vimeo.com/13377489.

35. "Honolulu Answers," hnlanswers.herokuapp.com. "Code for America 2012 Fellowship Projects: Demo Webinar Part II," Vimeo.com, October 10, 2012, vimeo.com/51157861.

36. Teke Wiggin, "New Orleans No Longer Most Blighted U.S. City: Detroit and Flint, Mich., Come Out on Top," AOL Real Estate, August 24, 2012, realestate.aol.com/blog/2012/08/23/new-orleans-no-longer-most-blighted-u-s-city-detroit-and-flint.

37. "2012 Code for America Fellows," Code For America, codeforamerica.org/2012-fellows.

38. "Providing Up-to-Date Information on Vacant Properties So That Communities Can Find Ways to Make Tangible Improvements to Local Spaces," Knight Foundation, August 21, 2013, knightfoundation.org/grants/20102537.

39. Supplemental information on the Presidential Innovation Fellows was derived from the following sources: Jennifer Pahlka and Dan Tangherlini, "New Round of Innovators Joins US Government to Tackle Big Challenges," WhiteHouse.gov, June 24, 2013, whitehouse.gov/blog/2013/06/24/new-round-innovators-joins-us-government-tackle-big-challenges; "The Presidential Innovation Fellows," WhiteHouse.gov, whitehouse.gov/innovationfellows.

40. "Bob McDonnell quotes Thomas Jefferson in his response about Barack Obama's State of the Union," Hark.com, hark.com/clips/prdwkjvcsn-bob-mcdonnell-quotes-thomas-jefferson.

Postscript

1. fbo.gov/spg/HHS/HCFA/AGG/Reference-Number-CMS-2007-0001/listing.html

2. IDIQ Contract Awardees (sixteen): Northrop Grumman, CGI Federal, EDS, CSC, IBM, Lockheed Martin, SAIC, ViPS, Buccaneer Computer Systems, IDL Solutions, Quality Software Services, Maricom Systems, 2020 LLC, iFed LLC, Alta Systems, DCCA. See also blog.dobt.co/post/63655420372/how-healthcare-gov-went-wrong.

3. fas.org/sgp/crs/misc/R40228.pdf

4. http://www.nytimes.com/2013/12/01/us/politics/inside-the-race-to-rescue-a-health-site-and-obama.html

5. http://fcw.com/articles/2015/03/27/dickerson-at-sxsw.aspx

6. http://www.fastcompany.com/3046757/innovation-agents/president-barack-obama-on-what-we-the-people-means-in-the-21st-century

7. healthdata.gov/data/dataset/healthcare-finder-api;health.usnews.com/health-insurance

8. http://www.wired.com/2014/06/healthcare-gov-revamp/; http://www.nationaljournal.com/tech/silicon-valley-startup-saved-healthcare.gov-20150710

9. https://personaldemocracy.com/media/us-digital-service-improbable-public-interest-startup

10. https://www.whitehouse.gov/the-press-office/2014/08/11/fact-sheet-improving-and-simplifying-digital-services

11. www.media.mit.edu/people/msmith

12. http://www.wired.com/2014/08/healthcare-gov/

13. http://foreignpolicy.com/2015/03/04/the-exchange-walter-isaacson-and-megan-smith-talk-tech/)

14. http://www.forbes.com/pictures/lmm45emkh/2-jeff-hammerbacher-chief-scientist-cloudera-and-dj-patil-entrepreneur-in-residence-greylock-ventures/

15. https://www.washingtonpost.com/news/post-nation/wp/2015/07/01/since-1976-the-fbi-hasnt-counted-more-than-460-fatal-police-shootings-in-a-year-weve-counted-461-already-in-2015/

16. https://www.whitehouse.gov/the-press-office/2015/05/18/remarks-president-community-policing

17. https://medium.com/@CoryBooker/the-role-of-reliable-data-in-reducing-police-use-of-force-incidents-6adb41d72f9a

18. https://www.whitehouse.gov/blog/2015/10/27/police-data-initiative-5-month-update

19. https://medium.com/@WhiteHouse/does-open-data-build-trust-49ee4d400ba

20. http://www.mychamplainvalley.com/news/burlington-police-no-longer-using-repurposed-military-equipment-for-policing

21. https://www.whitehouse.gov/sites/default/files/microsites/ostp/final_us_open_government_national_action_plan_3_0.pdf

22. https://www.whitehouse.gov/the-press-office/2015/10/21/fact-sheet-white-house-releases-new-strategy-american-innovation

23. http://www.opengovpartnership.org/blog/blog-editor/2015/10/29/ogp-next-level

24. http://www.hamiltonproject.org/multimedia/video/future_of_work_in_age_of_machine_panel_1/

25. http://economics.mit.edu/files/8514

26. http://larrysummers.com/2015/03/03/3977/

27. "Global economy: The case for expansion", Financial Times, October 7, 2015

28. http://www.mckinsey.com/insights/employment_and_growth/connecting_talent_with_opportunity_in_the_digital_age

29. https://governor.virginia.gov/newsroom/newsarticle?articleId=5787

30. www.nytimes.com/2015/06/10/opinion/thomas-friedman-how-to-beat-the-bots.html

Index